Baroness of the Ripetta:
Letters of Augusta von Eichthal
to Franz Xaver Kraus

Baroness of the Ripetta:
Letters of Augusta von Eichthal
to Franz Xaver Kraus

Robert Curtis Ayers

Baroness of the Ripetta:
Letters of Augusta von Eichthal
to Franz Xaver Kraus

Copyright © 2004
by Robert Curtis Ayers

Cover design by Trisha Hadley

All rights reserved. No part of this book may be used or reproduced in any manner whatsoever without written permission except in the case of brief quotations embodied in articles and reviews.

Published by

6137 East Mescal Street
Scottsdale, Arizona 85254-5418

www.CloudbankCreations.com

ISBN: 0-9651835-7-2 soft cover edition — $ 24.95
ISBN: 0-9651835-8-0 cloth edition — $ 36.95

Library of Congress Control Number: 2004107700

Printed by Lightning Source
La Vergne, TN

To
Hubert Schiel (1898–1983)
and
Christoph Weber

for their support

Corrections to Edition of 2006:

According to the distinguished historian of Bavarian banking, Dr. Franziska Jungmann-Stadler, the palace purchased by Aron Elias in 1806 was the Palais Piosasque de Non, Theatinerstrasse 16, and the name Eichthal was derived from his estate at Maria Eich bei Planegg, near Munich. Also in Footnote 73, the names should read "Khuen-Belasi" and "Hoesslin." [*Zeitschrift fuer bayerische Landesgeschichte*, 2004, Bd. 67, Heft 3, 841-843.]

Dr. Victor Conzemius helpfully drew attention to the lovely portrait of the baroness in the Kunstmuseum, Basel. [*The Catholic Historical Review*, July, 2005, 542-543.]

Emilie Linder, Portrait of the Baroness
Augusta von Eichthal, undated.
Oil on canvas, 66 x 51.5 cm.,
Kunstmuseum, Basel
(by permission) Painted 1855-60?

Table of Contents

Preface — i

Introduction — 1

Chapter One (1895-1896) — 37

Chapter Two (1897) — 43

Chapter Three (1898) — 87

Chapter Four (1899) — 117

Chapter Five (1900) — 149

Chapter Six (1901) — 195

Epilogue — 227

Appendix — 229

Bibliography — 240

Franz Xaver Kraus. Freiburg photo, about 1890.

Preface

The letters of Augusta von Eichthal (1835-1932) to F. X. Kraus (1840-1901) had not been examined with any special degree of care until Dr. Hubert Schiel, Director *in Ruhestand* of the *Stadtbibliothek* in Trier, drew my attention to them in May of 1978 as I was researching a dissertation. I had narrowed the subject of the dissertation down to the relation between Kraus and various Americans, most of whom were in Rome. Dr. Schiel knew that the letters had many references to Americans.

I photocopied the letters and gradually transcribed them from the antique script in which they were written into readable German and made use of some of them in my doctoral dissertation "The Americanists and Franz Xaver Kraus. An Historical Analysis of an International Liberal Catholic Combination, 1897-1898." (Syracuse University, 1981)

The Editor of the *Catholic Historical Review*, Father Robert Trisco, kindly allowed me to compose a précis of the dissertation which was published in October 1982, Vol. LXVIII, p. 726. Sufficient copies of the dissertation were ordered by scholars and libraries to produce a small royalty check.

When Christoph Weber published *Liberaler Katholizismus. Biographische und kirchenhistorische Essays von Franz Xaver Kraus* (Max Niemeyer: Tübingen, 1983), he stated in the foreword, "…wertvoll war mir die Korrespondenz mit Dr. theol. R.C. Ayers, ehemals Pfarrer der episkopalistische Studentengemeinde der Universität Syracuse, N.Y., der mich frühzeitig über sein Dissertationsthema zu Kraus und dem Amerikanismus informierte.…Ich hoffe sehr, dass Dr. Ayers seinen Plan, die Dissertation zu drucken sowie den Briefwechsel von Kraus mit der geistreichen Baronesse Eichthal zu publizieren, bald verwirklichen kann." [Page XXXIV.]

In 1984 I presented a paper titled "The Americanist Attack on Europe in 1897 and 1898." The paper made use of some of the letters of AVE. It was published in the volume *Rising From History. U.S. Catholic Theology Looks to the Future*, edited by Robert J. Daly, The Annual Publication of the College Theology Society, 1984, Volume 30 (Lanham, MD: University Press of America, 1987), pp.84-92.

In 1986, Rev. David Francis Sweeney, O.F.M., presented a paper at the Spring Meeting of the American Catholic Historical Association titled "Herman Schell: A German Dimension to the Americanist Controversy." In support of his thesis Father Sweeney opened his address that day by saying: "The complete history of the Americanist controversy remains to be written. With the publication of Robert C. Ayer's [sic] *The Americanists and Franz Xaver Kraus: An Historical Analysis of an International Liberal Catholic Combination, 1897-1898*, (Ann Arbor, Michigan, University Microfilms International, 1983), the German dimension to the Americanist controversy is coming into focus." [Citation from a typewritten copy distributed at the session on Saturday April 19, 1986.]

In 1998 Claus Arnold published a chapter titled "Frauen und 'Modernisten.' Ein Kreis um Auguste von Eichthal," in Hubert Wolf (Hrsg.), *Anti-Modernismus und Modernismus in der katholischen Kirche*, (Paderborn: Schöningh, 1998). In this chapter Dr. Arnold cited some letters from AVE which had been quoted in my dissertation.

Subsequently Dr. Arnold has published *Katholizismus als Kulturmacht. Der Freiburger Theologe Joseph Sauer (1872-1949) und das Erbe des Franz Xaver Kraus*, (Paderborn: Schöningh, 1999). Again, Dr. Arnold referenced my dissertation and quoted from the letters of AVE.

Very recently a published dissertation appeared in Germany: Michael Graf, *Liberaler Katholik – Reformkatholik – Modernist? Franz Xaver Kraus (1840-1901) zwischen Kulturkampf und Modernismuskrise*, (Muenster: Lit Verlag,

2003). The author cites my dissertation and makes use of similar terminology for the relationship between Kraus and the Americans. He also quotes from some letters of AVE which he examined at Trier.

The time seems to have arrived to make the letters available to an American audience. They offer useful information about many of the American clergy associated with the Americanist controversy. In the letters there are substantial references to the activities of Denis O'Connell, John J. Keane, John Ireland, John L. Spalding, and lesser notations about Thomas O'Gorman, Charles P. Grannan and John Zahm. Significant mention is made of Msgr Joseph Schroeder. I have added an appendix which details the friendship between AVE and Charles Warren Stoddard, an early faculty member at Notre Dame and the Catholic University of America, based on his letters to her and the dedication to her of one of his travel books, *Mashallah!*

I believe that these letters will be informative to persons interested in American Catholic history, the history of the Catholic University of America, the history of the American College at Rome, and the story of the Americanist controversy. The letters reflect the proto-feminist perspective of a spinster aristocrat of the day. They also bear broadly on European tensions within the Triple Alliance and at the time of the Spanish-American War. Finally, the observant and sarcastic lady, an ardent Catholic, was of direct Jewish origin.

I have translated the letters into English and annotated them extensively to identify persons and to explain details. While the letters <u>from</u> Kraus <u>to</u> AVE are rarely very informative, beyond time and place and arrangements, nevertheless Kraus' letters to her have been noted and summarized where needed. Occasionally a letter from some one of the Americans is placed in a note.

The letters from AVE to F. X. Kraus are in the *Nachlass Kraus* in the *Stadtbibliothek* in Trier. Kraus kept files of correspondence from more than a thousand individuals, noting the dates of each letter's reception and his replies. In addition he left a number of files and cartons in which he had placed notes and newspaper clippings for reference. In reproducing the letters from AVE I have omitted individual citation. All her letters are in the same file, marked Eichthal.

The letters from Kraus to AVE, and other letters to her from Americans, are in the *Nachlass Eichthal* in the *Bayerisches Hauptstaatsarchiv* in Munich. In the course of a very long life the baroness kept many letters from a great variety of friends, including Franz Liszt and Ignatius Döllinger. In quoting or referencing letters from Kraus I have omitted individual citation. Other letters received by AVE have been referenced for the file in which they are found.

I want to express my gratitude to the late Dr. Hubert Schiel and to Dr. Christoph Weber for their encouragement over the years. Dr. Claus Arnold has been very helpful and I owe him much thanks. The Rev. Robert Trisco of the Catholic University of America very kindly gave me opportunity to put notice of my earlier work before interested readers. I appreciated the hospitality and assistance I received at Mullen Library of the Catholic University of America and at the archives of the Diocese of Richmond. The staffs at the Bavarian State Library in Munich and at the City Library in Trier were always very helpful.

Finally I want to express thanks for the support of my friend Dr. William Portier, now of the University of Dayton, and formerly of Mt. St. Mary's College. His interest has kept my interest alive.

Robert C. Ayers
Cazenovia, New York

Introduction
The 1895 Trip to Rome

IN THE WINTER OF 1895 Professor Franz Xaver Kraus of Freiburg made a trip to Rome. As was his custom he recorded in his diary on the 17th of November a list of people he met, including, "I saw… Baroness von Eichthal." He obviously knew her previously for she wrote him at once on his appearance in Rome to invite him to visit her at her apartment on the Via di Ripetta in the next few days. Over the remaining years of his life, until the end of 1901, there are seventeen more diary entries about her. In the Kraus *Nachlass* in the Stadtbibliothek of Trier there are seventy-nine letters and postcards from her to Kraus. His meticulous records show that he wrote to her at least sixty-seven times. Most of the letters she received from Kraus are in the Eichthal *Nachlass* in the Bayerisches Hauptstaatsarchiv in Munich.

His diary entries and their letters provide an interwoven story of the life of two remarkable figures in the church-political struggles of the day. And while we know much about Kraus from other sources, we discover from the Eichthal letters the significant role she played in the intrigues of the time. Over the years she became the means for many people to meet and communicate with Kraus. Chief among them for American interests were the prelates who came to be associated with the 'Americanism' movement and related efforts to resist 'Vaticanism' during the last years of Pope Leo XIII. Through her, Kraus was able to meet John Keane, deposed rector of the Catholic University of America; John Ireland, the Archbishop of St. Paul and his loyal assistant, Bishop Thomas O'Gorman; John L. Spalding, Bishop of Peoria; and John A. Zahm, C.S.C. Through her, Kraus acquired the cooperation of Eichthal's busy young friend, the charming, mercurial, Monsignor Denis J. O'Connell, the dismissed rector of the American College, still however Cardinal Gibbons' agent in Rome.

The Eichthal letters also provide a glimpse into life in a "liberal" portion of Roman society, a pro-Triple Alliance, composed of German and Italian aristocrats and their adherents. This grouping was generally inclined to reform in church matters, and was conciliatory to the Kingdom of Italy in the great question of the day, the issue of the pope's Temporal Power. Her noble birth, modest but widely connected, provided association with the privileged whose activities appear in her letters. She was, as Kraus put it early on in their friendship, "sadly, possessed of a very gossipy tongue." But that is our fortune.

Franz Xaver Kraus

We meet Kraus in these letters fully advanced in his career, and in the last six years of his life. Born in Trier in 1840, he had opted for the priesthood and life as a German academic. After service as household tutor in important families, he first gained advancement to the faculty in Strassburg and then in 1878 to that of the University of Freiburg in the Breisgau. His appointment was for Church history and Christian art. He possessed both a brilliant intellect and a capability for making himself attractive to the highly placed. His specialty in archaeology, monuments and inscriptions, brought him into early contact with archaeological activities in Rome, especially the work of the famous de Rossi. His interests in Dante made him a favorite in Italian risorgimento circles. His devotion to Antonio Rosmini guaranteed him friends among the northern Italian advocates of ecclesiastical reform. His hesitations in 1870 about the first Vatican Council confirmed a lifelong tendency to resist the centralization of the church, and formed him as one destined for a career dependent on lay patronage rather than from the eccelesiastical system. For Kraus, 'infallibility' could mean the proclamation of nothing new, but only the protection of that attested by history and supported by the episcopate.

The events of 1870 were traumatic for Kraus, as it became clear to him that his scholarly profession would bring him into opposition with the dominant elements in the church. In 1863 at the Munich Congress of Catholic Scholars,

Ignatius Döllinger had inveighed against the "one-eyed" speculations of Latin scholastic theology, blind in the other eye to the unavoidable truths of history. The effects of this one-sidedness bore in on Kraus as he suffered from the consequences of his critical investigations into dubious relics and into erroneous attributions of ancient art. In 1870 Döllinger, writing as *Quirinus*, described how, at the end of the Vatican Council, as part of the minority delegation to plead with Pius IX, Bishop Ketteler fell to his knees before the pontiff, aghast and imploring in vain against the self-contented pontiff's impervious conviction and narrow lack of awareness of anything outside in the real world of the nations. Undone, the honorable bishop, possessed of an aristocrat's integrity, had collapsed in horror at the choice to which he was now forced, the choice between historical truth and the demands of constrained obedience to the letter of a definition which conflicted with historical reality.[1]

To survive, Kraus, like others, choked down the dogma of Infallibility but he was never at peace with it, never absorbed it into his faith. From 1870 onward his aim was to struggle for "reconciliation between faith and knowledge, with a serious recognition of the historical character of the Christian religion, with all the consequences that followed, and especially in the treatment of the history of the Church."[2] He was convinced that he "suffered for a noble and holy matter" and that the day would come when he would be proven right.[3]

From 1872 to 1879 Kraus brought out editions of a multiple volumned *Lehrbuch der Kirchengeschichte für Studierende*. A devastating revue from the Jesuit Hartmann Grisar of Innsbruck pointed out the textbooks to the authorities of the Roman Index and a bitter struggle took place from 1883 to

---

[1] Ignatius Döllinger, *Römische Briefe vom Concil von Quirinus* (Munich, 1870), pp. 624-627.

[2] Christoph Weber, "F.X. Kraus und Italien," *Quellen und Forschungen aus italienischen Archiven und Bibliotheken*, 61/1981, p.173.

[3] *Franz Xaver Kraus, Tagebücher, herausgegeben von Dr. Hubert Schiel* (Cologne 1957), p.290. [hereafter cited as *Tgb.*]

1886. Although the examiners at the Index found little fault with the work, a combination of ultramontane and Jesuit interests urged its condemnation. In 1883 a hitherto insignificant writer, Joseph Schroeder, aligning himself with ultramontane orthodoxy and the Jesuits, attacked Kraus with a one hundred and eighty-one page pamphlet, *Der Liberalismus in Theologie und Geschichte. Eine theolog. histor. Kritik der Kirchengeschichte von F.X. Kraus*.[4]

Kraus was accused of advocating "Gallicanism," or nationalism in church government, with less dependence by diocesan bishops on Rome. This was anathema to a Vatican which had fought the Kulturkampf and resisted any attempts to nationalize the German church. The universal primary jurisdiction of the Pope was a concomitant of papal Infallibility, and the accusation that he favored "Febronianism," a theory of autonomy for bishops, put Kraus' orthodoxy, and with it his career, in jeopardy.

Beginning in 1870 Kraus developed a firm friendship with the archeologist G. B. de Rossi and established a reputation in Rome for his archaeological knowledge. This had first brought him to the attention of Pius IX and later gained him serious recognition from Leo XIII. Leo had a positive regard for the Freiburg professor because Kraus had served in 1880 in the process of winding down the Kulturkampf. Kraus and de Rossi had enabled Leo XIII to communicate indirectly with the Grand Duke of Baden and through him, with the Prussian administration.[5]

Kraus was fortunate that Leo XIII personally intervened and allowed him to make revisions, humiliating to the author, in the *Lehrbuch*. An "edition for demoiselles" was re-published in 1887.

Archaeology was the key to Kraus' association with those who gathered at the salon of Donna Ersilia Caetani Lovatelli, at the Palazzo Lovatelli. Donna

---

[4] In 1889 an unwary Bishop John J. Keane recruited Schroeder from Cologne as a professor for the new Catholic University of America. Keane later became the target himself of Schroeder's accusations of lack of orthodoxy.

[5] *Tgb.*, pp.416-417. (April 11, 1880)

Ersilia, a vigorous widow with five children, was the daughter of the blind Michaelangelo Caetani, Duke of Sermoneta, sometime Minister of Police under Pius IX. She was a serious archeologist who began publishing in 1878 and who received honorary doctorates from the University of Halle in 1894 and the University of St. Andrews in 1906. In the 1890's her salon attracted important Italian scientists and politicians, as well as liberal Catholics from other countries such as Msgr Duchesne and Msgr O'Connell. Without doubt it was at Donna Ersilia's salon that Kraus first met Baroness von Eichthal.

By late 1895 Kraus was deeply involved with the policies and information processes of the German government. A consortium composed of the German Foreign Office, the Grand Duke of Baden and others, had purchased the *Allgemeine Zeitung* of Munich in order to provide an organ for their national and liberal viewpoint. Kraus had contracted with the paper to write a substantial monthly "report" reflecting his and their views on the outstanding church-political issues of the day. Signed "Spectator," and published in the *Beilage*, the "scientific" supplement of the newspaper, these "Letters" extended to the number of forty-eight over the ensuing four years.

More particularly, under the impetus of Leo's failing health and advanced age which made a conclave very likely, it had been arranged in 1895 that Kraus, at the behest of the Emperor and Chancellor Hohenlohe, should go to Rome for the winter to observe the forces building around an anticipated election, to confer with appropriate Italian politicians because the interests of the Triple Alliance were involved, and to represent the German government's position to those cardinals who were receptive. France had to be thwarted. The sympathies of that combination of forces which were oriented to German interests were to be delicately drawn together and encouraged. To cover Kraus' presence in Rome it was put about that he was engaged in archival research.

At this point in his life Kraus, who was a Privy Councilor (*Geheimrat*) to the Grand Duke of Baden, had been offered by Prussia as a candidate for Bishop of Trier (1880), and tentatively proposed by the Baden government as

Archbishop of Freiburg (1886). In both cases it was granted that he was respected in Rome for his knowledge, but was rejected because he was not dedicated to Roman policy, and was suspect in his ecclesiology. These hesitations had been greatly aggravated by the publication of Joseph Schroeder's book.

His 1895 mission to Rome was in keeping with a role Kraus had performed for various German administrations, writing *promemoria* or *Denkschriften* on subjects of a church-political nature. *Kirchenpolitik*, the politics of the manifold relations between German states and the Catholic Church, encompassed many matters, chief among them the appointment of bishops, in which the state had to concur, and the staffing of the Catholic portion of the educational system, particularly the higher education.

Kraus' lengthy reports to Berlin detail his experiences and conclusions on his 1895 trip, and show his activities at the time the letters from Baroness Eichthal begin.[6]

Purpose of the 1895 Trip

A conclave,[7] had it occurred in 1895, would have proved in significant part a contest between the interests of France and those of the new Italian nation. The Ralliement to Republican France, the prominence to which Cardinal Lavigerie had risen — he was openly talked of as a papal candidate —

---

[6] On the 1895 trip Kraus kept two diaries, a general one and one specifically recording his church-political activities and conversations. The two are interwoven in the 1957 edition of his many diaries, *Franz Xaver Kraus, Tagebücher, herausgegeben von Dr. Hubert Schiel* (Cologne, 1957.)

[7] A complete discussion of matters related to a conclave in that period, including the problem of a veto, can be found in Christoph Weber, "Italien, Deutschland und das Konklave von 1903," *Quellen und Forschungen aus italienischen Archiven und Bibliotheken*, 57/1977, pp. 199-260. There the pertinent entries from Kraus' diary in 1895 and 1896 are cited.

increased the possibility that the precarious Italian state might find the Vatican dominated by anti-Italian forces, pressing for the return of the Temporal Power and the reduction of the unity of the Kingdom of Italy. The Italian interests favored reconciliation between the Papacy and Italy, abandonment of the Roman Question, and permission for Catholics to participate in elections. Italian liberals and nationalists looked to Germany, possessed of a Cardinal Gustav Hohenlohe and a Chancellor Chlodwig Hohenlohe, as the guarantor for a united Italy. The Italian liberal nationalists expected Germany as a matter of policy to thwart France in Rome, to encourage Italian interests in Africa, and to stabilize the monarchy in Italy.

As Cardinal Lavigerie had made his famous toast to Republican France, so Cardinal Gustav Hohenlohe, in the spring of 1895, had made a toast which openly supported the Crispi government of Italy. These two acts were clear expressions of definite polarity within the Vatican; Temporal Power versus Conciliation, French versus Italian interest. But Cardinal Hohenlohe was not the man to lead, nor did he want to. Instead the Triple Alliance partners — Germany, Austria, Italy — put their hope in Cardinal Luigi Galimberti, the likely Secretary of State in any conciliationist papacy for which in a conclave a majority of non-French cardinals might vote. In this context the name of Cardinal Serafino Vannutelli began to surface, as an agreeable candidate for pope who would be guided by Galimberti.

When in 1892 the Italians began to fear that Republican France, favored by the new Ralliement policies of Cardinal Rampolla, might again threaten their hard-won unity, the question of a veto[8] of pro-French candidates in any future conclave had been raised and discussed in Rome, Berlin, Vienna, Madrid and Lisbon. Since only the last three of these represented 'Catholic' states who could actually lay claim to the controversial right of veto,

---

[8] Veto, a right of exclusion of a candidate for the papacy. Said to derive from the prerogatives of the Holy Roman Emperor, and in 19th Century to be possessed by France, Spain, Portugal and Austria, as the Catholic states which were successors to the Empire. Exercised by Austria in 1903 to exclude Cardinal Rampolla, it was outlawed formally by Pius X in 1904.

discussion in Berlin and Rome had to center around planning in concert with one or several of them.

It was well known that the French were contemplating a veto. By December of 1895 they had circulated a memorandum to their cardinals to exclude any candidate who would not uphold French rights of protection of the church in the East or who would not press for papal rights of restoration of some temporal sovereignty in Italy. This represented a use of the veto which went beyond previous examples and seemed to the other countries to do violence to the conclave. The veto was a relic from the days of the Holy Roman Empire, when the other rulers of the empire sought to influence the election of a brother sovereign, a Pope-King, a *papa re*.

As the long-term fate of the Italian government became more precarious in early 1895, Cardinal Gustav Hohenlohe, once called 'the only Italian in the Sacred College,' urged his brother Chlodwig, the Chancellor of the German Reich, to help Italy in the struggle with her French enemies. In this brother-to-brother diplomacy, Franz Xaver Kraus was sent as the secret "Special Councilor to the Chancellor of the Reich for Conclave Preparations," more as an exercise in the private church-political policies of the Hohenlohe brothers than in the official diplomacy of the Wilhelmstrasse. The secret mission was to be kept from the Prussian envoy to the Vatican, Otto von Bülow, who was regarded as inept, and so lacking in finesse and in a grasp of Catholic internal politics that he could be used only for the most routine matters.

In later years Philipp Eulenburg, a major advisor to the Reich, set down a Memorandum concerning Kraus. He described the value Kraus had for the government; "A liberal scholar of the Catholic Church, closely initiated in the secrets and circles of Old Catholics, very clever, very proper, not without vanity and ambition, he was the man who always knew exactly 'how the Roman rabbit jumped.' He was a form of walking reference work in matters Catholic…"[9]

---

[9] "Notiz betreffend Professor Kraus," written by Philip Eulenburg between 1913 and 1918. Reprinted in Christoph Weber, *Quellen und Studien zur Kurie und zur*

Thus it was Kraus' 1895 assignment to sound out the various factions in Rome with regard to the acceptability of candidates, and to learn the attitude of potential Italian governments — whether of liberal Crispi or conservative Rudini — toward the use of the veto. The intention to intervene on the part of the French government made the issue very pertinent.

From Baron Blanc, the current foreign minister, Kraus determined that the Crispi government would prevent, as it could, for the sake of its own integrity, the election of any pope who would seriously consider himself the pretender to the throne of Rome, a *papa re*. Nor would the government willingly allow foreign cardinals to participate in the election of one who considered himself to be a sovereign on the peninsula. Blanc, obviously anxious to deprive the French of any advantage from the veto, observed that the very concept of the veto was a bit ridiculous at the present time. While it perhaps ought to be declared null and void, Blanc said that if it were to be used by the Triple Alliance, then Germany ought to persuade Austria to exercise the privilege.[10]

Later the Freiburg professor conferred with Marchese di Rudini, who would head any government called to replace Crispi. Rudini cautiously said that the veto ought not be abandoned, since it might have some use. In the interviews Kraus correctly suspected that Rudini was already in contact with the pro-French Cardinal Rampolla, and that any collaboration in the use of the veto by the *Triplice* would be unlikely in a Rudini government. On March 1, 1896 the Italian army in Africa suffered a disastrous defeat at Adowa. In mid-March of 1896 the Crispi government fell, and Rudini was called to head a new one. Kraus' secret mission to a cooperative Italian government was thereby seriously hindered and he returned to Germany in April.[11]

---

vatikanischen Politik unter Leo XIII (Tübingen, 1973), pp. 443-445.

[10] *Tgb.*, p. 639.

[11] A complete account of Kraus' activities is recorded in his diary for the period. (*Tgb.* pp. 629-669.)

It had seemed reasonable for Kraus to make an appearance in 1895 in Rome for purposes of research. He was a professor of church history whose expertise in archeology and cataloguing monuments stretched from ancient Trier, Baden, and Alsace-Lorraine to Italy and Rome. In addition, he had, in the most recent years, developed a reputation as a scholar of Dante and had, to the delight of Italian patriots, emphasized the epochal significance of the great Florentine.

This wide range of interests made Kraus a welcome figure with the liberal Catholics of the Italian north, in Milan and Trent, and in the art and historical circles in Florence. In Rome, as we shall see, his presence was happily greeted by a wide circle of friends and admirers. The arrival of "*il professore* Kraus" was warmly welcomed.

We are indebted to Karl Bill, one of his students, for a vivid picture of Kraus as he lectured at the University of Freiburg im Breisgau, the 'Albertina.'[12]

The students and spectators, wrote Bill, regularly assembled in the great hall, the 'audi max,' of the university, filling it to the last place. At Kraus' entry an absolute quiet prevailed and the audience saw "a deeply bowed man, supported by a cane, limp into the room. If he had stood upright, [he was] of an average size, with a congenial expression seen from the side but which also showed that the terrible pain and suffering of his body had not overcome his spirit."

> Arriving at the front row of seats, he laid down his hat and cane, but always kept a light shawl thrown over his shoulders, to ward off the faintest draft, and with effort gradually and painfully climbed the step of the rostrum. There he seated himself slowly, in order not to have to move his limbs too rapidly, which, as is well known for arthritis sufferers, is the most painful, and next looked to see that all the windows were closed, and began his lecture in a light voice. Gradually he straightened himself up, a bit at a time, until his shoulders could rest on the back of the chair. Then

---

[12] Karl Bill, in *Freie Deutsche Blätter*, 1902, Nr.3, quoted in Hubert Schiel, *Im Spannungsfeld von Kirche und Politik, Franz Xaver Kraus* (Trier, 1951), pp.36-38.

>one could see the handsome, still majestic countenance, the forehead high and almost broad, which immediately revealed that behind it, mighty, world-moving thoughts dwelled.
>
>With his dark, sparkling eyes he swept the hall and poured out his soul...The nearly black and always elegantly combed hair, parted in the middle, emphasized the arch of his brow.

Walter Goetz,[13] at the time a young *Privatdozent*, recalled the stream of visitors in Florence who came to see Kraus when he resided in a pension. Kraus was visited by scholars, diplomats, priests, ladies and gentlemen from different nations, who came in friendship and to honour him, to seek advice, to pour out their hearts. After a visit with Kraus in Florence, the art critic Bernard Berenson, considered a brilliant conversationalist in his own right, wrote to him, "Permit me to say in writing what as a shy Anglo-Saxon I should find it difficult to say to your face, that you are altogether the most interesting and delightful talker — without prejudice to your other qualities — that I have ever met."[14]

The reform-minded novelist, Antonio Fogazzaro, twice described Kraus in his novels in the figure of the Abate Dane. "The celebrated professor Dane, in his garments half worldly and half ecclesiastical, always folding and closing his very delicate feminine hands under a cotton shawl, in perpetual adoration, exquisite in his turning to the ladies or to five or six of the more intellectual...renowned historian, profound connoisseur of painting and music."[15] "Abate Dane, with all his rheumatisms and his nerves and his sixty-

---

[13] A lengthy obituary by Goetz appeared in the *Münchener Neueste Nachrichten* in 1902, and is reprinted in Christoph Weber, *Liberaler Katholizismus, Biogaphische und kirchenhistorische Essays von Franz Xaver Kraus* (Tübingen, 1983), pp. 430-438.

[14] Bernard Berenson, 3 Via Camerata, Florence, to F.X. Kraus, March 30, 1900.[*Nachlass* Kraus, Berenson file.] Berenson was born in 1865 in Vilnius, Lithuania.

[15] Antonio Fogazzaro, *Piccolo mondo moderno* (Milan, 1901), p.277.

two years, possessed, in addition to a great knowledge, an indomitable vigor of spirit, a well-tested moral courage."[16]

This unconquerable spirit had manifested itself at points in Kraus' career as an inability to restrain himself from inappropriate comments. He cooked his goose in 1888, when, as a candidate for the bishopric of Trier, sensing that Bismarck's regime had swung around to the other candidate, the ultramontane Korum, Kraus published an article in the Augsburg *Allgemeine Zeitung*, alleging that the Prussian government after ten years of battle, had already entered the precincts of Canossa, where Bismarck had pledged never to go. It was the worst possible mistake. "Sensational utterances at an inappropriate time and the inability to conceal his feelings, were indeed a weakness of Kraus."[17] Once, when leaving a dinner party in Rome, the envoy Schlözer chaffed Kraus about some remark he had made before the ladies, and the professor snapped at him to the effect of "Don't tell me what to do, I know how to conduct myself." Schlözer later thought it motivated Kraus to seek his dismissal.

And while we shall see the baroness complimenting him on toning down his sarcasm in the Munich *Allgemeine Zeitung*, one of his last works, finished near his death, his *Cavour*, was described by Kraus himself as "a book that would cause great rage and trouble in the Ultramontane circles and in Rome."[18] Christoph Weber describes it as a very self-willed, indeed personal, interpretation of the politics of Cavour and Pius IX, loved by protestants.[19]

---

[16] Antonio Fogazzaro, *Il Santo* (Milan 1906), pp. 37-85.

[17] Christoph Weber, *Kirchliche Politik zwischen Rom, Berlin und Trier, 1876-1888* (Mainz, 1970), p. 52.

[18] *Tgb.*, p. 757.

[19] Christoph Weber, *Der "Fall Spahn" 1901* (Rome, 1980), pp.106-7

Donna Ersilia and Her Salon

In 1880, on a trip to Rome, Kraus, depressed by his failure to be named Archbishop of Freiburg, had been diverted by an encounter with a dynamic widow of great family, a fellow archaeologist, and a kindred spirit, Donna Ersilia Lovatelli Caetani. Born in 1840, she was the daughter of Michaelangelo Caetani, duca di Sermoneta. In 1859 she had married twenty-seven year old Giacomo duca Lovatelli, borne five children,[20] only to lose him to death in 1879. In 1878 she began to publish serious work about Roman archaeology. In his diary Kraus recorded that at a meeting of patrons of archaeology, he was happiest of all to be introduced to Countess Lovatelli, "one of the most educated women of Rome." Noting her widowhood and her family, he recorded "a certain youthful manner of approach" and estimated her age at "30 to 40," evidence of the fresh appearance of the vibrant forty year old. "She also invited me to call, and I did so the same evening and received a delightful invitation to dinner, in the Latin language…"[21] Only a year later he was recording that her letters to him were "filled with pain, warm friendship, dear sentiments."[22]

The Italian art historian Adolfo Venturi gives us a glimpse of Donna Ersilia, from his experiences in the same time.

> I had a genteel visitor in the Contessa Ersilia Lovatelli Caetani. Already the widow of Conte Lovatelli, she came to bring one or the other of her sons to the military school at Modena. I already knew of the fame of her Roman salon and how much was written about her polished manner: but I expected to see a wrinkled lady archaeologist in the studio, with a pair of gold-rimmed spectacles, and instead found a lady not quite young, but who had not ceased to look like

---

[20] Giovanni, born 1859; Kallista, 1860; Witold, 1869; Rosalia, 1872; Filippo, 1874.

[21] *Tgb.*, p.414. 6 April 1880, Rome.

[22] *Tgb.*, p.429.

> a beautiful Roman empress, smiling at the archaeologists, courtiers of the "lynxes" whenever they resemble them.[23]
>
> I accompanied her to see the best part of the Galleria Estense, but I found her indifferent, impassive; while I did my utmost to expound the beauty of the things, I observed the great lady hiding a yawn behind the lace of her handkerchief.

He relates how he showed her treasures, Veronese, Velasquez, bronzes, jewels, terracottas, enamels.

> In vain, I could not succeed to unlock the vein of her taste. And when we visited the Romanesque cathedral, she was not observed to open her mouth save to yawn... Modern art, like that of antiquity, was voiceless for the gentle lady; ... perhaps an education entirely literary caused her to investigate the subject of a relief or statue, to research iconography, without studying the form, as if the form were no more than the negligible garment of a concept, the simple envelope. That impressed me how that type of archaeological education, in a complicated example in iconographic judgements, lost sight of the horizon of the study.[24]

That Venturi's experience was not unique is borne out by the first encounter the young Joseph Sauer had with the patrician lady. In Sauer's diary he recorded "8 May 1902, through Baroness Eichthal I got to know... [Countess] Lovatelli, who on this occasion was immortally boring and scarcely said five words to me: however 8 days later invited me to lunch, apparently believing to repair the damage. I sat at her right hand and had her daughter at my right: it was mostly pleasantries, much about a young cat of Duchesne's"[25]

---

[23] Reference to the "Royal Academy of the Lynxes" [dei Lincei], the Roman scientific society which published Donna Ersilia's work, and to which she left her library.

[24] Adolfo Venturi, *Memorie autobiographiche*,(Milan, 1911), pp.73-76.

[25] Claus Arnold, "Frauen und 'Modernisten,' Ein Kreis um Auguste von Eichthal," in Hubert Wolff,ed.,*Antimodernismus und Modernismus in der katholische Kirche*, (Paderborn, 1998), p.248.

And that she was not without quick humour was recalled by Richard Voss: "Count Lovatelli was dead and the Romans smilingly related to themselves a charming story. When friends of the family decried the death of the Count, while extolling his extraordinary handsomeness, the Countess had exclaimed, 'But you should have seen him naked!'"[26]

In his 1904 book of remembrance about Kraus, Ernst Hauviller gives a description of Donna Ersilia's salon, drawing on Kraus' own Essay, "*Frauenarbeit in der Archaeologie.*"

> In a palazzo near to S. Maria in Campitelli lived a woman, who by Kraus' witness "today undoubtedly leads the round dance of the archaeological ladies." It is Donna Ersilia, Countess Caetani-Lovatelli, the daughter of one of the most illustrious families of Rome, descended from the sovereign Boniface VIII, a distinguished lady, in whose friendship and intellectual exchange Kraus recovered his own expanded self. Her salon became the rendezvous of all those whom spirit and learning drew together in Rome. Theodor Mommsen and Gregorovius were old and welcomed guests here. De Rossi, an old family friend of her father's, provided himself the evidence that one could be a great researcher of the past and yet a man of complete graciousness of demeanor.[27]

> The representatives of the French as well as the German schools met each other here on neutral ground. Le Blant,[28] Geffroy[29] and Duchesne, who took over in succession the direction of the Ecole francaise de Rome, were frequent visitors there. But in knowledge in the area of the sciences of antiquity as well as a specialist's training in the Latin and Greek languages

---

[26] Richard Voss, *Aus einem phantasticshen Leben, Errinnerungen*, (Stuttgart, 1923), p. 250.

[27] In contrast with the ill-tempered Mommsen, who was often a disagreeable guest.

[28] E. LeBlant, author of *Inscriptions chrétiennes de la Gaule,.*(Paris, 1856,1865,1892.)

[29] Mathieu Auguste Geffroy (1820-1895), 1874 appointed to superintend the opening of the *École française de Rome*.

and literature, the beautiful and majestic mistress of the house did not fall behind her guests.[30]

It was, as Kraus maintained in his Essay, a constant testimony to the abilities of a great list of female historians and archaeologists, Anna Jameson,[31] Luisa Twining,[32] Frau Dr. Schliemann,[33] Madame Dieulafoy,[34] Mrs. Elisabeth Lecky, the former Baroness von Dedem,[35] Sibylla Mertens-Schaaffhausen,[36] Frau Prof. Helbig,[37] and, crowning them all, Donna Ersilia. At the end of his Essay, Kraus

---

[30] Ernst Hauviller, *Franz Xaver Kraus, Ein Lebensbild aus der Zeit des Reformkatholizismus* (Colmar, 1904), p.49.

[31] Anna (Murphy) Jameson (1794-1860), art historian, travel writer, feminist, estranged from husband, supported herself by writing.

[32] Louisa Twining (1820-1912), tea heiress, social reformer and historian of Christian symbols.

[33] Sophia Engastromenos, at 17 married to 47 year old Heinrich Schliemann (1822-1890). In August of 1895 Kraus met the beautiful Greek widow and her children Andromache and Agamemnon in Baden-Baden. [*Tgb.*, p.626] Frau Schliemann had continued to dig at Troy after the death of her husband.

[34] Jane Dieulafoy, (1851-1916), widow of archaeologist Marcel Auguste Dieulafoy. She continued excavations at Susa-Persia after his death and in 1886 was awarded the cross of the Legion of Honour.

[35] Elizabeth van Dedem, Dutch noblewoman, married 1871 W.E.H. Lecky,(1838-1903) British historian. She contributed articles on historical and political subjects to various reviews.

[36] Sybilla Schaaffhausen (1797-1857), patroness of art and antiquities, at 19 married 35 year old Louis Mertens, her father's successor at the family bank. Until 1849 wealth enabled her to be the "Countess of the Rhine" with a salon at Bonn which was renowned for its habitués, including Anna Jameson.

[37] Nadeja Schakowskoy, wealthy Russian princess, wife of archaeologist Wolfgang Helbig (1839-1915). From 1887 they made the Villa Lante on the Janiculum into a salon of culture, frequented by literary and musical notables. Kraus wrote of his visit to the Villa Lante in February of 1896, of the "estimable inhabitants," especially Frau Helbig, "so distinguished, and wonderful in her acts of benevolence." [*Tgb.*, p. 655]

stressed that what was proved by all these women — who had participated in historical and archaeological research, and had been successful, and had found in this study invigoration, diversion, consolation, as well as in part protection against financial need — defended them forever "against the charge that their sex had entered into an unapproachable area, and should serve others as motive and stimulus to imitate their energy and power."[38]

After Adolfo Venturi located in Rome, he found himself a frequent guest, at the Palazzo Lovatelli, at what he termed the 'kaleidoscope' of historians, artists, novelists, poets, noble ladies, each of vital intelligence, (the kind he said who would awaken a husband in the night to read him a chapter of platonic philosophy.) After the day's work, attired in *'le smoking'*[39], he continues,

> We entered the salon of Donna Ersilia Lovatelli, frequented by a great number of writers, archaeologists, scientists, living in Rome regularly or just in passing. Often I have been table companion in the house of Donna Ersilia, with Carducci,[40] pleased with the good wine of Argiano, much too often splashed into his glass. ... We often left together and supported by fatigue started for home at the Passeggiata di Ripetta like a man of iron, but by the unfortunate generosity we were bent immediately like a twig of tin.[41]

"In the salon of Donna Ersilia one encountered Gregorovius,[42] who had already been my companion in research at Modena, and Mommsen,[43] who,

---

[38] Among the eight, four widows, an heiress, a spinster, an estranged wife, a rich wife and three notable salons.

[39] Dinner dress, tuxedo.

[40] Giosue Carducci, poet, politician. In February 1896 Kraus recorded, "I ate at Donna Ersilia's with Carducci…a congenial, very worldly type." [*Tgb.*, p.648.]

[41] Venturi, *op.cit.*, p. 75.

[42] Ferdinand Gregorovius (1821-1891), author of the great standard work, *The History of Rome in the Middle Ages*.

[43] Theodor Mommsen (1817-1903), author (1855). of *History of Rome*, 3 vols. Nobel Prize for Literature 1902.

always caustic, talked of the history of Rome in medieval times." Mommsen, Venturi continued, once remarked to Gregorovius, "What a good book could be written about that!" 'About what?' naively answered Gregorovius. "The history", Mommsen responded sarcastically, "of Rome in the Middle Ages."[44]

Kraus, who came to dislike Mommsen intensely,[45] recalled Mommsen's presence at Donna Ersilia's salon with a version of the same story.

> I saw Mommsen another time on Tuesday at Countess Lovatelli's. And here again I remarked the unpopularity of the great scholar. An Italian[46] told me how Mommsen one time said to Gregorovius in the salon of the Palazzo Lovatelli, "Don't you know that that would be a good task, which you would be able to do straight off, a history of the city of Rome in the Middle Ages?" To a French lady, by whom he sat at dinner, and after he had not spoken a word to her the entire evening and after she had invited him to come to the coffee, he said, "Yes, that's the only thing which the French know how to make well." When he mistreated the Countess' cat and she protested on its behalf, Mommsen replied, "If it had only been one of your children, you wouldn't have said a thing."[47]

A further view of salon life by the British diplomat Sir James Rennell Rodd gives an interesting view of Monsigneur Duchesne, a frequent guest in the salons.

> At such gatherings you would be almost sure to find the illustrious historian of the Church, Monsigneur Duchesne. Director of the French Institute in Rome, which occupied the upper floor of the Farnese palace. In a long and wide experience I have seldom met a more entertaining conversationalist than that

---

[44] Venturi, *op.cit.* p. 73.

[45] "Mommsen... [was] at pains to show me a pronounced discourtesy." *Tgb.*, p.662, March 29, 1896.

[46] Certainly it was Venturi.

[47] *Tgb.*, p.448, March 31, 1882, Rome.

eminent ecclesiastic whose caustic humour might in any case have been an impediment to his promotion to the highest dignities, even if he had not sacrificed professional ambition to his devotion to historic truth.

His softer affections were bestowed upon a family of cats. One of these, a special favorite, fell from a lofty window of the Farnese palace and was killed. Duchesne was greatly upset, and observed to a friend who expressed his sympathy, "It has been a great blow to me. I could better have spared five cardinals."

When certain conclusions in his ecclesiastical history were discountenanced by the Vatican... (Duchesne submitted). It was reported at the time that the question of transferring his activities from Rome to Egypt was under consideration. When asked whether there was any foundation for the rumour, Duchesne replied that he thought it might prove to be correct, it would, after all, be quite in traditional order. "*Après le Massacre des innocents la fuite en Egypte.*"[48]

Kraus found the companionship of Ersilia Lovatelli extremely sympathetic.[49] In Rome in March of 1896 he recorded, "I eat quite regularly with Countess Lovatelli, two times per week."[50] He dedicated Volume II of his Essays to her, and in his will he left her "the small framed picture of Dante which is on my writing desk."[51] It was the sole bequest to be sent outside Germany.[52]

But there was a much larger location in Rome for the meeting of broadminded German and Italian society and here also Professor Kraus was a welcome visitor. It was the Palazzo Caffarelli, the Embassy of the German Empire.

---

[48] *Social and Diplomatic Memories, 1902-1919*, by the Rt. Hon. Sir James Rennell Rodd, (London 1925) Chapter I. "Rome 1902," [no page, see www.lib.byu.edu]

[49] "Poor and noble Ersilia. Thou hast looked deep into my soul and divined a portion of my suffering." *Tgb.*, p.449. April 16, 1882.

[50] *Tgb.*, p.662.

[51] Schiel, *Spannungsfeld*, pp. 80-85.

[52] In contrast, there is no mention of Augusta von Eichthal in Kraus' will.

Palazzo Caffarelli, the Embassy of the German Reich

Today a reconstructed Palazzo Caffarelli belongs to the Comune of Rome and serves as an art museum. But its position bears witness to its role in the days of the German Empire and the Triple Alliance. Unlike much of golden Rome the Caffarelli has a darker impression of faded yellowish brick banded with deep green accents. It is accessible from the southern rim of the Capitoline hill by narrow roadways that follow the curve of the promontory. Two levels of balconies command extensive views, one to the southeast, across the oldest remains of Rome, to the Forum itself; the other, facing the southern sun toward the Teatro Marcello. The view from the balconies of the Caffarelli is commanding. The 'presence' of the structure is imperious.

Here in Rome before the Great War, in the days of the Triple Alliance, and in the time of the baroness and the professor, there assembled the Germans and their friends.

Dr. Sigmund Münz, the Roman correspondent for the Viennese *Neue Freie Presse*, described the Caffarelli in those days when it was the palace of the German Ambassador to the Kingdom of Italy, Bernhard von Bülow, with his wife Maria, the step-daughter of Marco Minghetti.

> Palazzo Caffarelli was a place of meeting for the most important Germans who came to the Eternal City, just as for the cream of Italian society. And when we say cream, that means not only the fashionable circles, Cavaliere, countesses, princesses and people of the court, who were to be seen in every embassy, but besides the social, also the top political, artistic, literary and scientific figures.
>
> The family connection of Frau von Bülow carried with it that primarily the affiliates of the old Right, men like Visconti-Venosta, Ruggero Bonghi, di Rudini, the Duke Caetani of Sermoneta, or earlier likeminded of this party, the habitués of the salon of Donna Laura Minghetti, all of them paid calls to

the Palazzo Caffarelli. Yet the Ambassador was independent enough from personal inclination or familial restraints not to fail to cultivate exchange with men of all political colors and directions. He had arrived in Rome at the very moment that Francesco Crispi was Minister-President, and so he held regular exchanges of opinion with the energetic Sicilian, whose element in all things was more the deed than the word — oftentimes more the unfortunate deed than the fortunate word. And thus matters set him together with Baron Blanc, under Crispi Minister of External Affairs, a frizzled bizarre diplomat of hot blood, whose lack of political wisdom not infrequently drew smiles from the Germans who listened to him.

The symposia were seasoned with deeply thoughtful conversation. Here German intellect came into contact with the Italian. At Easter, when Germany sent its flood of travelers, enthusiastic for Italy, one saw the best of them at the Embassy. The violin-king Joachim fiddled with Hungarian verve, the young Siegfried Wagner showed himself to be the hopeful son of his Nibelungen-strong father; the old Delbrück,[53] who had sat in the Imperial Council with Prince Bismarck and Bülow the Elder, refreshed remembrances about the heroic age of German political craft; Theodor Mommsen, the monarch in the empire of ancient Rome, from his delicate body proclaimed his great spirit, and with his thin voice gave forth his conclusions, dethroning gods and idols.

Franz Xaver Kraus, the Freiburg theologian, the Dante expert, who had written a monumental work about the great Florentine, held forth over literature and the Vatican and did not spare the clerical demi-gods."[54]

---

[53] Martin Friedrich Rudolf Delbrück (1817-1903) Bismarck's right hand, reorganized the *Zollverein*.

[54] Sigmund Münz, *Römische Reminiscenzen* (Berlin, 1900), pp. 87-89, quoted in Weber, *Liberaler Katholizismus*, pp. 29-30.

Whites and Blacks, Germans and French

While Kraus felt himself somewhat isolated in Germany from those who shared his outlook, it was far different in Italy. In upper Italy, where the memory of the philosopher Antonio Rosmini was still strong among those who hoped for reform within the church, he found in Milan, Rovereto, and Florence many fellow liberals who longed for the day when Catholics could participate in the political life of the new nation of Italy. In Rome, in the salons and gatherings, he could share his convictions with intellectuals and leaders who wished to end the stalemate between the Church and the Kingdom and to reconcile the Church with science and learning.

By the last decade of the nineteenth century the old papal families were divided into two factions, those who had remained completely loyal to the papal claim to the Temporal Power, and those who had elected to be conciliatory and cooperative with the united Kingdom of Italy. The former still held the Pope to be the 'pope king', the *papa re*, and therefore regarded the House of Savoy as usurpers. The latter grouping had decided that Italy seemed to be an accomplished fact and had entered into public life, taking positions of responsibility and seeking to enjoy the advantages which accrue to those who seize new opportunities.

The families who were loyal to the papacy were dubbed the "Blacks." They had their own club, the '*Scacchi*' [chess squares], and their own salons, the Aldobrandini, the Borghese, the Altieri, among others.[55] They never attended any functions of the Kingdom and assisted in the Vatican boycott of participation in the political affairs of Italy which forbid Catholics either to vote or to be elected. Since Italy had elections anyhow, this refusal had the effect of denying to conservative political movements of the right the numerical support of many Catholics, reduced the total of the electorate substantially, and thus favored the left. Blacks, like the Vatican, hoped that

---

[55] Weber, *Quellen und Studien*, p.458.

Italy would not survive its fragile youth, and waited for some collapse in which the papacy would be restored to Temporal Power, perhaps as the leading republic in a collection of republics. Meanwhile the Blacks kept their curtains drawn.

The families who had chosen to go along with the new Italy were called the "Whites." They were aware of the new opportunities afforded by the fact that Rome, formerly only the putrescent seat of an inefficient papacy, was now the capitol of a developing nation.[56] No doubt they had memories from earlier days. Napoleon had done away with the feudal system in the States of the Church, and when by 1815 Cardinal Consalvi had seen in France the system of prefecture administration, he set about to erect it in Rome and elsewhere. In so doing he put all the administrative posts and the legal system into the hands of clerics and made the clerical state necessary for entry into a 'career.' Not only was this detrimental to the spiritual values of the clergy but it turned public office over to those who had little experience of civil life. And the result was that clerics largely pushed the old Roman families out of jobs and influence.[57] After 1870 some leading Roman families had opted for the chance to take advantage of the new regime, among them the Caetani, the Buoncampagni, Ruspoli, Cesarini, Odescalchi, and the Lovatelli.[58] The overt activity which accompanied cooperation with the new government was the purchase of land.

As the capitol of the new Kingdom of Italy moved to Rome from its temporary site in Florence, it quickly was seen that the population of Rome would have a great increase. In 1870 the inhabitants were estimated at 220,000, but by 1910 the number is thought to have exceeded 600,000. In the land rush which had taken place there were two actions open to developers. One could buy land in the empty quarters or on the exterior of the ancient city and put in new streets and buildings, or one could acquire

---

[56] In his novel *Rome* (1896), Emile Zola called them "the Romans of the New Italy."

[57] F.X Kraus, *Cavour* (Mainz, 1902), pp.16-17.

[58] D.A. Binchy, *Church and State in Fascist Italy* (Oxford, 1941), p. 10.

lands and houses from the dispossessed property of the church for which the government of Italy had found no need. By 1874 many former Blacks, among them the Lovatelli, had done the latter. Since Pius IX had pronounced excommunication on those who bought former church property, these 'graying' Blacks executed deed covenants in which they made the promise to sell the land back if the pontifical government were ever restored.[59] It was an action which surely heightened their patriotic devotion to Italy.

The social distinctions between Whites and Blacks continued to be sharp throughout the pontificate of Leo XIII.[60] As Italy, by membership in the Triple Alliance with Germany and Austria, sought guarantees for its internal stability and its program of expansion in Africa, with all that that required for defence against France, 'the eldest daughter of the Church,' the Whites naturally developed a pro-German flavor.

The French-German polarity in Rome sometimes had great ferocity, exacerbated by what often seemed to the Germans an unreasonable French sensitivity. In 1886 Pope Leo XIII hoped to enhance the prestige of the papacy by inviting the Emperor of China to send an ambassador to Rome. This meant that in exchange the Vatican would establish an embassy, a nuntiature, in Peking. But such a proposal drew a great outcry from Paris, where Republican France, while engaged in an internal culture war with the Catholic Church in France, still claimed the old privilege of the kings of France to protect the Catholic Church in the East! The Parisian press began a battle against the prelates whose names had been mentioned in connection with the project, Antonio Agliardi, the designated nuncio, and Luigi Galimberti, the Secretary for Extraordinary Affairs, both of whom were known to be friendly to Germany. Taking aim at France, Galimberti publicly deplored the systematic mingling of colonialism with Catholic missions, while Leo secretly obtained German approval for the potential establishment. It was a battle between France and Germany for the greater prestige, and had not

---

[59] F. M. Underwood, *United Italy* (London, 1912), p. 252, and 248.

[60] See Vittoria Colonna, Duchess of Sermoneta, *Things Past* (New York, 1929). Born a Colonna (Black), she married Leone Caetani (White) in 1901.

much to do with China. When the French threatened to break off diplomatic relations with the Vatican, calling the matter a diminution of prestige and posing the question as 'Are they friends or enemies of France?' Leo XIII canceled the project.[61]

The uncertain balances of the Triple Alliance form a background to our letters. An exchange between Baron Blanc and the Chancellor of Germany, Chlodwig von Hohenlohe, illustrated the dependence of Italy and the Whites on German opposition to the program of the French and the Blacks.

Blanc, Foreign Minister of Italy from 1893 to 1896, sometimes found that his attempts to extract more from the French-German polarity were met with stubborn resistance in Berlin. In July of 1895, the unskilled baron implored German aid in the question of the Veto and was quickly snubbed by Chancellor Hohenlohe. In his importunity the baron threatened a bit too much. Pleading that France was doing everything possible to get Italy to abandon the Triple Alliance, that Abyssinia was proving no success, that France was creating trouble for Italy at home and abroad, that Italy might break apart, Blanc asserted that Italy might have to leave the *Triplice* unless the new nation received more aid. "The 'groupe Franco-Russe,'" he moaned, "exercise their armies, ours does not. They agitate and consolidate themselves, we do not." Fearing that a French veto in a conclave would weaken Italy, he blustered that he must have more help in Berlin.[62]

Instead of help, Chancellor Hohenlohe bluntly detailed all the troubles Italy would have if it undertook to leave the Triple Alliance. "What would Italy expect in church-political matters," replied the old prince, "from entry into the Dual Alliance of France and Russia? The loss of Rome and the end of the monarchy, when the Pope and France combine! If Italy abandons partnership with Germany and Austria the German government will concede to its

---

[61] Weber, *Quellen und Studien*, pp.154-155.

[62] Christoph Weber,"Italien, Deutschland und das Konklave von 1903," *Quellen und Forschungen aus italienischen Archiven und Bibliotheken*, 57/1977, p. 217.

Catholics their dearest desires — in the Roman Question neutrality, or perhaps positive participation in the restoration of the Temporal Power. And it might be that the Austrian border would be readjusted to the detriment of Italy."[63]

Origins of the Eichthals

Baroness Augusta Henriette von Eichthal, born in Trieste in 1835, was the great-granddaughter of Aron Elias Seligmann (1747-1824), the Court Jew of Maximilian I, King of Bavaria. In 1799, Seligmann, who came from a long line of *Hoffaktoren* and court bankers, moved part of his business to Munich from the family seat in Leimen at the moment when Count Montgelas began his work as the architect of modern Bavaria. As the enlightened count proceeded to reform Bavarian administration by, among other things, separating the rather feeble financial affairs of the Wittelsbach dynasty from those of the State, the talents and resources of the experienced banker to the royal Bavarian court became more and more useful. Taking advantage of the interlude of "Napoleonic liberalization" and the influence of his substantial loans to the court, Seligmann obtained complete civil rights for himself and for all his children. The latter is significant in a day when a Jew could perhaps purchase citizenship for himself that could be passed on to one descendant, but not for the rest of his progeny.[64]

---

[63] *Idem*, p. 222.

[64] "Only a limited number of Jews were allowed to be citizens. When a Jew died, another Jew would be given his place, but no new places were created. If a Jewish citizen had four sons...only the eldest had a future in a Bavarian town. He alone inherited his father's citizenship. As for the others, they could apply to the courts for citizenship, but the applications were costly, and permission was rarely granted." Ruth Gay, *Jews in America* (New York 1965), p. 43. For a detailed description of the issue see James F. Harris, *The People Speak! Anti-Semitism and Emancipation in Nineteenth-Century Bavaria* (Ann Arbor, 1994.)

In 1814 the court banker Seligmann was elevated, as an unbaptized Jew, to the Bavarian nobility, as were each of his ten children. Designated "*Freiherr* (Baron) *von Eichthal*" after their estate "*Eichthal*" (Valley of Oaks) in Leimen, near Heidelberg, the new dynasty of Jewish nobles adopted an easily interpreted coat of arms which featured a pair of six-pointed stars of gold rising in a blue valley (Thal) formed by two silver mountains.[65]

In time the enormously wealthy banker to the crown established an impressive palace in Munich at Residenzstrasse, 26, near the *Residenz* and the *Feldherrnhalle*. Contrary to prevailing usage Aron Elias waited five years to follow several of his sons in Catholic baptism, taking the additional name of Leonhard. His wife, Henriette, remained in her Jewish tradition and they are buried separately, he in the Southern Cemetery of Munich at Thalkirchner Strasse and she in a Jewish cemetery at Wiesloch near Mannheim.[66]

With fortunate timing, Leonhard Aron Elias, first Baron Eichthal, passed from this life in early 1824, well before the death in 1825 of his king, Maximilian I, thus avoiding the accession of Count Montgelas' opponent, the new King Ludwig I. And though his son Simon continued banking activity in Munich, other members of the family dispersed into the new wave of merchant banking and financial activity made possible, especially in France, by the breakup of the Rothschild monopoly of international credit. Adolphe d'Eichthal was one of the founders of the Credit Mobilier in 1852, accounted among its backers as a "Bavarian Jew."[67]

After 1815 the need for international credit from the Jewish banking houses turned from war to industry. Auguste von Eichthal (1795-1875) was the

---

[65] "Eichthal Coat of Arms, Bavaria 1814: Azure, two rocks argent from the base of the shield, accompanied in chief by two stars or. Lambrequins: argent and azure." Image and citation in "Coat of Arms," *Jewish Encyclopedia.com*.

[66] "Traces of the Jewish-Christian Banker Family Seligmann-Eichthal at Munich's Old Southern Cemetery," http:/home.t-online.de/home/RIJONUE/eichthae.htm, Article and Photographs by Susanne Rieger, October 30, 2001.

[67] "Banking," *Jewish Encyclopedia.com*

grandson of Leonhard Aron Elias, and the firstborn of Leonhard's oldest son Arnold (1772-1838). Auguste followed a career in industrial credit and development. And so it was in 1835, in the same year and place as the genesis of the great Jewish insurance firm, *Assicurazioni Generali*, that his daughter, Augusta Henriette von Eichthal, was born in Trieste, the natural outlet and commercial hub of the Austrian empire.

Auguste von Eichthal returned to Munich as a developer of the new gas light industry, a utility made possible in much of Europe (Hamburg in 1825, Berlin 1826, Vienna 1845) by the Imperial Continental Gas Association, directed from London by Sir Moses Montefiore and Sir Julian Goldsmid. In 1847 Auguste gained the concession to build and develop the gas plant in Augsburg.[68] The financial backing of the gas light industry was so clear that the new service was known on the Continent as "English Lighting."[69]

Baroness Eichthal seems to have had an unhappy youth, or so she told the playwright Richard Voss.[70] Her mother, Elise Krings, who came from Heidelberg near the family estate at Leimen, was the daughter of a very minor university officer, a "beadle," and died in 1860 when the baroness was twenty-five. From the letters to Kraus we learn that she was very attached to her brother Emil and traveled with him. That she was on poor terms with his wife is clear. At the time of Emil's death a sister, Luise, of whom we know little,

---

[68] Heinrich Schnee, "Die Familie Seligmann-Eichthal als Hoffinanziers an den süddeutschen Fürstenhäusern," in: *Zeitschrift für bayerische Landesgeschichte*, Vol. 25 (1962), pp. 163-201.

[69] See the many references on the internet to "Imperial Continental Gas Association" and the article in the *Jewish Encyclopedia.com* "Sir Moses Montefiore."

[70] "Her cleverness was wisdom and her sharpness the result of most bitter experiences, which she had had in earlier youth." Richard Voss, *Aus einem phantastischen Leben* (Stuttgart, 1928), p. 237.

Augusta von Eichthal (1835-1932), kneeling, with the painter Wilhelmine von Stein (born 1823). Between them a portraitof their dear friend Franz Liszt. Roman photo taken about 1870. Bayerisches Hauptstaatsarchiv. Munich, Eichthal Papers.

appears in the death notice published in the Munich paper.[71] None of the siblings had any children.

In 1876 she made an excursion by boat up and down the Nile, fortunately for us in the company of the American writer, Charles Warren Stoddard, whom she had met in London in 1874. In 1881 he dedicated to her his book describing the trip, "*Mashallah!,*"[72] later writing to her as "Lovable but exceeding cross and very spoiled person!"

Augusta's brother Emil married a Countess Bronska, and starting with the older cousins, many of the third and fourth generation of Eichthals joined in marriage with a variety of titled families.[73] This web of relations provided the baroness with a great selection of friends and places to visit and contributed to the panache she enjoyed in Rome and Munich. Her "connections" were widespread in the family and in the noble houses of South Germany.

It is not difficult to guess at the nature of the inheritance which was her means of support. Her brother operated a vineyard and winery in France and at his death there was an estate to which the baroness felt herself partially entitled. To negotiate matters pertaining to the contest with the widow she had to go to London, probably with regard to investments tied up for the siblings in international credits. While her income was not lavish — she was careful with vacation expenses — she seems to have been able to travel as she wished. She was in a position to lend or grant money to her protégés and friends, as we

---

[71] More details in article "Eichthal, Augusta Henriette Baronesse v." by Claus Arnold, *Biographisch-Bibliographisches Kirchenlexikon*, Band XX (2002), Spalten 453-457, found at www.bautz.de/bbkl.

[72] Charles Warren Stoddard, *Mashallah! A Flight into Egypt* (New York, 1881)

[73] Heinrich Schnee reckons that the prosperous Eichthals were related to the counts Oettingen, Armannsperg, Berchem, Bossi-Fedrigotti, Khuen-Belani, Leyden; and to the baronial families Weichs, Seckendorf, Godin, Moreau, Gumppenberg, and Freytag-Loringhoven, as well as to the distinguished families Brentano, Huesslin and Forster. Schnee, *op. cit.*, p. 198.

learn from the matter of a loan to Charles Warren Stoddard[74] and from her correspondence with Joseph Sauer.[75] At least until the war of 1914 she was able to live in comfort in Rome and to entertain in a suitable style.

She possessed a command of the English language which she put to use in her relationships with the Americans. If her pronunciation was as good as her spelling, she was clearly communicative in English. She was not fond of the English themselves, as we learn from her tiff with Kraus during the Boer War, her resentments of the English "snob" with whom she has to deal in settling her brother's affairs, and her mockery of the antics of the Gibsons. The World War naturally intensified her feeling about the English, and lowered her love for the Americans too, one suspects. She was a German patriot without reserve.[76]

The Jewish background to the prominent and possibly Sephardic family of Eichthals, could have scarcely escaped anyone in southern German society. In 1803, Augusta's grandfather Arnold had taken a prominent role in pleading for Jewish rights in Baden, asserting that Germany had become a new fatherland for the Jews. Throughout the early 1820's her great-uncle David von Eichthal, by refusing to pay the customary assessment for membership in the Jewish community, made his Jewishness a matter of public discussion. Baron David did not convert until 1831, after the death of his Jewish mother and the death of his Jewish in-laws.[77]

---

[74] See Appendix "The Baroness and the Genteel Pagan."

[75] Claus Arnold, *Katholizismus als Kulturmacht. Der Freiburger Theologe Joseph Sauer (1872-1949 und das Erbe des Franz Xaver Kraus*, (Paderborn, 1999), p. 273.

[76] Although outside our time frame, her views during World War I are made clear in Arnold, *Katholizismus als Kulturmacht.*

[77] Details in Schnee, *op.cit.*

Augusta von Eichthal's Jewish origins — she was certainly "half-Jewish"[78] — would have brought her great grief when the anti-Jewish laws of the National Socialist government caught up alike those in Germany who were the descendants of Court Jews or of cattle dealers, and for whom neither baptism nor Christian faith nor patriotism could provide exception from the program to destroy the race. It was therefore her good fortune that she died in Munich, approximately 97 years old, in April of 1932.

The Nature of the Circle of Baroness Eichthal

In her life and activities in Rome Augusta von Eichthal exercised her independent character. An aristocratic spinster of Jewish race and of independent means, nurtured in Bavarian particularism, she drew notice in Rome at the time of the first Vatican Council as an advocate for that 'Liberal' group which opposed the definition of infallibility and an increasing centralization of the Church. She served as a correspondent for the distinguished dissenter, Ignatius Döllinger. A complete description of her associations then and later can be found in the excellent article by Claus Arnold, "Frauen und Modernisten, Ein Kreis um Augusta von Eichthal," published as a chapter in the 1998 work edited by Hubert Wolf, *Antimodernismus und Modernismus in der katholischen Kirche*.

By the close of the century, her salon, her circle of invited guests, was ranked by many among the most important vehicles in Rome for the promotion and circulation of liberal ideas. Richard Voss has described the matter in detail:

> A salon, which deserved this name in the best sense of the word, was the salon of the Baroness Eichthal in Via Ripetta. She was an unusual woman: acerbic almost to visible hardness, with astonishing knowledge, acquainted and friendly with the most important people of all leading countries, most of all maintaining connection to the aristocratic and intellectual world. Whoever came to know

---

[78] Grandfather Arnold's wife was a cousin, Henriette Maria Seligmann.

her in her true essence, whomever she allowed to get to know her, had not only to think highly of this frequently misunderstood lady but to marvel at her as well!

Her cleverness was wisdom and her sharpness the result of most bitter experiences which she had had in earlier youth. It was these experiences which enabled her to function with deep mistrust against all falsehood, against every pretense. She was a friend to me in the finest meaning of the word and I alone know how much I thank her: she has made my life richer and given me the strength to carry on the battle of life.

In the salon of this remarkable lady, there gathered at that time everyone of intellectual significance that Rome contained. The high-ranking Catholic clergy visited her home; and the diplomats of all leading countries were in regular exchange with her. Observing the guests with a sharp discernment, she received them all, in order later to make her selection, so that to her next session only those would be invited whom she believed worth acknowledging.[79]

The influence of her salon with its circle of liberal guests is also attested by Lorenzo Bedeschi. Deriving his information from the correspondence of Paul Sabatier, whose publication in 1896 of the Italian version of the *Life of St. Francis* served to coalesce those who opposed what they viewed as the stultifying intransigence of the Vatican authorities, Bedeschi suggests a series of salon vehicles for liberal propaganda. He includes that of "Baronessa D'Eichthal" among a list of renowned Roman salons drawn from many national and religious backgrounds.[80] The list provides a strong sense of forward-thinking feminists who struggled for liberality and progress in the

---

[79] Richard Voss, *Aus einem phantastischen Leben* (Stuttgart, 1928), pp. 237-238.

[80] "Bastarebbe citare a Roma, desumendo i nomi della correspondenza sabateriana, i salotti della contessa Pasolini,… della russa Helbig,… dell inglese Maud Howe Elliot,… della tedesca Alice de Schlegel, della contessa Caetani Lovatelli, dell'inglese Edith Munro, delle signorine Mac Crackett, della baronessa D'Eichthal, dell'americana Margaret Chamber, dell'israelita Alice Franchetti, della contessa Spalletti dei conti Morichelli d'Altemps, di Dora Melegari, ecc." Lorenzo Bedeschi, *Modernismo a Milano* (Milan, 1974), footnote 25bis, p. 13.

social and civil culture of Italy, for progressive schools, and for the foundation of "Il Consiglio Nazionale delle Dame Italiane" in 1903. A separate treatise on feminism in Italy could be composed from an analysis of the list. Certainly a proto-feminist streak can be observed in her letters to Kraus, the indignation at the treatment of Soeur Marie, the exhilaration with which she receives the views of Bishop Spalding on the education of women. And Kraus also had his feminist sympathies.

By the time the exchange of letters with Franz Xaver Kraus begins in 1895 her salon must be seen as the gathering place of an intellectual liberal minority. Her associates were principally composed of the discontented who moved in an atmosphere of resistance to the dominant church-political trend of the day. Many of them had been of the party of the minority in 1870, advocates of the attempt to resist the doctrine of Infallibility on historic and other grounds – and that cause was lost.[81] In the ensuing concerns for some national (German, Italian, American) liberty within the Church they resisted "Vaticanism," with its dependence on French democracy, its intransigence, its concentration of power in the Roman center.[82]

In this circle of friends we find the omnipresent Abbé Duchesne, witty and irreverent, frankly an opportunist, whose upward climb had been slowed by his learned sarcasm. Like Kraus, his career had been adumbrated by conservative resistance to his historical findings.

The brother cardinals, Serafino and Vincenzo Vannutelli, ancient Romans, were well connected in the Italian civil service,[83] and secure in their visible

---

[81] Arnold, "Frauen und 'Modernisten,'" p. 243.

[82] Kraus said the Vatican "suffered from cerebral congestion." Cardinal Hohenlohe quipped that every time Leo XIII seemed weaker the Curia " broke out in an epidemic of infallibility."

[83] Rennell Rodd, *op. cit.* Ch. II.

strength, but they had had to resist attempts to restrict their careers.[84] Openly advocating conciliation with Italy, they were essentially curial diplomats whose clerical state rested lightly upon them and was reputedly not absolute.[85] Augusta herself was an irreverent idealist, sceptical of superstition and wishing fervently for a less political exercise of Catholicism. While she shared her "utopian" hopes for the Church with the Schleinitz sisters, nevertheless she was realistic enough to urge Kraus to bend to get what he wanted, citing the supposed dissimulation of the South American bishops as a way of survival.

In this group there appeared the leonine form of Baron von Hügel, blessed with ultramontane faith and a calling to study and reflection. He hinted at embodiment of Döllinger's call for the scholarly stereoptical vision which sees with both the speculative eye of theology and the eye of history and philosophy.[86]

Ersilia Lovatelli, hostess, archaeologist, imperious Caetani, easily bored and cold toward lesser mortals, was nevertheless drawn to the learning and sociability of the indomitable Kraus. Eichthal, aware of the contessa's occasional lack of empathy, seemed a bit jealous of the woman Kraus so admired.

---

[84] Details in Weber, *Quellen und Studien*, pp.416-427.

[85] *Tgb.*, pp. 646, 657-8. Cardinal Hohenlohe told Kraus that Vincenzo had received a thrashing from a jealous husband after a "gallant adventure in the Via Sistina." Kraus thought the brothers were of average ability but somewhat *frivole*. The muck-raking ex-Franciscan, J. McCabe, maliciously repeated that in 1904 "one of the chief American consuls in Italy" pointed out to him the supposed Roman home of the mistress and children of Serafino Vannutelli, "the leader of the 'German faction' at the election of Pius X." Joseph McCabe, *The Totalitarian Church of Rome*, (Girard, Kansas, 1944) (www.textfiles.com/conspiracy/mccabe)

[86] "The scholastic divines...could not construct a system corresponding to the harmony and wealth of revealed truth, and without the elements of biblical criticism and dogmatic history they possessed only one of the eyes of theology." Summary of Döllinger's address to the Munich Conference of Catholic Scholars in 1863, John Acton, "The Munich Congress," *Home and Foreign Review*, No.7 January 1864, pp.209-244..

The emblematic personage in this grouping was Cardinal Gustav Hohenlohe, a German prince whose Roman career was marked by high position and low achievement. Identified with the anti-Infallibilists in 1870, he had gained some influence by voting for Leo XIII. But even in 1878 he was wrapping himself in the air of persecution and danger with which he dramatized his life.[87] His career in the church reached a peak in 1878 and 1879 when he was first appointed Archpriest of S. Maria Maggiore and then Cardinal Bishop of Albano. In 1883 he relinquished the bishopric due to conflict with the Curia. His anecdotes of church gossip and a constant fear of poisoning were recurring themes. Richard Voss remembered him, as "not the owner but well indeed the occupant of the Villa d'Este in Tivoli" who invited Voss in 1883 to use the vacant upper – the "Liszt" – apartment in the Villa.

> He [the Cardinal] was a fine ironic spirit, of truly princely bearing. Something of him alienated me ever anew, his all too frank remarks about Vatican circumstances, indeed about the person of the Holy Father himself. He hated the Jesuits and was hated by them in return. He frequently spoke to me about that: "They will yet have me murdered.' And further, 'I know I shall someday fall victim to their hatred."
>
> So it must have happened. From sources, about which I must remain silent, I was assured that the death of the cardinal had not been a natural one, but at the instigation of his enemies was accomplished through a functionary who had been showered with kindness by him.[88]

For this group of disciples and friends the pious and unsullied Kraus knelt in their Gethsemane. His learning and wit gave focus to their company. His moral life was irreproachable. Though after ordination he had fallen in love and had struggled to be faithful to his priesthood, still his sincere affection for women and his devotion to his calling was easily observed. His constant illness, with physical agony, made him the object of true sympathy. His strength of purpose drew them together.

---

[87] He was the only cardinal at the conclave of 1878 to have his meals prepared at his residence and sent in.

[88] Voss, *op.cit*, p. 150.

His determined opposition to the "Vaticanism" that followed on from the events of 1870 made him the opponent of any political use of religion which subordinated the weal of his German church to an ultramontane obsession with a return of the Temporal Power. Such subordination, in his experience, had resulted in the preferment of docile party-followers to an intelligent and independent minded clergy who were required to maintain faith in the souls of the educated Catholic citizens of Germany. Kraus was convinced that the well-being of the Catholic Church within a given nation-state would be advanced by letting it develop in harmony with the nature and progress of that state.

In advocating understanding for the Catholic Church in Germany and freedom from ultramontane manipulation Kraus took the opportunity to work together with the American prelates who labored in Rome and in America for similar treatment of the American Catholic Church.

In the correspondence which follows we learn some more details of that combination, as Kraus produces his "Spectator Letters," particularly the "American" ones, and as the combination of liberals loses its potential leader John Ireland and experiences a depressing blow in the condemnation of "Americanism." While both Kraus and Eichthal come to admire the talented Bishop of Peoria, John L. Spalding, he plays no permanent part in their program. The death of her brother and the consequent financial problems depress the baroness understandably. The final illness of Kraus brings the correspondence to an end.

1895 and 1896
Chapter 1

(To FXK at Eden Hotel, Rome)

November 14, 1895
175 Ripetta
Thursday evening

Honored Privy Councilor,
What a joyful surprise to know that you are here![89] I myself have just returned and have made no visits yet. In the morning I am obliged to be away from home. Should you desire however, tomorrow in the course of the afternoon, about four o'clock, to afford me the pleasure of your company, you will find your appreciative, admiring, welcoming

    A. v. Eichthal

---

[89] Kraus had written her a note that day, or left his card. His record of letters written to the Baroness (he kept continuous records of all the letters he wrote) begins with November 14, 1895.

January 29, 1896
175 Ripetta
Wednesday early

Because, my dear Privy Councilor, I am with sincere thanks returning your highly interesting Spectator Letters, I add several numbers of Castagnac's <u>Autorité</u>. You will find all sorts of things in them useful for your purposes. Fontecan (Bishop of Albi) is the prelate referred to, whose speech, <u>in extenso</u> as abbreviated, you will find underlined in blue. General Grandin will be delighted to meet you here, and he puts himself and his influence at your disposal in case you want any sort of expression of opinion to appear in any French newspaper you prefer. If you should be well enough to come Thursday evening after your supper, you would meet the General in a intimate tête-a-tête at the home of your most admiring

A. v. Eichthal

[P.S.] Saturday afternoon between four and five the General always visits me, but I think he chats better in the evening.[90]

---

[90] Kraus replied immediately.

October 12, 1896
Chateau de Saint-Selve
Par Castres-Gironde
Monday

Dear friend!
For a long time I have wanted to haunt you by letter in order to renew the pleasant hours of conversation of last winter in Rome and to feel your pulse as to your condition. How often my thoughts turn to you and put a thousand questions to your ever quick-witted knowledge, wanting news of your acutely interpreting spirit! That I have nevertheless spared you that in reality, surely secures me your warmest gratitude?

After your departure I sent you, by your wish, various newspapers. As I later learned to my surprise from the Schleinitz sisters, you not only made a fib out of my notice to them that you would visit, but that you were unknown in the Hotel Austria, (at Obermais-) Meran, from which the ladies would have snatched you away, and I saw that my dispatches had been purposeless.

Why did you give up on Meran? How did you take this wet summer? God willing we will see each other soon in Rome, because for your rheumatic constitution not only does the warm sunshine of the Roman sky answer better, but also so many of your warm friends wait for you!...a propos of these, have you found my translation of Donna Ersilia's[91] "Chiostro di S. Paolo" in the *Beilage* of the *Allgemeine Zeitung* of September 30th? Since I have been under way the whole summer, the *Allg.* has never come to sight and I consequently don't know anymore about the progress of the Spectator...does he proceed with his Letters or did he over the summer let his church-political pen rest?

---

[91] Countess Ersilia Lovatelli Caetani. Kallista Lovatelli, mentioned later in the letter, was her daughter.

What does he say about Leo XIII's click-clack snip-snap breakoff of all unionistical dreams of our idealistic Baron Hügel and his co-worker Lord Halifax? The Anglican bishops have answered firmly enough and the resentment appears great about the collection-bag dangled by the pope and Cardinal Vaughan as bait for the so rudely repulsed heretical divines.[92] This stingy pope, how so Italian he is in every fibre, and nothing more! To believe that with his collection-bag offer to the independent proud English he could work like a magnet! Good gracious! I can see from here Abbé Duchesne's sarcastic smile as a commentary thereon!

What has not happened since we saw one another. In Turkey, which sadly is no more <u>back there</u>, where the races fight one another, the blood flows unhindered in streams as ever, and an unimportant young man of absolutely no experience roams Europe as master of the fate of two worlds![93] Emperors and kings bow to him and listen intently to his words…Not content with that, an entire great nation which brags about its democratic principles and structures, stands on its head before this autocrat and honors him with the cleverest somersaults, only to gain from him a smile!

On the trip here from the sea-shore, at the end of September in Paris I saw the beginning already of this lunatic asylum which increased in the celebrations all through France, all schools were closed, and with my own eyes I saw all Bordeaux flagged, publicly and privately. That's the way it was <u>everywhere</u>!

---

[92] In addition to enlarging the Collegio Beda, founded by Pius IX in 1852 for converted Anglican clergy, Leo XIII had announced that any financial difficulties encountered by Anglican convert clergy would be assisted with papal funds.

[93] Czar Nicholas II had just succeeded to the throne and together with his consort, a princess of Hesse, was making a round of the courts of Europe.

I am here until the end of the month, visiting my brother,[94] whose wine harvest was very productive. If you, dear friend, should want to put away reasonably some <u>absolutely pure</u> Bordeaux with great taste for future satisfaction, my brother (who generally gives his production to the wholesaler) would be happy in that event to send you a *barrique* of his excellent '93. In a double barrel, delivered, you would have 225 Liters for 350 francs. His year '94, because lighter, ready to drink, on the other hand would only come to 250 francs for the same amount, that is, about 300 bottles of Bordeaux, or 225 Liters. My sister-in-law, born Countess Bronska,[95] caused my brother to take over this winery which belonged to her, and so he is a winegrower body and soul and won't leave the cellar until all is pressed and in barrels so that nothing may go wrong.

I only bring this up in order to give you friendly advice, because today unblemished Bordeaux is almost impossible to get in the trade, to say nothing of price.

On the Baden celebrations, because you are so close personally to the Grandduke, did you perhaps take any heartfelt part?

The Montenegrin wedding of the Italian crown prince was almost fairy-tale in its makeup. Kallista Lovatelli wrote to me, very amused, the solemnities in Rome seemed put together in completely Montenegrin fashion in their scanty simplicity![96]

I imagine you are still in Freiburg. Hurry over the Gotthard before snow falls and your poor arms and legs have to suffer again.

---

[94] Emil, Freiherr von Eichthal, (1827- 18 Sept 1900).

[95] Marie Christine, Gräfin Bronna-Bronska, married Emil von Eichthal in 1851, died at Sevre 1929.

[96] The future Victor Emmanuel III married Elena of Montenegro.

With a heartfelt grasp of your hand, your admiring,

A. v. Eichthal[97]

---

[97] On October 26, 1896 Kraus responded to this letter. He inquired after Denis O'Connell, "the former Rector of the American College," and observed that the deposition of the Rector of the "Washington University" [Bishop John Keane] was undoubtedly likewise a strike at Archbishop Ireland. Apologizing for his failure to pass through Meran, he explained: "I came back from the trip to Rome in April and May with such a heavy cold that I had to abandon the side trip to Meran and so I did not get to meet the Schleinitz ladies. It is hard for one like me, who has to be governed by such a miserable state of health, to make definite plans."

1897
Chapter 2

January 4, 1897
176 Ripetta
Rome

Dear friend,
Along with a number of French papers and news about Diana Vaughan,[1] I replied to your welcome letter immediately from the Gironde. Did you get it all? In the course of this, thank God, finally concluded year, such a quantity of letters went astray that a number of friends only write me when I indicate receipt.

Loaded with problems of travel, as soon as I had Genoa behind me, I got back to Rome in the course of December and found the same infamous weather here again that I had left in France. As a result I took cold, am just now normal with the return of the old Sun God to his long frightfully gloomy fields; however thereby just now once more in contact with the human race.

(Three Kings.)[2] There, you see how everything gets interrupted! To wish you, as the year begins, strengthening of your precious health, is first in my heart…in the meantime your blood-red catacomb sketch with the Latin wishes has brought me a welcome sign of your thoughts.

---

[1] Diana Vaughan was the imaginary woman in the Leo Taxil/ Dr. Hacks/ Bataille hoax that had fooled the gullible of Catholic Europe with a tale of a Masonic conspiracy with Satan.

[2] January 6.

Last evening at the table of the admirable von Hügels,[3] naturally the regret at your present distance was pronounced and sincere; so quickly people get accustomed to good things! The excellent Hügel regaled me with the news in the Parisian sheet *La Croix*, about the shameless mystification of the public which a certain "X" wanted to get away with in the so-called Memoirs of Diana Vaughan. After that this man revealed to Leon Taxil that it was all a trick, that he scribbled off the Galimathias to make fools of the world.

No sooner had I returned than I looked up someone (who knows exactly everything and everyone in the Vatican) for a report on the disappointment over Macario's Abyssinian mission.[4] I knew back in June the hopes which those in the Vatican had placed on the <u>doubtless</u> known success. <u>How far</u> Leo XIII was extended in his great delusions and really thought to succeed, I have yet to learn. Imagine this, that he set up the whole plan, in case, as was to be expected, Menelik demanded ransom, the pope would have appealed to the entire Italian people to make voluntary contributions; naturally the millions would have so poured in that as a consequence – after the papal liberation of the Italian prisoners – there would have been such clever threads spun out and it would so work on the charmed population, that the helpless royal government would have had to abandon Rome and retreat to Piemont. Rome would be – without a stroke of the sword – once more given into the hands of the pope and the rest of Italy become a federation-republic. <u>Isn't that too much</u>! [in Italian. Ed.]

For 14 days now the dethroned Rector of the Catholic University of Washington, Bishop Keane, abides here. The pope had invited him under

---

[3] Baron Friedrich von Hügel (1852-1926), English philosopher of religion. Kraus had just met him in Rome in December 1895.

[4] On March 1, 1896 an Italian expedition of 21,000 in Abyssinia was set upon at sunrise by an army of 100,000 natives armed with French and Russian rifles. Italian losses at the Battle of Adowa numbered 6000 dead and 4000 taken prisoner. Leo XIII proposed to obtain the release of the prisoners and sent Monsignor Macario, the Coptic Catholic Bishop of Egypt, to the Negus, Menelik, to negotiate. Menelik held out for direct arrangements with the Italian government and received a ransom of Lire 400,000.

<u>formal assurance</u> of a position, which should make good to him here for the one he lost out on there. What happened? Summoned to an audience, Leo XIII clasps him to his bosom with inarticulate noises and begins as follows: [in French. Ed.] "My well-beloved son, you know how much I cherish you – How much is the salary of your rectorate at Washington?" "3000 dollars" "Oh well, wouldn't it be possible for your successor to grant you 100 per month?" "With 3000 dollars a Rector at Washington doesn't have a sou to spare." "And the American college at Rome? Wouldn't it be possible for them to maintain you?" "It wouldn't be appropriate to draw on business there."

Thereupon, repeated inarticulate gruntings! That's called His Holiness keeping his solemn promise.

Naturally I have gotten to know Keane — of honorable open appearance. He told me about the grisly attacks which Schroeder[5] (your archenemy) made upon him, after he in all innocence had called him to his university, and how he had fallen victim to his intrigues and that of his fellow conspirators. [*franz compagnons*] He said very straightly, "Ireland[6] has been branded by these obscurantists as an enemy of the Germans; but it absolutely does not concern a nationality which he as well as I love and highly prize, but it is simply about the opposition of progress to backwardness, of liberal [*freisinnige*] Catholics to the Ultramontanes."

I believe that Ireland will soon attempt to clear up this unholy misunderstanding, so that the artificially erected barriers between likeminded people of different descent drop away, so that they might unite in common understanding. For here so much political-religious mischief is produced that

---

[5] Monsignor Joseph Schroeder, sometime professor at the Catholic University of America, had years earlier delated Kraus' church history to Rome, charging it with unorthodoxy. Kraus had been forced to make humiliating changes to the work to save it from condemnation. In America Schroeder became the clerical leader of the German Catholic faction.

[6] John Ireland (1838-1918), Archbishop of St. Paul, Minnesota.

the hour compels all rightminded and well-intentioned ones to unite in an unbreakable, flexible community in order to place a dam around this Jesuitized church and give her back her old <u>universal</u> mission! What do you say to that, dear friend.

Keane is filled with deep regret that he doesn't know you until now. Hopefully that will still happen. He speaks German and reads it fluently. When the pope doesn't keep his word, he goes home.

In general for now Russia rules the world and vice flourishes; still the world hasn't thrown up and virtue sits there to one side, groveling in the dust, beaten black and blue. What does Spectator say to all that?

How gladly would I follow your lectures and gossip again with you by the hearth! When I hear from you, then there will write to you, your, devoted in all things new and old,

A. v. Eichthal[7]

May I ask you to drop the enclosed in the nearest letter-box?

---

[7] To this letter, mailed after January 6, Kraus immediately replied on January 10, 1897. The mention of Jos. Schroeder and the Americans had riveted his attention. He wrote: "Hearty thanks for your letter of the 6th, which I answer at once. It is in many respects <u>very</u> important that in Germany a correct insight into the American matters be made clear and especially the circumstances about Msgr. Keane. The Spectator has the intention to communicate such things in the March Letter (which has to be ready at the beginning of Feb.) He has taken trouble to gain connections to good information in America, but nevertheless would like a detailed elaboration of the situation and the reasons which led to the dismissal of Msgr. Keane, particularly about the intrigues of the otherwise insignificant Schroeder."

Kraus asked her to go directly to Keane, and quickly to get a written account from him in French, which Kraus discretely could use. He further asked her to invite Keane to come to Freiburg, impressing upon Keane that it would be very advantageous to gain a powerful organ to publicize his version of the events. And he informed her that the forthcoming February letter of Spectator would be devoted to Diana Vaughan.

January 14, 1897[8]
Thursday early
Rome

My dear friend,
I have just come from Msgr. Keane, to whom I hurried to convey your card with its hospitable invitation. He was deeply touched by both and bid me thank you warmly, but – so he added at the end of his detailed exposition – write to friend Kraus as is appropriate, "I regard it as more probable to welcome him here by me than that I should go over the Alps and be in the situation to take advantage of his good offer."

And now to business: The official letter of Leo XIII to him was given by Keane along with his answer on the 5th of October last year to be printed by all American papers. In Europe the English <u>Tablet</u> brought it out and still other Catholic publications. That contained only the official reason; it should not be maintained that a Rector is guaranteed for life. Since Keane had already filled this post since the founding of the University (1887), he should give it up. For that the pope offered him elevation to Archbishop, and as circumstances allowed a post in America or one in Rome as advisor at the Propaganda with a solution appropriate to his rank. Keane submitted without argument, gave on the 6th of October both documents to his University and set out at once for California: there his former student Archbishop Riodurn [sic] is devoted to him.[9]

As one of the trustees of the Catholic University, Ireland came along in this matter to Washington for conference. The council put to Satolli[10] the

---

[8] This letter was not mailed until after January 22, 1897.

[9] Patrick William Riordan (1841-1914), Archbishop of San Francisco 1883 – 1914, was a good friend of Keane's, but not his former student.

[10] Cardinal Francesco Satolli (1839-1910) was the first Apostolic Delegate for the United States, and was resident at the Catholic University of America at the time of Keane's

justifiable question about the exact grounds for Keane's removal. "Why only," offered His Eminence, "Keane is not enough of a Thomist, has on trips and speeches at missions, etc., taken liberties with explanations of our doctrine and — besides there are three million Germans here against him."

"What?" protested the supervisory board, "Keane has always strenuously taught Catholic dogma. At most it may be that in haste on his trips his speeches may have lacked exterior polish. But how can anybody make his position as Rector dependent on the veto of fanatic masses, led by a pair of insubordinate intriguers, who have never contributed a penny to the support of the University?"

This had been, easily understood, Schroeder's work on behalf of the German mass element, as well as the – clinking – influencing of Satolli, who earlier had shown himself inimical to this alignment. However – after the white cows were all milked out, why not relieve the black ones of their abundance? "After all," as Princess Altieri[11] once said of the [Italian] regime, "their money is just as good to spend as the others."

A protest against the grounds given by Satolli, with <u>total</u> rejection of Keane's lack of orthodoxy, was sent to the Nuntius by the united Board of Trustees. Keane stayed six weeks peacefully in California, spoke to Riodurn [sic] in San Francisco, learned from him about the Washington goings-on, and on the return trip in Chicago heard further reports from Ireland, how the universal activity in the U.S. on his behalf had Rome dumbfounded and alarmed. He showed him a letter of Satolli's from Rome, overflowing with affectionate recognition of Ireland (while here we know that at the same time he spoke at the nastiest about the same Ireland and sought to overthrow him at the

---

dismissal. At first he seemed well disposed to the Americanist prelates, but later supported their adversaries. His American experience allowed him to play a large role in the fortunes of Eichthal's American friends.

[11] Mathilde Theodolinde, Princess von Urach, Countess of Württemberg (1854 – 1907), married (1874), Paolo Prince Altieri, Prince di Viano (1849 - 1901).

Vatican.) That last didn't succeed, still the pope was taken aback by the remark: [that] Ireland's socialistic teachings and republican opinions served in Europe to spread the socialist weeds.

Ireland strengthened Keane enough in his intention to justify himself personally in Rome, showed him how through such strong support by public opinion his cause could yet be won, to put the cause ahead of the personal element. However this required a fearless representative in the Vatican and he ought to establish himself as such. In 1882 Ireland had already shown to the pope how it would be impossible for the Holy See to know the requirements of all Catholic peoples without having a representative of the same at his side <u>as counselor</u>. Leo XIII, agreeing with that, added, " that's why I now have even three German cardinals at my side." "It's not a matter of whether they are cardinals," replied Ireland, "but of better, independent, well instructed clergy."

So Keane arrived back in Washington to a ceremonial farewell to his institute. In these last words, the sentence stood out, "I betake myself to Rome to give account of my conduct and to work there without fear of man or the devil." Naturally these last words of Keane flew before him, torn out of context, to prepare his reception here! This act of love was provided by friend Schroeder, who still teaches in Washington. He is trying to pick up a mitre, but the diocesans fear his lust for power, wherever he has until now applied as candidate on that side of the water. In the Vatican, where they are accustomed by centuries old traditional power to walk unpunished through a docile credulous world, where every manly resistance has been nipped in the bud by the seminary-training, they were not prepared for this American's fearless, upright, arrival. After Leo XIII, as I wrote you, attempted to put Keane off in that first audience by just breaking his word, or by delay, Keane quietly proceeded to set out his requirements in a written memorandum to the Secretary of State and to recapitulate the papal written promises. It did not take any three days for the pill to work! With a *Breve* Keane was at the same time named as Archbishop of Damascus (*in partibus*!), as assisting Prelate of His Holiness, and as an active canon of the Lateran.

Lots of sand in the eyes, one prebendary in the pocket, but practicing activity? Nihil! How truly Jesuiticallly national!

My American, not lazy, appeared by Rampolla,[12] who embraced him sweet as sugar, himself assured him of his on-going affection and that of the pope and, astounded, heard – 'he was still not satisfied.' Dear heart, what more dost thou crave? Why the <u>practical</u> effectiveness promised to me! "And that would be?" "To be named as advisor for the American affairs at the Propaganda according to the papal pledge. <u>That's what</u> I am here for, not for the reception of empty titles, much I care about that!"

The deuce! <u>This</u> talk was new! A few days after that, they bit into the apple, and therewith, since day before yesterday, Archbishop Keane has arrived at his goal, energetically and systematically to serve at the Holy See, as a fearless, candid, informed judge of conditions at home. Under such circumstances he is very right to put a firm foot where he can make good use of his experiences, sheltering his homeland, and, with a small phalanx of likeminded, work *in loco*, so that the Congregations gently be divested of their Italian coloration and returned to more universal comprehensions.

Remarkably, in this sense, right under Steinhuber's[13] nose in the Index, just such a breach has been made through the appointment of Father David[14] a progressive sharpminded Irish Franciscan, who looks so young, who for a long time enjoyed great respect in England as † Manning's confessor, and who, in his outlook, has his whole Order behind him. When Vaughan took over the Archbishopric of Westminster, he called out in his vain exalted opinion of

---

[12] Mariano Rampolla del Tindaro (1843-1913), Cardinal Secretary of State 1887 – 1903. Generally conceded to have been pro-French, and opposed to the new Kingdom of Italy and its connections with Austria and Germany in the Triple Alliance.

[13] Cardinal Andreas Steinhuber, Prefect of the Index Congregation.

[14] David Fleming, O.F.M.

himself; "Now it's the end with pater David!" Pater David just continued peacefully on his way, strong in his upright personality, and when his Order's General proposed him as the English advisor with the Index, Cardinal Vaughan was the most eager one to recommend him. Will he hold his own? Will his spirit not become crippled by working as a Roman mole?

Friday, January 22nd. My pen has rested till now to await the fulfillment of Keane's promise in regard to the written description of the pre-history of his removal, which you wanted. He gave it to me day before yesterday to look over. One sees from his speech and writing that he is still too moved by the experience to put himself in the position of a newcomer, so he presumes much, and thinks it well said. With this marginal comment I returned the piece yesterday, so that <u>today</u> it might go off to you directly from the archbishop. He wanted also to thank you <u>directly</u> for your invitation. He will live on via Meridana in the Palazzo Brancaccio, just as the American owner has arranged, where he may stay for some time. Did I tell you that he also belongs to the Congregation "Per I Studi Dei Scritti Sacri?"

Satolli brought with him an adept of Schroeder's, the Westphalian Minkenberg, as secretary, and thought this honor should satisfy him instead of payment! I know that the Cardinal Archbishop of Cologne in his time reported to Rome about this Minkenberg: he suspected this priest would become insane!

"Pater Hyacinthe Loyson"[15] is in passing here with his wife on the way to Palermo. In his time Döllinger[16] sent him to me. The man is too illogical, vain, and fantastical to be of any sort of significance; therefore I have refrained

---

[15] Charles Jean Marie Loyson, (1827-1912), sometime Carmelite and famous preacher at Paris' Notre Dame cathedral. After openly opposing the Doctrine of Infallibility in 1870 he entered into marriage with an American widow, Emilie Meriman, in 1872 and continued clerical activity in the Old Catholic Church.

[16] Johann Joseph Ignaz Döllinger (1799-1890), German theologian excommunicated for refusal to submit to doctrine of Papal Infallibility, lived in Munich.

from renewing old connections. His newest whim appears to be — Mohammedanism!

Do you know that here I cannot provide myself with both of your *Beilage* to the *Allgemeine Zeitung*? I am very cast down about that. Couldn't you – against sure return – send them to me?

I am hurrying to the end of this sweeping to and fro. It makes me happy to have been able to fulfill your request so quickly and I hope these pages find you up and about and victoriously happy?

Indicate to me, please, my accurate accomplishment in this letter as well as the missive of Keane, and be convinced with a friendly handshake of my highly respectful participation in your work.

A. v. Eichthal

[in Italian]
January 25, 1897
176 Ripetta
Rome

Two single words to inform you that I succeeded in procuring the journals which they did not have at the *casino tedesco*. For me, think no more of it.

My letter dated 21st and 23rd will be delivered yesterday at the latest and the other correspondence document received today or tomorrow from Archbishop Keane,[17] who came to see me Saturday toward evening, telling me that he would prefer to avoid in your connection, as much as possible, the personal matters; about which there will be no more. I agreed and I well understand — I didn't want to insist. Already therefore the report is clear enough to make out the rest with sharp eyes as much as....[illegible.][18]

---

[17] Keane mailed his account of events at the Catholic University, 16 pages in French, from Rome on January 28, 1897. Kraus saved the envelope, pre-stamped with two cents American postage, bearing the Italian postage as well. The reverse of the envelope is stamped in red wax with a maltese cross, the seal of the Archbishop of Damascus *in partibus infidelium*. In an accompanying brief note in French, signed – Jean Joseph Keane, Archev. de Damas. — Keane asks Kraus to refrain from personalities. [*Nachlass* Kraus, File Keane]

[18] A note to AVE from Denis O'Connell in the same week says, "Keane finishes his dainty work this evening." [*Nachlass* Eichthal, O'C to AVE, Saturday, Jan.23, 1897.]

February 28, 1897
176 Ripetta
Rome

My honored friend,
Your lines,[19] which I personally handed to Archbishop Keane, pleased him uncommonly. He has, which I find very reasonable, taken rooms in the Canadian College and is therewith relieved of all earthly cares, for a very small payment. I brought him at the same time the Spectator letter of the 1st of this month, which satisfied him highly, and he looks forward eagerly to the next one. Since the two next ones, which for the purposes of publication in the U.S., will be translated by a close friend of Keane's and mine, a religious, will not however be obtainable here, I ask you in this regard each time without delay to set on the right road a copy to me for this purpose.

The Jesuits, namely in America, who maintain that the south German press including the *Allgemeine* is in cahoots with them, ought to have their untruthfulness proved to them, through the publication of these Letters, *coram publico*.

Satolli (the sly gold-milker) works (in the most recent period) headlong – to procure the purple for Abp. Corrigan of New York! The consistory has on this account been put over to June to give time for these intrigues. You grasp what a blow this designation would be for the party Keane-Ireland-Gibbons! Corrigan's anger that the cardinal's hat went away from his archdiocese to that of Baltimore lies indeed at the bottom of the whole retrograde war which this worthy man of God made against Gibbons and the whole progressive movement in the American Catholic Church! Eve lost Paradise for an apple… in our church the apple has become the red hat!

---

[19] Kraus wrote her on February 5, 1897, "A thousand thanks… for the worthwhile information and particularly for your good arrangements with Dr. Keane… please ask him to keep my authorship out of any discussion… I will treat of the American goings-on in two dispatches – first , examples, and second, the principal matter."

This devil of a fellow, Corrigan, maintains constantly since the death of [Cardinal] McKlosky [sic] and he became his successor, that the purple should stay with the seat which he then took over, and as the opposite occurred, he threw himself into that obscurantist movement of the German priests' association in the U.S., which rules over the lower German element there, and tries to keep it in Egyptian darkness.

Your intimate enemy Schroeder also plays his unholy role there and now is at the bottom of things as the chief laborer for Corrigan's elevation. The 50,000 dollars which the Abp. of N.Y. gets yearly makes it child's play for him to satisfy Satolli's greed in exchange for plentiful services. *Sapienti sat!!!*

Since that well-known nun, who said to the pope that she offered up her life for the prolongation of his, is now taken at her word and called into the Beyond, Leo XIII is happy as a lark, presumes on this marvelous life insurance and considers himself pretty near immortal.

The Jesuits still have the upper hand and with them, the nice Satolli, who ceremoniously overwhelms Ireland with love letters, and ... while he works for his deadly enemy, assures him of his unchangeable devotion!

With regard to the library of our dear † Cardinal Hohenlohe,[20] nothing can be gotten from there except by way of the auction which will be held on March 10th by the antique dealer Innocenti in Babuino, along with all the effects of His Eminence. The books are specially catalogued and I will send you the catalog when I get it. Anything you want from it, please underline for me and you will have it (that is, according to the established limits you set.) Our poor cardinal was, as we know — sadly no judge of men and ensnared by miserable fellows among whom his so-called Secretary and general heir occupied no respectable place. Beside what during the lifetime he sucked up,

---

[20] Cardinal Gustav-Adolf Hohenlohe, , died October 30, 1896 at the age of seventy-three. He was created cardinal before the first Vatican Council and had served in Rome for half a century.

he took over the inheritance only "for the benefit of an inventory" and therefore brings under the hammer what he has not previously been able to put aside quietly for himself.

How right you are to make a pilgrimage to Meran in March and in noble nature to recover from winter and its hardships. I will announce you to the Schleinitzes, who are very disturbed by the death of Princess Hatzfeldt[21] in Venice and who want, these days, to get back to the Villa Rosenberg at Obermais. Here we have May weather. Awaiting your commission — about the books, I press your hand, as your ardently appreciative

A. v. Eichthal

---

[21] Princess Marie Hatzfeldt-Trachenberg, who died at Venice on January 25, 1897, had a protestant funeral. Princess Hatzfeldt, born (13 April 1820) Marie von Nimptsch, was the second wife of Friedrich, Prince of Hatzfeldt, Duke of Trachenberg (Lower Silesia). The Schleinitz sisters were raised as protestants, but converted to Catholicism as grown women. [*Nachlass* Eichthal, Hatzfeldt Death Notice in Schleinitz file.]

April 13, 1897
Tuesday
176 Ripetta
Rome

Dear friend,
(Above all, please, please speak to me in your letters in German and not in Gaulish, all right?)[22] Your second American Spectator is a masterpiece of clear consistent presentation and development of the circumstances.

I read it with mounting satisfaction, and gave to friend O'Connell, who visited me that same evening, a pointed translation of the best part, since he to his sorrow understands not a word of German.

O'Connell is – as I have already well given you to understand – the motive power and support for Abp. Keane on this unsteady Roman ground; besides that, he brings together with him once a week in the afternoon a number of likeminded to discuss church matters. Von Hügel, Abbé Duchesne are never missing, and indeed two Jesuits (but Bollandists from Holland)[23] have found their way, to give expression to their indignation at the [...] transactions of their Roman fellow Jesuits.

---

[22] Kraus had written to her on March 4, March 10, and April 5, 1897, the last from Meran. In these notes, in which he unguardedly addressed her as "chère amie," he provided her and Keane with the "New York" letters of Spectator which were being published, and said that in Germany everyone was convinced that the author was "on the other side of the ocean." Kraus expressed great concern that any letters from him might show up in the Hohenlohe auction and offered to buy them up in advance.

[23] Hippolyte Delahaye, a Belgian Bollandist arrived in Rome in 1896. His fellow Bollandist Francois Van Ortroy came later in 1897. They frequented Denis O'Connell's weekly gatherings. David G. Schultenover, S.J., "Louis Martin Garcia, the Jesuit General of the Modernist Crisis (1892-1906) On Historical Criticism," *Catholic Historical Review*, Vol. LXXXIX, (2003), No.3, 447-448.

O'Connell is fire and flame for you and hopes for a golden future for the church from your courageous and clever coming forward, for which Keane, Ireland from beyond the ocean, want to add their work as they can. The one newspaper clipping shows you how Ireland has already taken the first step to union. The other should give you the latest example of Schroeder's vehement hatred for any freethinking Catholic tendency. O'Connell wants you to know in connection with that, that Schroeder, when he was first in America, came out just as powerfully <u>against</u> the Germans whom he is now stirring up and judged that: they were estranged from the Holy See. In that sense he even put together a letter to Cardinal Rampolla. O'Connell authorizes me to inform you of that, with mention of his name, because he could add even more.

Now O'C has asked me to procure <u>yes six</u> of the American Letters in the *Allg. Z.* to distribute to friends in America. The *Allgemeine* – as you noticed at the bottom – puts the price however at <u>one Mark</u> for each copy for a re-order! Wouldn't it be possible, best friend, to get them more reasonably and have them sent <u>to me</u>, <u>for him</u>, or, <u>to him directly</u> from the dispatch office, by parcel? This could happen collect, or whatever is usual.

One could wait a while until the printing of the <u>May</u> letter to send the 18 numbers all together here, don't you think? Since O'Connell's successor as Rector bears the same name,[24] it would (to guard against a mistake) be the smartest thing simply to direct his order to me at <u>176 Ripetta.</u> Since I in the meantime have been surprised by my brother and been chased half to death between here, Naples and Monte Cassino, so that as a result I was totally miserable – I could not yet, sadly, translate Donna Ersilia's essay to the finish, but hope to do it this week and then send it right off.

Innocenti has mounded up a number of the books for you and will send them to you with the little figure you bid on. Everything reached such enormous prices that, unfortunately, he was not able to comply with your wishes in the

---

[24] William O'Connell was Denis O'Connell's successor at the American College, but was not his friend.

greater part. Since the auction of the furniture fell at the time of my brother's presence here, I could not attend. Innocenti assured me however that there was such a pressing crowd that his duties cost him bitter sweat and he never had seen such rubbish sell so dearly.

Then what was it otherwise, with but few exceptions? It was never a matter of the Cardinal's correspondence; that was immediately taken away from the nice Cav. Nobili by court order. (Otherwise there was no way to make an impression on the rogue.) Now however the court also seized, thank God! at the last moment the letters from Liszt, advertised with so many trumpet flourishes, as well as all the <u>photographs</u> furnished with inscriptions from German and Italian gentlemen. This happened at Berlin's special request, whereupon Koenigs here set about quickly to comply.

Innocenti told me the books brought <u>12000</u> lire, the furnishings, etc. <u>53 lire</u>!!! And with that the Cardinal's priceless cross and chain[25] along with several other pieces of jewelry were <u>not</u> included since Nobili held them back because they didn't seem to him to go high enough. You possibly knew this heir of our poor Cardinal as well as I?

Why did you only stay in Meran so briefly? Didn't the air please you? That really makes me sorry! Indeed the Schleinitzes are a very choice pair of sisters! <u>High-minded</u> as you so accurately remarked and <u>well educated</u>. With that kind of Catholic material to work with a person could be very content and with that sort of ingredients might hope for an upturn of events. What do you think?

What do you say to the Greek-Turkish buffoonery? And to Europe as the expected bulldog? Isn't that enough to shame the eyes right out of your head, or just laugh?

---

[25] "This very vain little princely cardinal, who with so much coquettery wore upon the purple of his cassock a large bishop's cross with emeralds and so loved to display on his delicate white hands the large emeralds of his episcopal ring..." Philip Eulenburg, quoted in Weber, *Quellen und Studien*, p.444.

Buona pasqua! Frohe Ostern! best friend. May I soon learn that your trip made you stronger!   In friendship

   A. E.

Do you know that Hügels had their second daughter at death's door? Now she recovers in Anzium, accompanied by a Sister of Charity.

to Franz Xaver Kraus   61

May 20, 1897
Rome

Dear friend,
The date of the adjacent lines[26] of the honorable Archbishop explains to you my long silence in letters and dispatches. Yesterday evening he wrote me and early today my letter is off to you. We all are electrified over the Spectator's accomplishment and Duchesne expressed to me his regret that the Letter could not be made available to his compatriots in a more universal language (that's supposed to mean French.) O'Connell has already taken care for the translation in America and the remaining copies Keane and he have distributed to designated places. A note from the latter[27] shows you <u>privately</u>

---

[26] Sending the final one of the three Spectator Letters of 1897 (March 1st, April 1st, May 1st) which had to do with America, Kraus wrote to AVE on May 4th. The May 1st Spectator Letter had Keane as the source of the first four pages.

Starting on the last blank page of Keane's note to her, AVE wrote this May 20th letter to Kraus, and so sent him the following original note from Keane as well as the note from O'Connell which is in the next footnote.

Baroness Auguste von Eichthal, Rome, May 19th, '97.

My dear Baroness:
I beg that you will convey to "Spectator" my sincere thanks for his three articles on the Church in America. While it could not be expected that he would be in entire sympathy with our democratic ideas, or that he could fully grasp the meaning of some movements and questions of an entirely local character, still he has treated the whole matter in a fraternal and friendly spirit and with much judiciousness. I pray most earnestly that a similar spirit may be granted to all parties in America. It would go far toward removing misunderstanding and bring about peace & unity.

For the great kindness of his judgments concerning myself I am specially thankful. Believe me, my dear Baroness, sincerely and gratefully, Yours in Christ, John J. Keane

[27] Baroness Auguste von Eichthal, Rome, Friday [14.4.97, dated by AVE]

My dear friend:
I hope to see you soon and we will arrange the time.

Keane's delight over Spectator's discernment, because <u>chuckled</u> means to relish something heartily with a slight smile.

Since Keane was asked by the Irish College, for the 50th anniversary of the death of their great patriot O'Connell, to give the memorial address in their church in which O'Connell's heart has reposed for 50 years, this required weeks-long preparation to acquaint himself with those times and to evaluate in short form all the massive materials for a foundation for a speech in O'Connell's memory. Keane succeeded <u>masterfully</u>. Instead of, as he likes to do, letting himself be transported by the feeling of the moment into rich improvisation and then flood on, each word here was thought out and delivered with personal warmth, and the enthused speaker so aroused the emotions of his hearers that many eyes were moist. It was a masterful speech, which should appear soon in all languages.

Of course the audience could scarcely form any judgment from Keane's presentation about the Irish <u>people</u>; because the strength which O'Connell had by reason of his powerful personality, was of no use to the otherwise drunken quarrelsome "Paddy," who can only be agreeable and sober momentarily, never permanently.

Keane has repeatedly assured me of his satisfaction that Spectator, as much as he keeps his independence, and in so much is of an other opinion than he [Keane] is, yet by that increases the value of his presentation all the more. Ireland naturally judges exactly the same.

Schroeder seems, over there, to have lost out significantly with his compatriots, since he didn't succeed – which he promised the pope here last summer – in eliciting from the Germans over there the donation of a chair for German Language at the Catholic University of Washington.

The Archbishop will preach tomorrow morning. The Mass will begin at 10:45 and "post hoc," the Sermon.
How he chuckled over Spectator's last letter! A bientot, Always sincerely, D.J.O'Connell

A propos: do you know that in initiated circles Satolli is considered to be a son of Leo XIII? Satolli lately has suspiciously made friends with the General of the Benedictines, Abbot Hemptinne[28] (sometime Zouave of Pius IX.) As you know the Benedictines are anything but edified over this papal unification and centralization of their Order under Hemptinne. They see it as the overthrow of their age old independent confederacy and a slap in the face for their founder who wanted neither seclusion [*Klausur*] nor centralization. Hemptinne, as an old officer of the pope, knows only obedience and accommodation; still, they say, when the pope vanishes then his unification of the order with its central seat at S. Anselmo on the Aventine will also disappear. Two million has that construction cost the Vatican and two further million Leo XIII made the Benedictines contribute to it!

Pater Semeria (Genoese Barnabite),[29] whose Lenten sermons at San Lorenzo in Damaso excited so much attention, has taken himself away from Rome, disgusted by the Roman-Jesuitical atmosphere. He was tracked and watched like a wild beast in order to catch him in a net. The air has become absolutely Jesuit.

What do you say to the new crown which the Chapter of St. Peter's presented to the Child Jesus on Ara Coeli?[30] The feast to honor this crowning lasted a full eight days! Each day the high mass was held by a different cardinal and

---

[28] Hildebrand de Hemptinne O.S.B. (1849-1913), born in Ghent, 1893 Abbot General.

[29] Giovanni Semeria (1867-1931), Barnabite, Preacher and writer, worked for religious renewal. Later suspected of Modernism.

[30] The Franciscan Church of Ara Coeli possessed a small statue of the Infant Jesus, which was sometimes carried to the sick for their restoration. "The Bambino came in a carriage with two horses, and the people in the street went down on their knees as it passed. One of the friars in priest's surplice carried it in a box with the lid open, and two friars in brown habits walked before it with lifted candles. But as the painted image in its scarlet clothes and jewels entered the Countess's bedroom with its grim and ghostly procession, and was borne like a baby mummy at the foot of her bed, it terrified her, and she screamed. 'Take it away,' she shrieked......Its visit had lasted thirty seconds and cost a hundred francs." Hall Caine, *The Eternal City* (1902), p. 257.

the evening Benediction was likewise parceled out to another Eminence! Worthy prelude to the beatification next Thursday, the 27th; the throng should be enormous. St. Peter's stands prepared in its scarlet brocade trousers and glitters like a village church with all sorts of exaggerated hangings...The Emperor of Austria contributes imperially to the expenses. *O tempora! o mores!*[31]

Your health, valued friend, has been improved by the lovely sun, God willing, since I hear through Venturi[32] that you harbor a plan for a trip to England? Protect yourself from the wet foggy air of that attractive island kingdom, which is <u>poison</u> for your rheumatic constitution! I remain here until the end of June, am thereafter without plans (only headed first for Munich). What do <u>you</u> contemplate? Please, occasionally, a sign of life for your faithful

A. v. Eichthal

---

[31] See the Letter of June 5, 1897, below.

[32] Adolfo Venturi, art historian.

to Franz Xaver Kraus

May 22, 1897
Rome

This postcard follows my letter of the 20th at the request of Innocenti who wants to know: whether the shipment he sent off to you as freight to your address (from the estate of Card. v. H.) has finally been received. He hopes you will soon indicate this to set his mind at ease.

Just now Duchesne left me, who charged me with his very best compliments to you, most worthy sir.

Here *scirocco* and *tramontana* change so unbelievably fast and variably, with rain and sunshine, wind and counter-wind, that a rhinoceros could scarcely hold up without nervous fits.

How goes it with you, God willing, a little bit better? Which subject will June 1st bring us? One is very anxious to learn that here.

For a sign of life, soon and gratifying, all right?

In friendliness,

AVE

June 5, 1897
Saturday
176 Ripetta
Rome

Worthy friend,
Ere I watch for your dear letter, probably sent off already,[33] this sheet flies to you to say that this morning I reproached Innocenti for his sloppiness and *nolens volens* convinced him of it. When he finally saw it, he begged for forgiveness. To him the German book No. 511 appeared far more worth reading – but of course for him unreadable – than 512! Of the pictures he maintained they were already in bad condition at the Cardinal's, and that's why they were so cheap. He still has not received the money, in spite of your notice; will likely do so soon.

These days I have read Schell's brochure[34] and last evening have spoken about its content with friends, who like so many parched Catholics, languish in this Roman formal unreality and are as open to a mighty rising of the <u>interiorly</u> religious portion of the Catholic population as once Noah was to the dove's return with an olive branch.

Anyone who knows the present terrain would find it no wonder that the Jesuits have sworn to bring Schell down. To this end his <u>Dogmatics</u> has been taken up, in order – which will naturally be child's play – to discover a pretext for persecution by the Index. They are determined to drive him out of the church so that they can triumph over this heretic and be able contemptuously to overlook his objections, as stigmatized <u>heretical</u>.

---

[33] Kraus wrote on May 24, 1897, but the letter has not survived.

[34] Hermann Jakob Schell (1850-1906), 1884 Professor, Würzburg. His chief works were placed on the Index in late 1898. The brochure, *Der Katholizismus als Prinzip des Fortschritts*, published at Würzburg in 1897, went to seven printings by 1899. Schell was aroused by Isaac Hecker's ideas and called for reform in the church.

"He is going the way of Döllinger," they whisper around and scornfully rub their hands together.

May God grant that the intelligent man has enough self-control and self-denial <u>not</u> to fulfill their wish for the Jesuits. For this is really the historically noteworthy thing about our sadly misguided church – the most important spirits, the most highly regarded individuals, just as soon as they let themselves express an idea outside the circular walls of the church, they stand isolated and without <u>any</u> influence on the purification or any kind of improvement of what they care about.

To whom do I say this? Don't you hope this a thousand times more? Meanwhile <u>warn</u> Schell and let him know about these sub-surface decisions so that he may be able to get on firm footing.

How gladly I would meet with you this summer, but <u>sulfur baths</u> I don't need! Am already a sulfur match! Need mountain or ocean air!

At the end of the month Msgr. Keane travels for three months in America.[35] O'Connell wants to learn German properly this summer and would most like to come to Freiburg for that. Should he carry out the plan, for which I have much encouraged him, may he surely count on a helpful hint from you in relation to choosing an instructor as well as appropriate acquaintances from your circle? You will be at home until the 15th of July, not so? Anyway please write soon a little word about my request for Msgre. O'Connell.

---

[35] Keane wrote her a note of gratitude upon departure, "Rome, June 21st, [1897]; My dear good Baroness: How can I thank you, dear friend, for all your kindness? Rest assured that during my vacation my talks with you will be among my pleasantest souvenirs of Rome, and that a renewal of our pleasant relationship will be one of my pleasantest anticipations in returning. May God abundantly bless you. Yours in Xt, John J. Keane" (*Nachlass* Eichthal, File English Letters)

The canonization[36] was a fitting pretext for the deification of Leo XIII. What a holy hovel! How many caricatures inside!

Get thoroughly better! In sincere friendship

A. v. Eichthal

---

[36] The canonization, reported in full in the *New York Times*, May 28, 1897, page 7, was of "the Blessed Zaccaria and the Blessed Fourier de Matincour." Anthony Mary Zaccaria was the founder of the Barnabites and Fourier was styled 'the Apostle of Lorraine.' AVE's announcement of the coming splendor was borne out in the events. "Since the Absolution of the Pope's Temporal Power No Such Scene Has Been Witnessed There – The Façade Illuminated." Forty thousand persons were admitted by ticket to formal seating for ceremonies featuring Cardinals Mazzella and Oreglia, offertory gifts of decorated candles, two loaves, a gold cask of wine, a silver one of water, and three cages of assorted doves. In the evening, for the first time since the Italian occupation of Rome, there was a grand illumination of St. Peter's. The ceremonies were reported to have cost four thousand dollars, recalling, said the *Times*, the words of Prince Falconieri, nearly bankrupted by the costs for the canonization of Giuliana Falconieri, "My dear ones, be angels as much as you want, but never saints. It costs too much."

June 29, 1897
176 Ripetta
Rome

My dear friend,
If I delayed until today with answering your friendly lines,[37] it was to be able to report to you something definite about Msgre. O'Connell's and my travel plans. Last evening he came with his friend the General-Procurator of the Order (of the Holy Cross) Pater Zahm[38] (an American of German descent) to say definitely how uncommonly he regrets not to be able to follow up on your intriguing offer. He cannot leave Rome before the end of July, since Zahm is tied down here until the holiday period of the religious pupils of his order. And then both of them want to attend the Catholic Congress in Freiburg i.d. Schweiz. After that they want to be in the Schwarzwald.

O'Connell thanks you with the greatest sincerity for your valued invitation and hopes very much to make your acquaintance soon. Also Zahm, an eminent thinker who, last year strongly accused of heresy, left America because in a sermon he observed: the books of Moses were not always to be taken literally, especially in connection with the days of creation, but figuratively – also he, energetic evolutionist, counts very much on a personal exchange with you in a – as God allows, not too distant future.

Our excellent Keane has in mind, after little calling stops in Savoy, France, and Belgium, to take himself home from there for the summer. In the fall we will all be back here together. He charged me, before his departure, with the heartiest wishes for you.

---

[37] Kraus wrote to her on June 7, 1897. He offered advice on where to stay in Freiburg and told her the July Spectator Letter would deal with Schell's accusations about Catholic inferiority, and Diana Vaughan.

[38] John A. Zahm, C.S.C. (1851-1921), 1896 – 1898, Superior of the Order of the Holy Cross in Rome, 1898 – 1905, Provincial in the United States, author in 1896 of *Evolution and Dogma*.

In order to give the turbulent patriotism of the Irish the proper leadership, the Jesuits set up in the Irish College – a few weeks after Keane's epoch-making memorial address about O'Connell – a second memorial celebration in the same spot. Pater Zarzi had to explain to the pupils in fulminating words how their great patriot <u>never</u> would have taken into his head to acquire <u>freedom of conscience</u>, still less would want to do something that the Holy See had not ordered him to do! Who failed to think thereon of the famous outcry of O'Connell's, as Rome wanted to take possession of him with its advices: "In matters of <u>faith</u> I am the most devoted son of the church, in <u>political</u> advice I would rather be a son of St. Petersburg than of Rome."

Schell's brochure continues to agitate the spirits…with what result? In any case recently a Dominican explained broken-heartedly from the chancel in Freiburg i.d. Schweiz, "Now we have received statistical proof of the subordination of Catholics. Now we know it. And are warned…"

Have you undertaken your excursion to Baden? As a sign of your improvement, I would be specially pleased to hear that. How I deplore that you must go to boiling hot Hungary in these hot days to be insulfurated.

Imagine this – even though my departure is definite for the middle of next week – (circa July 7), I still have made no decision about the particular "where." Can you recommend to me a – not expensive – mountain resort of about the height of the Feldburg? It is unbearable there because of the plank partitions and the tobacco smoke. If I were not in uncertainty because of a possible meeting in Munich with my brother, nothing would hold me back from still greeting you, dear friend, before your further travel to the sulfur pool, and for that, traveling over the Gotthard.

This dependency on brotherly decisions constrains me most of all. Is there – in any case a good thing to know – in your vicinity a decent pension or quiet guest house – at which to put up? A postcard would quickly educate me about that and give me a sure connection.

In the innermost chambers of the Caffarelli[39] there reigns painful confusion over the Ambassador's new employment![40] As Chancellor? – well! To be utilized as a Marshall? – better not that! His spouse[41] scarcely knows how to control her grief.

Papa Bülow beams over the appointment of his son[42] to the International Court at Cairo, where his irritating little wife will be right at home.

God be with you. In true friendship –

A.E.

Unfortunately I don't see the *Allg. Ztg.* any more. Couldn't you let me see the Spectator for July 1st?

---

[39] The Palazzo Caffarelli on the Capitoline housed the Embassy of the German Empire to Italy.

[40] In 1897 Bernhard von Bülow was recalled to Berlin as State Secretary of the Foreign Office.

[41] Bernhard von Bülow's wife was Maria Beccadelli di Bologna, who, in 1886, had her marriage to Count Karl von Dönhoff annulled in order to marry Bernhard. The second marriage of her mother Laura was to Marco Minghetti, sometime Minister President of Italy. Thus in 1897 the wife of the German Ambassador to Italy was Minghetti's stepdaughter, who naturally would hate to leave Rome.

[42] Otto von Bülow, the Prussian Envoy to the Vatican, had a son, Otto (the Younger), born in 1859, who in 1895 married Elsa Schricker, born in 1874. Otto the Younger, having served as *Regierungsrat* at the German Embassy, the Caffarelli, was transferred to the International Court of Justice in Alexandria, Egypt. While Kraus referred to Elsa in his diary (January 1896, *Tagebuch*, 646) as Otto Senior's "lovely little daughter-in-law," it is obvious that Baroness Eichthal did not care for the youthful bride.

July 7, 1897
Wednesday
Rome

My dear friend,
I hasten to thank you cordially for lending the Beilage of the 1st of this month.[43] I read the contents with the greatest interest and can only congratulate you at the masterful handling of the two subjects.[44] But if you fancy to hide the author behind his nom de plume, I must finally relieve you of this illusion. I guarded it for a long time, but now hear it confirmed from all sides that the author's name is an open secret, that is, known to everyone really interested these questions.

In a strange manner, there now appears to be staying in Freiburg i/Br an American clergyman who raves over Spectator without knowing anything about the author. The man is named Grannan,[45] teaches scriptural interpretation at the Cath. Univ. in Washington, is repeatedly in Germany because of his studies, and because of his interpretations stands on uncertain footing with the Curia. Msgr. O'Connell has asked me to indicate Prof. Grannan as possessed of the most exact knowledge of North American conditions, wholly

---

[43] Kraus, saying he would have to miss seeing the Americans, sent the *Beilage* (Spectator Letter) to her on July 3, 1897, with the request to send it back.

[44] In this issue Kraus reviewed Hermann Schell's *Der Katholicismus als Princip des Fortschritts* (Würzburg, 1897). In the pamphlet Schell stressed Catholic educational inferiority and Kraus confirmed it with details about the gullibility with which the Diana Vaughan swindles had been received.

[45] Charles P. Grannan (1846-1924), Professor at the Catholic University of America. The sly and cautious Grannan had been known to Kraus since 1894. Kraus wrote to him in late May of 1896 to get news about Keane and Schroeder. He supplied Kraus with two sets of anti-Schroeder materials in May of 1897 and in June had already written to say he was coming to Freiburg. (*Nachlass* Kraus, Grannan File)

secure in conversation, and asks you to receive him confidently when he makes himself known in a day or two.

O'Connell adds: "the nearly fifty year old is as bashful as a child and needs to be pumped a lot until he gets up courage to come out of his shell. <u>Courage</u> generally is not his thing, although from complete conviction he belongs to the party which strives toward the light."

O'Connell asked me to send you the enclosed, so that you may read for yourself the idiocy which under Schroeder's agitation is published over there by the Germans. Spectator's depiction of the nobody should have undone him completely. O'Connell enticed away from me the *Beilage* for Zahm and heard with dismay that he had to give it back because he doesn't know how he can come by a copy here for America.

Hastily I inform you that hopefully we can meet in Munich. I leave here about Sunday-Monday, stay a couple days in Bruneck with friends and hope to be together with you accordingly in Munich about July 17th. There I stay in the summerhouse of the Pension Landes 30/31 Theresienstrasse. Let me know from you please <u>if</u> and <u>when</u> we can talk comfortably. I'll bring your *Beilage* then.

So, as God wills! For a good reunion soon in Munich! With the handshake of friendliness, your

A. v. Eichthal

July 15, 1897
Bruneck (Pusterthal)
Baron Bossi-Fedrigotti's[46]

My dear friend – Since yesterday here for a visit, I recover in this fresh mountain air from the Roman bake-oven. Tomorrow I wanted to go to Munich, but had to put it off until Sunday the 18th because my pension hostess begged me intensely, since otherwise she couldn't take me at all. Today she writes moreover that I might wait patiently until the 20th. That I can and will not, <u>on your account</u>, otherwise I fear to miss you.

Therefore I wrote right away: she must take care of me elsewhere for Sunday the 18th, since I arrive in the afternoon with the (5 hours and 18 minutes) express train.

I hasten to let you know this, so you don't slip away. Please, in any case, let me know your plans, at the old address: Theresienstrasse 30/31 Summerhouse, till Sunday, and where we – in case you are in a hurry – can meet either Sunday about 7 p.m. or otherwise Monday. *Buon revederci!*[47]

AVE

---

[46] The Bossi-Fedrigottis were related to her.

[47] Kraus replied promptly on July 16, 1897.

October 3, 1897
Pension Washeim
34/II Theresienstrasse
Munich

My very dear friend,
After your departure I sent you various newspapers from America. But since you gave no further signs of life and on that account I didn't know whether you remained in Pystian [sic] I let it pass for uncertainty, all writing stopped, all the more because I went to the seaside and needed rest. I found it in Wittdun on Amrum[48] in the sand dunes at the sea shore, where I knew no one, and only took walks.[49]

Very diligently, the American friends wrote me there, and they were not at all unhappy with the Freiburg congress, in so far as they got in touch with others and learned that it seems more hopeful in the future.

O'Connell delivered a little exposition there, "what is Americanism,"[50] which, printed by Herder, naturally you have already seen? Apparently as innocent as childhood, its significance lies in what it is silent about, but what is the logical consequence of the simple explanation of Americanism – the clearing away of the ossified, the useless!

As he always likes to do the contrary thing, O'Connell, and Zahm, naturally, in your absence went toward the Breisgau and <u>then here</u> to Munich, since I

---

[48] One of the North Frisian Islands off Schleswig-Holstein.

[49] AVE wrote to Denis O'Connell from Wittdun, Sept 9, 1897 (Archives of the Diocese of Richmond).

[50] She means Denis O'Connell's address and pamphlet, "A New Idea in the Life of Father Hecker."

remained in the North! Schroeder has mismanaged himself with the Germans in the United States.[51]

In Schleswig, where I visited the dear Liliencrons,[52] I brought away for you the nicest greetings from the spirited youthful master of the house, and also from Donna Ersilia in her letter, and my eighty-six year old sharp minded old friend von Hefner-Alteneck[53] sang your praises over a glass of sparkling wine.

Now I have not yet as usual asked <u>how</u> your cure suited you? Hopefully I will soon learn exactly how. Naturally I wish all the best results for you, nevertheless that there be no illusions sufficient to hinder you from wintering over with us in Rome. On the 27th of September there arrived my translation of the 'Armilustrium' in the *Beilage*. I find it one of the most well done episodes of ancient life from the pen of our lady friend.

In Freiburg Prof. Dove[54] will breathe a sigh of relief to be relieved of his editorial efforts. What an existence! Wearing, I fancy, in every way.

Please give me exact instructions about your room in Rome. On what day may I expect to see you? I leave here on the 8th, and first, for 8 days go to Switzerland to old friends on the Zürichersee, with Oberst Wille in <u>Feld-Meilen</u>, in case you had anything to say to me there. After that it's over the

---

[51] "The American Ultramontanes have dropped Mgr. Schroeder. He compromised them and made them odious."(Denis O'Connell to Eichthal, Milan, August 13, 1897. *Nachlass* Eichthal, O'Connell File)

[52] Rochus Freiherr von Liliencron (1820-1912), 1876 Provost of St. John's Cloister, Schleswig.

[53] Jakob-Heinrich von Hefner-Alteneck (1811-1903), 1868-1886 Director of the National Museum in Munich and General Conservator of the Art Monuments of Bavaria.

[54] Alfred Dove (1844-1916), Historian, 1874 Professor in Breslau; 1891-1892, and 1895-1897, Editor of the *Beilage* of the *Allgemeine Zeitung*; in 1897, he was made Professor in Freiburg.

Gotthard and <u>at the latest</u> I hope to settle in at 176 Ripetta on the 24th of this month. Be reasonable and come soon!

In cordial friendship, your, highly devoted,

    A. v. Eichthal

Count Erbach wrote me highly pleased over your Letter and is on fire to get to know you personally, which needs to happen next spring in Rome.

November 7, 1897
176 Ripetta
Rome

How is it, my dear friend,
that you really want to treat your health so badly and once more expose it to that infamously "ultramontane" climate, which last winter already proved to you how little it does you good? That "otherside the mountains" doesn't suit you at any time, be it physically the North or theologically the South![55]

This recent unwelcome information met me the evening before my departure from Munich. In response I could only read O'Connell's brochure, of which I suppose you also received a copy, as I hear, direct from the author. Since I devoted October to a series of friends in Switzerland and Tuscany, I just arrived here three days ago and found waiting for me a request from O'Connell: when could he see me? This was effected last evening.

First of all he expressed to me his and Zahm's regret that they did not meet up with you in Freiburg. After that he told me of his satisfaction with the Catholic scientific Congress, at which Schell's call for freer inquiry had been repeated by the most respected divines. As a significant indicator he reported to me how Mons. Baumgarten's invitation to meet next in Rome, which he made on the highest authority, was simply declined and Munich was designated as the next location to hold the Congress. The pope's blessing (about which Baumgarten[56] made much), when invoked, could be sent by telegram; on the contrary, in Rome any real discussion would be impossible. Well, what do you say to this poke in the nose?

---

[55] Kraus had written on October 4 that he was not coming to Rome right away.

[56] Paul Maria Baumgarten (1860-1948), Priest, Biblical scholar and publicist, lived many years in Rome.

But now listen to this: On the 22nd of October the fourteen member committee which oversees and decides about the Catholic University in Washington unanimously resolved that Msgr. Schroeder, on grounds of an absolutely private nature, should hand in his resignation, otherwise they would, short and sweet, discharge him. Archbishop Corrigan – his previous protector and Ireland's bitterest opponent – was completely in agreement with the others, because it was about moral lapses, for whose confirmation the witnesses stood assembled in the next room!

Schroeder at first dared to put on a show with a letter of Steinhuber's[57], in which the pope's wishes might be read: he ought to remain firm in his position. When this didn't help, he got Rampolla to telegraph to the committee the pope's order in the same sense. Who is Rampolla to be mixing in our affairs? cried the indignant Americans. They had more than enough of last year's proceedings to which Keane had fallen victim, and so they stood firmly together to protect their prerogatives.

With regard to the Vatican telegram, which was laid aside <u>ad acta</u>, they stepped around it as if it had been an April Fool's trick. When Schroeder now saw that all was lost, he had to bite the sour apple, and hand over his resignation, but he pled to be allowed to remain on the University faculty till spring, that is, to get paid, which was granted. Previously he had tried, with the most miserable bowing and scraping, to get close to the Ireland whom he so poisonously hates, in order to entreat his protection! A wretched toad!

Tell me: would the Jesuit Schroeder, the rector of the Collegio Germanico here, be his brother? Because you said to me once that he has a brother here in an Order.

---

[57] Andreas Steinhuber (1825-1907), Jesuit, Cardinal and Prefect of the Index Congregation.

Since the above is still as good as unknown in Europe, I don't need to suggest the greatest discretion in handling this news. Schroeder has now played out in America and will probably try to come home.

Whether the Jesuits will not turn to their old tactics with him: to expel members grown insupportable? The General of the order I know begins to have second thoughts, for stormy petrels fly away and one asks oneself if the decree of Clement XIV couldn't be renewed? Leo XIII however lies totally in the hands of Steinhuber and Mazzella, these fanatical Jesuits. While the papal newssheets were filled with the Milanese Catholic Congress, not one syllable was divulged about the one in Freiburg.

The pope himself – according to famous old patterns – is already treated as half dead by the College, since he deliberates so long about dying! He, on the contrary, thinks only to live and to haggle things together. Like <u>Satolli</u> he has also warehoused everything of value in his room in order to feast his eyes upon it; also surely because an ancient usage awards to his family all that is found in the death chamber of the pope. Which doesn't keep the servants from steadily plundering everything as the eyes of the pope close!

For the confirmation of the above, at the dedication of the Catholic university at Anagni – the papal city – for which three million was donated by the pope – there appeared – besides the two Jesuits – scarcely <u>one</u> cardinal. All reported themselves sick! "All Rome was ill on that same day," exclaimed one acquaintance, sly, with a wink.

On the trip back I visited Bishop Bonomelli[58] in Cremona, who sends greetings. He sighed and groaned over the muzzling of the episcopate, 'the very Jews in Babylon could have had it no worse.' [No ending]

---

[58] Geremia Bonomelli (1831-1914), 1871 Bishop of Cremona. Advocated reconciliation of the Church with modern culture and an understanding between the Vatican and the Kingdom of Italy.

December 3, 1897
Friday
Rome

My dear friend,
Barely in possession of your welcome news[59], I gave myself over to the room-search for you. Convinced that you can only find in a guest house your indispensable comforts, I fixed an eye first on two houses for you: On Trinità dei Monti, Hotel New York, Hassler's German guesthouse, and in Due Macelli the always well occupied Victoria. The latter is just recently gone over into German hands and offers, in the garden building (christened Villa Aegir!), besides absolute quiet, full southern exposure.

The host, Herr Thiele, guided me around and showed me on the first floor itself a spacious, two-windowed salon, with a hearth, lengthy, and therefore comfortably can be so rearranged with a bed screen, that one room supplies you as a sitting- and visiting-room also. If not, a little bedroom next door could be connected with it.

Thiele noted the prices for me on a card which I enclose and added that he would be prepared to make small reductions for missed meals, provided that he knew of it the day before. He showed me on the ground floor an extension to the social areas through a smoking room and a second small sitting room where he thought you could always receive visitors undisturbed. I have indicated on the card the room proposed for you. The prices remain the same as on the ground floor for the first and second floors.

At Hassler's I saw a balcony room (No.19) in the second floor with a view toward St. Peter's, a cute three-cornered annex (however *'wachilir arm'* as the

---

[59] Kraus wrote to her on Nov. 21, 1897, to say he was coming to Rome. He added that he would deal with Schroeder in the January letter of Spectator and in a happy mood he inquired about Duchesne's cats and their owner.

Austrians say), a coal stove sits in the fireplace. The restrictedness of this space, stuffed nevertheless with two beds, is compensated for by a dark closed-off anteroom that serves as a wash cabinet and wardrobe and is partitioned with a curtain, so that direct passage to the door and stairs is completely free. The electric light in both areas eases this division significantly. There is also a lift there.

Hassler wants, for full pension with this little balcony room, <u>before</u> February, 13 lire, from Feb. 1st on, 14 lire per day. Since however I know him, that lets me speak with him, and the headwaiter thought that, when a <u>definite</u> inquiry came – a reduction would certainly be arrived at.

Countess Lippe[60] was right satisfied last winter in the Molaro (corner of the Gregoriana and Capo le Case). There I know the Italian owner also and can – as you wish – talk to him.

In your place I would restrict my choice to these three reliable and well managed houses, which are all three near the Spanish Place. Since last year an elevator affords direct communication every five minutes between Trinità dei Monti and the Spanish Place. The fare is payable for half the service, that is, five cents for the trip <u>up</u> from below. Besides that, carriages always stand at the hotel door.

The Pension Lermann is in other hands, in that Lermann has established the Hotel Germania in the Via Boncompagni (a long way behind the Ludovisi and the Palazzo Piombino). The electric streetcar luckily goes over there, otherwise the Hügels would have become totally inaccessible, since two winters ago they settled over there with Lermann.

The above mentioned are back here again since fourteen days ago and rejoice about you no less than the Lovatelli and our American friends, who all together heartily greet you and send their devoted compliments.

---

[60] Carole von Stillfried, born 1847, married Count Egmont von Lippe-Biesterfeld-Weissenfeld, of the Catholic branch of Lippe (b.1841) on April 16, 1879.

I send congratulations on the conclusion of the Dante![61]

Duchesne is here again, though he supposes me still far away and up till now has shown no sign of life. Next thing I'll shake him up. To Lovatelli he has – God knows why? – since last year – been totally aloof and doesn't visit her any more. I know that from <u>her herself</u>.

Brunetière's[62] audience at the Vatican – as was not otherwise to be expected – proceeded with mutual admiration. The pope bid him to go forthwith and smooth the way for him in *chère* France and Brunetière found it flattering, just too admirable. He left together with Guillaume[63], who – with one and three-quarters feet in the grave – goes expressly to Paris to candidate for the Academy! Who besides a Frenchman would possess the energy of such vanity?

Archbishop Keane is not only back again in the best of health, happily exalted by the colossal banquet which they gave him in Washington, but also he already has his audience behind him! It happened last Monday. As usual the Servant of All Servants embraced him unctuously, rejoiced in overflowing expressions over his return, his sure help at the Propaganda as Referent for the American affairs (which up to now despite his appointment has remained a dead letter) and added: "We have relinquished Schroeder to the American decisions, we support him no longer."

O'Connell and Zahm ask you urgently <u>at first</u> to remain strictly silent about this; so that if Schroeder yet opens his mouth, he can without mercy be stopped cold. I think the Jesuits – true to their old methods – will, along with the pope, let him fall, since he brings them only damage instead of usefulness.

---

[61] Franz Xaver Kraus, *Dante. Sein Leben und sein Werk, sein Verhältnis zur Kunst u. zur Politik,* (Berlin, 1897.)

[62] Ferdinand Brunetière (1849-1906) French historian of Literature, from 1893 Editor-in-chief of the *Revue des Deux Mondes.*

[63] Jean Baptiste Eugene Guillaume (1822-1905) From 1890 Director of the Academie de France in Rome.

After Satolli at the beginning opposed Keane's appointment to New Orleans, which Keane later refused <u>in order</u> to work here, la Chapelle[64] has gone there.

Corrigan's altered stance toward his protégé Schroeder was a mistake. He still always stands up for him, and thus is isolated from the whole American episcopate.

Ireland's esteem rises again in Rome after his indestructibility has proved itself so brilliantly in America and so he will arrive here sometime in February for further strengthening of the same.

How can you stay away from that? Get ready <u>soon</u> to come and stay a long time!

Since I never see that insane thing the *Civiltà*, I don't know Grisar's[65] article. However Baron Hügel made a note of the exact number for your man.

---

[64] Placide L. Chapelle, born in France, educated at Baltimore, close associate of Cardinal Gibbons and Archbishops Keane and Ireland; as Archbishop of Santa Fe was named Archbishop of New Orleans, Dec. 1, 1897.

[65] Hartmann Grisar, S.J. (1845-1932), Church historian, 1871-1895 Professor in Innsbruck.

> The article appeared in the *Civiltà Cattolica* of July 11, 1897. Kraus noted that it was an "enraged attack on my *Kunstgeschichte*...wherein I was summoned to God's throne of justice...to think about the obligations of my calling..." (*Tgb*, p.692, September 28, 1897)

Friend Venturi[66] has been down with a severe cold for two weeks. He told me above all of his regret that a letter from you which his wife forwarded to him in Madrid, remained inaccessible for him in spite of repeated attempts to reclaim it from the post office there. I write that to you to avoid any misunderstanding.

From Schleinitzes I have indirectly the disturbing news that Adele, because of a small hemorrhage in the brain, requires the greatest care and her doctor says: I think a recovery would be very slow. I <u>fear</u> that only comes with death in such cases! You grasp how deeply this troubles me and affects me also for Alexandra who lives for her sister. What an affliction!

Command me as 'master of the house' and soon make your decision known to your

A. v. Eichthal

---

[66] Adolfo Venturi (1856-1941), Italian Art Historian. Director of Galleries and Museums, author of an exhaustive history of Italian art. Sometime Inspector at the Este Gallery in Modena, Venturi moved to Rome in 1889, where he and other civil servants urged the State to purchase the art held by the Doria Pamphilii, etc., who preferred to sell abroad. Gabriele D'Annunzio added to the complications. See Giacomo Agosti, "Adolfo Venturi and the Roman Galleries Fideicommission, 1891-1893," *Roma Moderna e Contemporanea,* Vol. I, No. 3, Dec. 1993.

December 19, 1897
Rome

Dear friend,
Immediately after receiving your commission[67] I hurried right then to the Victoria where the proprietor after much hemming and hawing wrote out the following: from the 1st or 15th of February, for No. 47 and No. 48 in the Villa Aegir, 15 lire per day. Deduction for lunch 1.50, for dinner 2.00. Included, two candles per week. One lamp per week – 2.50.

He said it was the most visited period, in February, March, and April, and so he must set these prices. I bargained and thus got one lira off per day. Why do you not want to be fully satisfied with the one room at 11 lire per day? You can look later and speak directly.

Dr. Zahm has unexpectedly been called away to inspect the Holy Cross filiale in <u>Bengal</u>, and unfortunately goes away in January, to return home from there by way of Japan.

Hügels and Duchesne rejoice wildly about you. To the latter I yesterday supplied the last two Spectators for a look-through. O'Connell and Keane impatiently look forward to your acquaintance and are happy about the ant. Canserie [sic] on January 1st.[68]

Happy holidays and a healthy beginning of the New Year – wished to you from the bottom of the heart by your
                                A. v. E.

---

[67] Kraus wrote to her on Dec.5, 1897, choosing the two rooms in the Hotel Victoria annex. He suggested that "Herr Thiele will make me a more reasonable price when you tell him I am an habitué." He reported that he had read O'Connell's *New Idea* and that he would handle Washington matters with great care. In subsequent letters on Dec. 17 and 21, he confirmed his arrival in Rome on Feb. 15th, repeated his desire to see the "Americans," and promised a "New Year's present" in his January Spectator letter.

[68] The immediate reference here is unknown, but it promises the American revelations in the January 1st Spectator Letter. See the next Eichthal letter of January 7, 1898.

1898
Chapter 3

January 7, 1898
Rome

Valued friend,
You have delivered a masterpiece! My head is still buzzing from the verbal translation which I immediately worked out yesterday for the benefit of the enthusiastic O'Connell. He jumped up, ran around, and exclaimed over and over again [in English] "good! excellent! how concise! how profound! He has rendered the meaning of it all in a nutshell." He expressed to you his most venerating thanks and will try to collect a number of copies for his distribution. Do you think that in consideration of the number a price reduction might be obtained? Say a dozen or more.[69]

Today Archbishop Keane will read it, he can do German admirably. The gentlemen are excited on account of your coming. Only don't hold back so long. Every day is a day gained here.

The reports out of Meran about Adele von Schleinitz sound <u>somewhat</u> more favorable; God allow that it indicates true improvement!

May this year bring good luck for you in every way and grant us many pleasant hours united together! Amen!

---

[69] Kraus had written on January 4, 1898, to say that he was packing for a February 15th arrival in Rome. He included his latest Spectator Letter, datelined, "Berlin, January 3, 1898." It made extensive reference to Denis O'Connell's speech delivered at the Congress in Fribourg, Switzerland. The Letter also asserted the futility of German-American resistance to American ways, and using material supplied by Professor Charles P. Grannan, gave the damning details of Msgr. Joseph Schroeder's dismissal from the Catholic University.

AVE

Please indicate day of arrival.[70]

---

[70] Kraus wrote from Nervi on February 15, 1898, to say that he was delayed.

February 22, 1898
Shrove Tuesday
Rome

[To Kraus, Hotel Eden, Via Ludovisi[71]]

Dear friend! Are you <u>finally</u> there? The last time I galloped over to the Eden in vain; that's why I am cautious this time and ask first.[72]

Are you at home this afternoon or do you want to come to me? Or I to you, right after lunch, between 2 and 3 o'clock? Should I invite Keane and O'Connell here for tomorrow for you, or for this afternoon at 4 o'clock?

Decide. Your will shall be done!   AVE

Until we happily meet again!

---

[71] Choosing the Hotel Eden over the Victoria, Kraus signed boldly in the 1898 guest Register, where his signature can still be seen. In 2001 the ancient register was on display in the lobby of the Hotel Eden, open at the October 1898 signature of Gabriel D'Annunzio.

[72] Kraus was very eager to meet O'Connell and Keane, sending greetings in a Feb. 15th note from Nervi and telling her of his hoped-for arrival in Rome on the 17th. He enjoyed the friendship of the two Americans from late February to early April. (*Tgb.*, pp. 697-700)

April 2, 1898
Saturday evening
176 Ripetta

To Kraus, Hotel Eden

Dear friend,
Archbishop Keane came here this afternoon from your hotel in the vain hope of finding you. He wants you, asking urgently, to grant him a rendezvous here, Monday (the 5th) around 5 o'clock since he fears otherwise not to see you anymore on account of the sermon…

[illegible]

April 8, 1898

To Kraus in Florence

Dear friend,
Last evening I parted from you sorrowfully and can only earnestly hope that the greater quiet of Florence may quickly strengthen your health.[73] I send along a pair of lines to my distinguished old friend Stallo[74] (for whom on the address his judge's office serves as a title according to American custom). His villa lies about 5 – 7 minutes from Porta Romana (can be reached on foot and also by carriage.) With Brentano[75] the Stallos are very good friends.

Give me news of yourself and may the future winter bring you to us longer.

In true friendship, your   A. v. Eichthal

---

[73] The cold wet spring in Rome was very hard on Kraus who was largely confined to his hotel. He left for Florence at the end of the first week in April.

[74] John Bernhard Stallo (1823-1900), United States Minister to Italy, 1885 – 1889. One of the 'Ohio Hegelians,' born in Sierhausen (Oldenburg), the '48er Stallo achieved prominence in America as a philosopher of science, educator, jurist, and statesman. Author of *The Concepts and Theories of Modern Physics*, he foreshadowed general ideas later formulated in the theory of relativity and quantum mechanics by observing that concerning light, heat, electricity and magnetism, each should be treated "as different manifestations of the same fundamental energy."

[75] Franz Brentano (1838-1917), philosopher and psychologist, left the priesthood in Würzburg in 1873 in disagreement with Papal Infallibility and taught at Vienna, 1874 – 1895, where his students included Freud, Husserl and Tomas Masaryk. Married in 1880 despite Austrian denial of his lay status. Retired to Florence in 1895.

April 20, 1898

To Kraus in Florence

Dear friend,
In vain I sought you out early on that Holy Saturday <u>before</u> 9 o'clock – evenso you were gone. You received my note I know[76] – and with the enclosure for Stallo. I am deeply anxious to know how you are. And if Florence fulfilled your hopes? Schleinitzes send their very best and ask: please visit them in Meran, as it fares much better with Adele. In March Alexandra published in the *Neue freie Presse* a memoir of the year '48 when the Prince and Princess of Prussia[77] fled to their parents and her father brought the noble party to safety to Spandau.[78]

We think of you in loyal circles here and <u>I</u> miss you indescribably! O'C. greets you ardently. Countess Kinsky[79] lets me know that she works on your photographic copies but can only achieve one per day. Of the twenty-four promised, one will be brought to me for proof-reading.

---

[76] In a diary notation of April 18, 1898, in Florence, Kraus wrote that he had been with "Franz Brentano, who took me to the former Ambassador of the United States in Rome, Mr. Stallo, a very highly educated, magnificent, old man." (*Tgb.*, p. 702.)

[77] Wilhelm Friedrich Ludwig (1797-1888), Prince of Prussia , (future Wilhelm I, King of Prussia and German Emperor,) married in 1829 to Augusta of Saxe-Weimar-Eisenach. In the revolution of March 1848 Prince Wilhelm was dubbed 'Prince of Grapeshot' (*Kartätschenprinz*) for his advocacy of military force. After an extended vacation in England he returned to Prussia in June 1848. Became King of Prussia in 1861.

[78] The name of von Schleinitz is associated with Prussian army service in the nineteenth century. Spandau was a fortress in a Berlin suburb at the time of the 1848 revolts. Alexandra von Schleinitz (whose memories of 1848 were that of a six year old child) converted to Roman Catholicism, with her sister Adele, in 1892.

[79] Marianne Countess Kinsky, born 1854, married 1877 Michael Baron Nicolics de Rudna, 1880 divorced and resumed maiden name.

In the Vatican dispatches fly hither and yon and Ireland threatens to fall between two stools into a sorry situation through his intermediary role, as well as through the publication here (despite his protest) of his dispatches, which hurt him there.[80] Everything is in an uproar...

[illegible][81]

---

[80] Archbishop Ireland attempted, on the initiative of the Vatican, to mediate in the American-Spanish conflict. His efforts were late and accomplished little.

[81] Kraus replied from Florence on April 23, 1898. He had moved to Lungarno Corsini 6, the weather had been nothing but rain, and bad for his health. He planned to leave on the 26th by Milan to Freiburg, or via Munich. Sending greetings to all in Rome, especially O'Connell and the Crown Princess of Sweden, and 'the good Venturi,' he added, "Brentano and Stallo I have visited. The latter is a most highly interesting old gentleman. I would have liked to be with him longer."

May 17, 1898
176 Ripetta
Rome

Now, beloved friend, how and by which route have you reached home? Hopefully in better health than you predicted? How often your name sounds from our lips and we long for the return of the wonderful hours of last March. Donna Ersilia, Friend O'Connell and Duchesne have these days commissioned me with wholly special greetings for you. The last paid me a productive visit yesterday and said to me word for word, [in French. Ed.] "Salute friend Kraus – and congratulate him – on my part, on the ascension, so fortunate, of the new archbishop to Paradise before he could once more make his entrance into his diocese! What a relief!" He spoke to me from the heart. On reading the newspaper report, I tipped up very ceremoniously in the easy chair and thought, "the much decried finger of God!" Won't the Ultramontanes suspect in this case, since he belongs to them, that this finger points at them?"[82]

In the meantime the pious successor to St. Ambrose and Charles Borromeo has performed an edifying stunt with his negative courage and his positive flight in the days of greatest need.[83] Naturally you know of the exchange of

---

[82] On the 10th of May the new and decidedly ultramontane Archbishop of Freiburg, Georg Ignaz Komp, died suddenly in Mainz the day before his scheduled enthronement in Freiburg. Kraus had thought his acceptance as archbishop by the Baden authorities an act of 'unbelievable stupidity.' (*Tgb.*,p. 700) Kraus repeated this 'finger of God' expression in his diary, May 29. (*Tgb.*,p. 704)

[83] In May of 1898 troops were sent to Milan to quell bread riots over increased prices caused by high tariffs and the Spanish-American War.

letters between Archbishop Ferrari[84] and General Bava.[85] The lapidary answer of the latter deserves to live in literature among the masterpieces of appropriate brevity and annihilating content. The general indignation at this intransigent peasant's son's cowardice will perhaps purge him forth from Milan! Yet here, even through all levels of the clergy, only one voice has been raised in disapproval of his disgraceful conduct. And it only asks that for politics' sake the pope should dismiss him.

Also, Don Albertario,[86] the steely feather hero (steel pen hero!) has vanished from the scene of his ink wars and Stoppani[87] battles.

Rudini's fainthearted making of pacts and flattering of the extreme Left, with Cavalotti as Speaker, proceeded from powerless ambition, that is the hallmark of these May days. In regard to the Left's death march here[88], the outlawed funeral looks and the unheard-of banner slogans – they appear to be unhindered – there dawns on one a bloody suspicion of the rapid realization of danger to country and regime. The first fright made Rudini courageous – for how long? Already in slight fluctuations the see-saw government begins to show itself again.[89]

---

[84] Andrea Giacomo Cardinal Ferrari (1850-1921), 1894 Cardinal and Archbishop of Milan.

[85] General Bava-Beccaris, whose shelling of working class districts of Milan in 1898 is said to have added impulse to the anarchist movement.

[86] Don Davide Albertario (1846-1902), fiery priest, fierce opponent of the reforms proposed by Antonio Rosmini, editor of the belligerently intransigent *Osservatore Cattolico di Milano*. In the aftermath of the bread riots Albertario was sentenced to three years in prison but was amnestied and released.

[87] Antonio Stoppani, leading advocate of Rosminian ideas.

[88] The May Day parade of the Socialists.

[89] The second premiership of Marchese Antonio di Rudini (1838-1908) began with the defeat at Adowa in March 1896. His domestic policy could not prevent serious rioting in 1898, nor could he deal successfully with threatening Socialist revolution. His

What do you say about England? My predictions, since this disastrous war came into prospect, will I fear be confirmed: those storm clouds conjured up in the East will explode over Europe from the West ... Spain serves as the first miserable lightning rod – for how long?

Can you enlighten me about <u>Paul Garin's</u> nationality and character, he who published the April 12th article on <u>Dogma and Science</u> in the *Beilage* of the *Allg. Ztg.*? Is he Catholic or Protestant?

Friend O'Connell would gladly see his little brochure on Americanism, which you know, translated into German and brought out by Herder, who printed the original. Have any advice?

Recently I had <u>here</u> a great Cardinals-reception, enlivened pleasantly by many of the worldly. The nice young Saurma[90] enjoyed himself like a child. Also Keane naturally was there, only I could scarcely exchange a word with him and thereby lack his salutations for you.

That Dutchman Van Eyck, whom you once snubbed here at my place, is off to the completion of his theological studies in England, where Cardinal Vaughan thinks to turn him to use after that.

It would be very nice of you, dear friend, if you would make subscription propaganda for Venturi's recently produced art magazine, *l'Arte*. The first volume (consisting of two issues) is followed these days by the second for March-April-May, full of well-done illustrations to the text. For foreign delivery 34 lire, domestic 30 lire yearly.

---

government fell in June 1898.

[90] Anton Baron Saurma von der Jeltsch (1836-1900), Councilor, later Ambassador in Rome. "Young" is apparently in jest. Saurma died at 64, in 1900.

Alexandra Schleinitz's request to come to Meran – didn't reach you before you left Florence? Have you seen Bulle[91] since then? Where sits Donna Ersilia's article about the ancient fire brigade? Extinguished in the Isar? That Stallo would reply to you, I knew. I take pleasure in this gift of divination and plead earnestly for a report to your devoted

   A. v. Eichthal

---

[91] Oskar Bulle (1857-1917), in 1897 became the new editor of the scientific supplement, the *Beilage*, of the *Allgemeine Zeitung*.

June 7, 1898

My beloved friend,
To know[92] that lately you are so full of pain is heart-rending. All your friends learn it with great sympathy and through me express to you the hope that the final arrival of warmer temperature may disperse the swelling as well as the pain!

Your June Letter[93] betrayed – by God! nothing whatsoever of all these physical hardships. You lift yourself this time <u>far</u> above the tone of the earlier Letters and you work in certain moments just like a seer, filled with holy wrath, like a new Dante: "Gaze upon the Roman disorder, which has from old grown too closely intertwined with the abode which produces it, ever to be otherwise." Every Catholic must acknowledge this at present.

As I translated for friend O'Connell last evening the chief points (especially about the results of the Cuban war),[94] he jumped up astounded and

---

[92] Kraus had written May 29, 1898, to thank her for 'affectionate lines.'

[93] Spectator Letter of June 1, 1898. A major portion of the Letter (with flattering reference to Msgr. Denis O'Connell), is devoted to Hermann Schell's latest broschure, *Die neue Zeit und der alte Glaube.* Kraus also commented on Abbé Maignen's criticisms of Isaac Hecker which were appearing in French newspapers.

[94] The part that pleased O'Connell the most reads:
"In one point, I believe [Schell and I] agree together, that is the conviction that the future of mankind and that of the Church is caught up in the Germanic or Anglo-Saxon world. If that was not clear to anyone, such a person can now be instructed by the most recent events, The deplorable collapse of the Romance peoples which we experience in these times has thrown a terrible flash of light on the situation. In succession, those states which are openly ruled or secretly managed by the statutes of Jesuitical Catholicism have gone the way to the grave, particularly because the Catholic principle within them has been covered over by Ultramontanism and the peoples have lost the thread of all ability to cultivate civil interests or to hold fast to them.
"The Cuban War has just destroyed…the last remains of this system. With preternatural force the American giant raises itself in the West. Its ascent will give the European nations a fearful jolt and compel them to an interior renewal and self-composure, out of

exclaimed, " almost word for word – exactly the same that I recently wrote to Ireland." Thus noble minds concur.

Let me express to you my thankful admiration about this lofty tone, honored friend! This time your ironic flights occur with such wide separation that, like sound seasonings, instead of irritating and burning the gums as is the case with an oversupply of pepper, they work powerfully through fine moderation. This time <u>no one</u> can question the deep source from which your irony as well as your holy wrath wells up and froths, <u>and that's the way it should be!</u>

Oh, dear fellow, your office is so singly important that I might contest every hour in which you turn your mighty spirit to other things! As useful as is your art history…other qualified men can do it! For God's sake concentrate yourself on that which <u>none other</u> than you can do! Last night O'Connell and I were so completely of one mind in that, that I promised to press you to think about it.

A propos of Art, before I go on to other things: Friend Venturi, greatly pleased to hear from you, returns your greetings many times and asks you right truly for the following help: Whether you can hunt up for him in Freiburg (where it is printed) Pater Beissel's "Vatican Miniatures," and, upon payment, have it sent? He finds himself in the fatal situation of having borrowed it from the Casanatense[95] and is unable to find it again, so that he has to think about replacing it. The poor man recently lost a younger brother in Modena very suddenly, with a surviving consumptive widow and <u>six</u> ill-bred children <u>and not a red cent</u>! You grasp what that means for Venturi!

---

which, from the religious side of the victory, the Germanic principle will raise itself." Spectator Letter, *Beilage, Allgemeine Zeitung*, June 1, 1898.

[95] The Casanatense Library founded in 1698 by Cardinal Casanate. Via di S. Ignazio, 52, Rome.

In the meantime père Meignan in Paris (with the cooperation of Periviez) [Ed. Périès] has given himself the luxury of giving libelous vent to his friendly feeling for the Americans. The item carried the highly suggestive question mark as a title, "*Le père Hecker, fut-il un Saint?*" and in touching devotion is dedicated to the Sacred Heart of Jesus, to which it brings an eye-rolling invocation and appeal.[96] Hecker is not alone as the subject of attack … Ireland, Gibbons, Keane, and O'Connell are also gleefully chopped up for the frying pan with coarse invective. When the product of these two noble souls came up to Cardinal Richard[97] for the <u>imprimatur</u>, and this man of God saw what it was about, as a decent shepherd of souls, he declined approval. Now what did Meignan and Company do? Hastily they came right here and acquired the necessary permission without further ado!

When our friends saw the publication, they learned simultaneously that of the fifty copies deposited here, twenty-two of them were gone immediately! Keane betook himself in the highest possible dudgeon, armed with a fulminating written complaint, to Cardinal Rampolla, who naturally played the astonished innocent, swore neither he nor the pope had heard anything about it and assured "immediate remedies." Yes indeed, [like] snails with a crane! A week has passed since then, with neither the *Voce* nor the *Osservatore* having said the least single word about it in the sense of a papal disapproval of what happened.

That has so shaken Keane out of his anxiety that he is even grateful for this step by the opponents, because of which the American phalanx, pushed to the wall for defense, to resist this gang, <u>can</u> and <u>must</u> develop their powers. *Eppur si muove!*

---

[96] Charles Maignen, *Études sur l'américanisme, le père Hecker — est-il un Saint?* (Paris, 1898.) The book bore the Roman imprimatur of Alberto Lepidi, O.P., Master of the Sacred Palace (court theologian to the pope).

[97] Francois Cardinal Richard (1819-1908), Archbishop of Paris, 1886; Cardinal, 1889.

Close by this there runs the satyr's play of one des Houx,⁹⁸ who having decided to vent his spleen on the pope, has lovingly investigated among the family papers and other things at Carpineto, in order to evaluate the desirable worthwhile materials for a — biography of His Holiness! He asserts that he has turned up *Carmina* from the pope's youth and learned things about the conduct of his life back then that would number among the most scandalous things possible, especially the Latin poems! And he is in good standing with that double-dealer Parocchi,⁹⁹ this des Houx! Rabble— foes one minute and friends the next!

I am sending you at once, commissioned by O'Connell, a copy of the Catalog of Relics which you wished to have. Since then, in Donna Ersilia's parish church of S. Maria in Campitelli,¹⁰⁰ there has indeed occurred a new enrichment of miraculous pictures through the eye-winking of a painted Saviour.

Would that in your vicinity I knew a mountain resort that suited me both for air and finances. Feldberg, never again, and otherwise? Everything too low, right?

O'Connell rejoices and longs like you for a reunion in the course of July before your trip to the baths and salutes a thousand times! He and Keane come to me day after tomorrow to relish your Letter *viribus unitis*!

---

⁹⁸ Henri Des Houx, pseudonym of Henri Durand-Morimbeau (!848-1911); *Histoire de Leon XIII – Joachim Pecci (1810-1878)*, Paris 1900. (See Weber, *Quellen und Studien*, p. 84.)

⁹⁹ Lucido Maria Parocchi (1833-1908), Cardinal 1877.

¹⁰⁰ The church , on the Piazza Campitelli, is just a few steps from the Palazzo Caetani-Lovatelli in the corner of the square.

On Corpus Christi at 8:30 P.M. I sup accordingly with Donna Ersilia. God be with you, precious friend! Hopefully, soon a line says that everything has come around all right to your

A. v. Eichthal[101]

---

[101] Kraus replied on June 16, 1898.

July 17, 1898
Saturday
Munich

Honored friend,
Today for the first time I can say something definite, because since being here I have been dependent on my brother,[102] who goes with me in the morning for a two-day visit to Princess Leiningen.[103] On the 21st we are in Baden-Baden. There I ask you to inform me at <u>Frl. Luise Siefert's, Langestrasse</u>, where in Freiburg (not too far from you), be it in a quiet pension or in a small clean guest house, I can put up for several days. Since I accompany my brother as far as Strassburg, I may scarcely get to Freiburg before evening on the 22nd. O'Connell also comes soon? There is much to tell and to think over. Infinitely rejoicing at the happy prospect of seeing you soon again, I am, your highly admiring

A. v. Eichthal

---

[102] Emil von Eichthal.

[103] Marie Amalie, Princess of Baden (1834-1899), married (1858) Ernst Leopold Emich, Fürst zu Leiningen (1830-1904). The two-day visit implies a side trip to Waldleiningen.

July 22, 1898
Friday
Baden

Dear, honored friend,
Your friendly lines I found here[104] and I thank you very much for the addresses. My brother would like the honor of being presented to you, and consequently has decided to accompany me <u>tomorrow Saturday</u> on the express train which gets to Freiburg at 11:47 A.M. I will put up at the hotel garni (over Café Thomann), which you recommended, as my brother wants to travel on home to the Gironde by way of Strassburg. While with the Geymüllers[105] I have already most affectionately thought of you and I am indescribably glad that tomorrow I will clasp your hand. Your

A. v. Eichthal

---

[104] Kraus replied, "Happy to see you here," on July 19, advising the Café Thomann or the pension Beau Sejour.

[105] Heinrich, Baron von Geymüller (1839-1909), Architect and Art Historian, lived in Baden.

July 22, 1898
7 o'clock in the evening
Baden

Dear friend, unfortunately it appears that due to a special matter (relating to the grave of our mother), we will not be able to come tomorrow early. My brother, in consequence has to give up on Freiburg and hurry straight home. But I hope to catch an express train in the course of the afternoon which takes me to you so that no postponement to the following day will result. Until a speedy reunion I send you my kindest regards.   AVE

October 12, 1898
Wednesday
Villa Friedheim
Meran (Obermais)

My dear friend,
Did you receive my Constance newspaper greeting? How I thank you for the advice[106] to travel over Triberg-Donaueschingen! It was marvelously pretty; in Triberg I found waterfall and forest surroundings of a true Schwarzwald mood, while the mere view of the little Fürstenberg palace served to satisfy my curiosity for the rest of my time on earth. I had imagined the situation far more romantically.

In Gossensass I delayed going to Innsbruck for a full week, and walked with rapture in the evergreen-spiced forest paths of this magnificent mountain world, while the comfort at Groebner's allowed me philosophically to bear several rainy days. Steam heat, electric lighting…! In a Tyrolean alpine village!

Also in Klausen I stayed for the night and that afternoon immediately climbed up to the Cloister Säben.[107] That morning there had been no less than three nuns clothed, one a Hohenzollern, one a Swabian. When I asked for the abbess, she received me at once in the visiting room, in the company of the novice mistress, separated from me by a simple grating.

The abbess impressed me more as a two-footed ruminant than as the superior of a Benedictine cloister, while the younger novice mistress, by her reserve, struck me more as an educated intelligent person. Although a Stuttgarter, she

---

[106] Kraus wrote, with apologies, on August 16, 1898, saying he had been delayed in Baden-Baden.

[107] Augusta von Eichthal at 63 must have been in good physical condition. These are serious uphill excursions in Klausen.

didn't "schwäbel" in the least. I learned that she is the daughter of a senior teacher there. Her example has likely kindled the hearts of the eight other Swabians who have followed her. Fifty-three nuns, of whom twenty-four are lay sisters, live up there according to the exact statement of the abbess, (lost in blissful idleness!)

In the old comfortable tavern below I noticed quiet astonishment that I had actually spoken with the abbess. And when I incidentally mentioned it to the Schleinitzes they couldn't conceal their amazement. They assured me that it is absolutely unheard of, since <u>no one</u> ever gains entry and even the cloister gate is scarcely attainable for laity.

Another morning I looked around in the Loretto Chapel of the Capuchins[108] at the Spanish legacy of Queen Anna Maria (born Countess Palatine) which contains a great many things uncommonly worth seeing, and after that met the Schleinitzes in Bozen, who came directly from the Talsergena and the castle of their aunt, the wife of the Austrian ambassador in Paris.

Both of them asked about you and received your picture with the greatest and most thankful joy. Your "Dante" shines forth from their library table, your Savonarola Letters[109] are devoured by them and overall they are devoted to you in boundless admiration. Adele, praise be to God and thanks, looks once more as she did; only suffers from frequent headaches, can scarcely get about after each time rain hangs in the air, is generally a sensitive person of most unusual sort. She, as well as her sister Alexandra, are both equally enraged over the present Jesuit control of the church, over the horrifying abuses which, demoralizing and silencing any other tendencies, set the present tone; so

---

[108] Also in Klausen near the Benedictine cloister. Today the former Capuchin chapel is a museum which houses the gifts of the Spanish queen, Maria Anna.

[109] Four of the Spectator Letters, Numbers 37 to 41, were devoted to Savonarola, the last one appearing in October 1898.

much so that Adele assured me she has already been tempted to turn her back on the whole church.

What she told me about the domination of Pater Abel[110] in the Viennese court and government circles is certainly hair-raising. This Jesuit appears to have become all powerful there for about ten years, to have the conduct of affairs as well as the Emperor under his thumb and to be the most ominous advisor in the present complications.

What makes my friends totally beside themselves is the newly founded society Of the Divine Saviour. What do you know about it? Schleinitzes assured me that it was an Italian importation; founded some years back (probably I think under the name il divin Redentore) as an affiliate of the Jesuits. They intrigued and insinuated themselves everywhere, say Schleinitzes. I myself have repeatedly encountered here an odious looking, slickly decked-out, highly elegant, dark young priest in Jesuit hat and gown, of whom Adele remarked that that would be the dress and the manner of the juniors of the Divine Saviour! O thou heavenly forbearance! Why doesn't it finally snap? If only you could tell me!

Adele would like to know how one can get hold of the authentic list of the titles of all the books that have been put on the Index in our century. Do you have any advice for me, or even moreso, us? Where to turn? It must surely be printed?

Friend O'Connell left you yesterday on the 30th of September like he thought? And you after that made the contemplated ramble to Baden? How did it suit you? How does the fall climate suit you? Oh, valued friend, determine to turn your back over the winter to that surely murderous cold home of yours, all the more so since your substitute can jump in for you and the Grand Duke authorizes every furlough!

---

[110] Heinrich Abel S.J. (1843-1926), Viennese preacher to the public in the days of Karl Lueger.

Your life is more valuable to us all than what you can always produce there. Think that your home is indeed the source of your production but that must eo ipso decline if you become incapable of writing. Therefore: come to Rome! Work there on your most important things, for which you can dispense with your library treasury and which <u>above all</u> it is your holy obligation to maintain. I implore you for this on bended knee!

What say you to France? Quelle débâcle!

Here in Meran it is already cold and damp, fall-like. Toward the end of the month, about the 24th or 25th, I will return through Florence to Rome. But before that, all right? make happy, by a dear reply to here, your faithful

A. v. Eichthal[111]

---

[111] In his reply on October 14, Kraus said he had heard nothing new about Pater Abel.

October 27, 1898
Villa Friedheim
Meran (Obermais)

Dear friend,
In haste a request from A. von Schleinitz: besides most admiring compliments: whether the History of the Popes by Schulte is worth reading? Which would you generally recommend, besides the well known Ranke and Pastor?

And another: whether the history of St. Ignatius by Prof. Gottheimer is trustworthy?

In contrast I can report to you that that short gripping story of Ferdinand von Saar of which I told you, is called <u>Innozens</u>.[112]

How might it be with you? Here divine weather prevails. They can't recall such a mild fall here for 13 years. If only you were here! How we would spoil you!

Eperjesys,[113] on furlough from Teheran, have telegraphed me a rendez-vous for tomorrow.

---

[112] Ferdinand von Saar (1833-1906). The 'story' is his first novella, published in Vienna in 1866.

[113] Albert Eperjesy von Szaszvaros und Toti, Austro-Hungarian diplomat (died 1916), married 1881 Armgard Bettina Countess Oriola (born 1856), daughter of Eduard Count Oriola and Maximiliane von Arnim.

Rotenhan[114] in Bülow's place is called "neither the one nor the other." [*weder gehauen noch gestochen.*]

I leave on the afternoon of the 31st through Florence and plan to be in Rome on Nov. 3rd.

Here may I still learn something comforting about your condition, which concerns us all so deeply?[115]

With sincere thoughts of you, always, in friendship,

A. V. E.

---

[114] Wolfgang Baron von Rotenhan (1845-1912), 1898-1907 Prussian Envoy to the Vatican.

[115] On November 14 Kraus apologized that he had been occupied in Baden and advised that the Gottheimer book was 'one-sided.'

December 6, 1898
Tuesday
Rome

My dear friend,
There is so much going on here, but in the embryonic stage, that I wanted to wait a little for its development to more concrete form before I wrote. At the same time I wanted a free moment for finding out about Hotel Europa on your behalf. Yesterday I was there, the entry has been rearranged toward piazza Mignanelli, fully south – which make a more comfortable impression. The owner (who has leased his house on Silenzi for 15 years), has now taken over the management personally and noted down the prices on his card. In full south there is, mezzanine and first floor both, only one sleepable room, which would be too narrow for your requirements. The pension of 13 lire (all included and electric light) applies to this room.

As you see a similarly situated <u>double</u> room would be calculated at 12 lire [more], which is enormous. In the court he could make other arrangements for spacious rooms which have the afternoon sun, since the south side has been turned into noisy private salons.

Hotel de Londres would be even more costly. An elevator is naturally present, so that you could certainly live economically in the inner court in a higher location where the sun, as Francesolini says, shines in from mid-day on. At a nod from you I will go in, inspect the rooms off the court and report thereon. <u>Reductions</u> in the pension are not to be had.

Keane and O'Connell send fond greetings. I have seen both this morning; they are in good fettle and that speaks wonders for Keane's sound nature, for another person would have been irritated into yellow jaundice after all that has happened to him.[116]

---

[116] Keane's ill treatment coincides with the rise of anti-American feeling noted in the next letter of January 15, 1899.

Not enough, that a circular letter to the collective seminaries in Rome <u>indirectly</u> forbids the alumni to attend Keane's sermons (in that they were redirected to their theological studies, which made the hearing of sermons superfluous), Keane in the end had his sojourn at the Collegio Canadense revoked, <u>because he corrupted the youth there</u>!

The embarrassed rector served in the matter only as the mouthpiece for the instigators. Why didn't they let Keane know this in the summer, to avoid the appearance of such a throwing-out? You grasp how this matter, hawked about from college to college, must be painful for Keane.[117]

O'Connell has secured him an accommodation near by at St. Sulpice and worked it out that he also counts as a papal guest. Naturally this stroke originates from Satolli and Company, for Ledochowski[118] (who detests him) is far from this kind of malice.

They wanted to deny the pulpit generally to Keane in roundabout ways. In S. Silvestro he nevertheless preached on the Advent Sundays on — <u>Christ</u>, (at O'Connell's clever advice). May one ever so dearly want here to render our Saviour speechless, if only in order to extol his Lady Mother, and to tend to worldly matters, so no one <u>dares</u> get upset about <u>that</u> subject as unorthodox or liberal!

While that goes on, the exorbitant protests from Ireland, and <u>totally</u> extraordinarily from Gibbons, have given Leo XIII such a wholesome fright

---

[117] Keane first lived briefly in the Palazzo Brancaccio on the Via Meridana, then at the Canadian College, and finally at St. Sulpice. He thought his eviction from the Canadian College originated in Montreal, "I have moved...there was Montreal spite in it." Keane to Zahm, Dec. 10, 1898, Rome, Archives of the University of Notre Dame. (Cited in Patrick Ahern, *The Life of John J. Keane,* (Milwaukee, 1954), p. 294.)

[118] Cardinal Ledochowski, Prefect of Propaganda, was regarded by AVE as an honorable man.

over the possible alienation of the American church, that the decretal which has been prepared for months to nail up Hecker's Life and Doctrine on the Index, remains lying <u>unfinished</u> on Leo's desk. <u>This however is said only to you in closest confidence</u>. With that also is added the politically gigantic success of the United States, their possession of the Philippines upon which the future of the monastic orders hangs in most ticklish suspense, so that far less than before would it be asked to behave harshly toward the religious Americanism whose help becomes so important.

So Leo had prepared an encyclical which, treating the subject of Americanism cautiously, desired to glide colorlessly between Scylla and Charybdis and which was supposed to appear the next day. Suddenly he decided to put off its publication.

O'Connell however travels to Paris this evening for eight days, to cheer up Klein and also to get closer to the Christian Socialists there. He hopes to steer them on to wider pathways and to divert them from their narrow nationalism.

There he ought to begin first with Keane, whose narrow Jingoism could infuriate a sheep. How differently my wonderful Stallo conceives the situation! Every inch the statesman jurist and reflective sage! When I saw him in Florence he asked eagerly about you and asked me to let you know how he struggled in vain to find your address so he could visit you. That is a real wonder for otherwise he, so to say, doesn't visit. You were just as much a kindred soul for him as he was for you. It is always a special pleasure to me to bring people into mutual trust and love, when I feel in advance that it will really work out.

Do you know that the French have asked Archbishop Ireland to give the main speech at their Joan of Arc festival in Orleans in the spring? Here that is very fatal because Ireland's boundless glorification of the French at the banquet in Paris six years ago still sticks in my craw. He accepted, flattered, immediately, and so it is the duty of friend O'Connell to supervise the speech and to lead its content into other than chauvinistic reflection.

Recently Ireland's voice sounded from the pulpit in America to call out a 'Salve' to congenial fellow combatants in Germany. Hertling[119] may scarcely be numbered among these elect, as I suppose. Here he traveled in the most ultramontane channels and only came to table with Duchesne, Keane and O'Connell. The day after that he visited me and remarked his regret that he does not yet know you personally and expressed very correct German sentiments. Unfortunately his vanity and diplomatic inexperience played a trick on him, as he widely gossiped about the content of political discussions with cardinals like Agliardi and Vannutelli, and as it seems even to that fresh indiscrete newspaper writer Dr. Barth![120] With that he spoiled everything here for himself and what's more, was laughed at. Too bad, since he does have eloquence and according to circumstances, could give the Center [party] reasonable advice. Yesterday he left for home.

Your words of recognition have done uncommon good to our dear old Bülow[121], all the more since he stands in holy awe of you and worries that you are not especially favorable to him. Now your well-wishing made him all the more happy.

I report to you generally and with inner joy, how by everyone the benign milder tone in your Essays is recognized and finds loud approval. "The embittered way of writing has indeed, God be praised, disappeared," I hear

---

[119] Georg Baron von Hertling, after 1914, Count, (1843-1919), 1880 Prof. of Philosophy at Munich, 1912 Bavarian Ministerpresident, 1917 Reich Chancellor.

[120] Dr. Hans Barth, 'correspondent of one of the leading journals of Berlin,' published *Guida spirituale delle osterie italiane da Verona a Capri*, Rome, 1910.

[121] For a time there were two von Bülows operating in Rome; Otto, called 'Black' Bülow, because Prussian envoy to the Vatican, and Bernhard, 'White' Bülow, because German ambassador to Italy. Otto retired in 1898 and Kraus mentioned him positively in a Spectator Letter. Kraus noted in his diary that Otto was very pleased with the good mention, but added, "It was not particularly deserved." (*Tgb.*,p. 714) Otto had always been very wary of Kraus, who had been the moving force in the downfall of his predecessor, Kurd von Schlözer. Otto von Bülow died shortly after his retirement.

from all sides. "How much more usefully the present style works! One sees that he has overcome his severe trials and, purified, has risen above it."

Dear friend! You see how this self-control repays itself? A propos: do you know that Baron Hügel has been operated on in a London clinic for God only knows what?

I had much more to say. But enough! You are coming, thank God! Hurry to us, we want to take care of you. The weather is heavenly!

In true friendship, your

A.v. E.

1899
Chapter 4

January 15, 1899
Rome

My dear friend,
Your letter of admonition[122] has so shaken me yesterday out of the steady Platonic intention to write you that I even send you this sheet of paper from bed. Since Thursday when I went out toward evening in the horrible wet, I have the mode-influenza. With care I hope to overcome it soon. Friend O'Connell also had it for a longtime, since his return. That then his first stroll was to see me, and was above all to report on his excursion to you, for that you may be thanked!

Your inquiry, worthy of a Reinecke,[123] in your dear first letter, accordingly entertained me not a little.

In the meantime the storm against the 'Americanism' gathers strength, filled with hate more and more critically. Satolli is naturally the soul and chief architect of the contention which finds a ready hearing - that through America's boundless dishonorable management of unforeseen circumstances at an armistice or further peace treaty, about which every upright frere, – we also say (because we are observers), every man without a conscience, – is

---

[122] Kraus, wrote to her on Dec. 28,1898, received no reply, anxiously wrote again on Jan. 13, 1899. He wanted to know if O'Connell had returned to Rome, when Archbishop Ireland was expected, and if she would find for him a hotel for March 1st.

[123] Reference unclear.

excited, [the church will lose.] The very word America irritates the ear-drum in the blink of an eye!

But who besides a few insiders knows what it is about? That is water for the mill for Leo, who proposed to a correspondent of the Freeman's Journal last week that there are many sorts of Americanism: 1) the political, of the United States, which only deserves acknowledgement; 2) the French, embodied in Abbé Charbonnel;[124] 3) a German, which ties into Luther's revolt against the church; and 4) the Italian, which repeatedly sides against the church in politics!

O'Connell, whom I have repeatedly warned that our good Keane with his irrepressible Jingoism, without surmising it, pours oil on the fire, assures me that the movement in Europe has unfortunately slipped out of his hands and that he can only sadly look on and observe what will develop out of it.

If the pope up till now has had a tight rein kept upon him through Gibbons' threatening address, and refuses a decisive proceeding against Hecker, Zahm and Co., so also is the Spanish influence increasing through a little Msgr. Merry del Val[125] who treacherously, in hour long contact with Leo XIII, is active to discredit everything American. In this way, to our talkative Keane was ascribed the most dishonorable table conversation about all Spain right up to its poor queen, which has caused him such hostility from the Spaniards that their embassy left his calling cards unanswered! Under such circumstances there can be no more talk about shipping him off to the Philippines! First, as you know, tossed out from Canada, he next found the best reception at the Sulpicians and can now converse there with that good but anxious man of God, Cardinal Richard, about Saint Maignen, etc.

---

[124] The ex-abbe' Charbonnell had left the priesthood, and, writing in the *Revue de Paris*, was urging a Congress of Religions at the coming Paris Exhibition of 1900.

[125] Raffaele Merry del Val (1865-1930), Spaniard born in England. 1888 entered Vatican diplomatic service, 1903 elevated to Cardinal Secretary of State.

Ireland embarked on the 14th of this month, arrives here at the end for, at most, a three week stay. If therefore my dear friend, you don't accelerate your arrival, you won't see him still here.

Your justified concern on account of Ireland's festal speech in Orleans I share so much that I at once offered my hesitations to O'Connell when I learned of the matter. He wants to assure you that you may depend on the influence of one who has already set out the main points of the politically colorless, purely religious speech, so that Ireland can make himself precisely familiar with it.

Your coming is necessary and important. On Montecitorio[126] is also the well-known good Hotel di Milan. When I am mobile I'll look around there for you and at some others, also Hotel Marini also in Tritone Nuovo.

O'Connell bestows upon you his warmest admiration and greets you cordially. Bülow[127] was at point of death, gradually recovers, and remains living here, moved over to the Palazzo Venona in the Corso, almost opposite Rotenhan who has set himself up in the Palazzo Odescalchi (Corso). The Crown Princess of Sweden[128] is already present – now – what's wrong with you! Everything is ready for your reception! The overworked Venturi thanks you most warmly and [will comply with] your wishes.

Always yours,

A.E.

---

[126] The Piazza Montecitorio, site of the Italian Chamber of Deputies, represents the closest of the various hotel locations to AVE's residence on the Via di Ripetta.

[127] Otto von Bülow.

[128] Sophie Marie Victoria, Princess of Baden (1862-1930), married 1881 Crown Prince Gustav of Sweden who became King in 1907. She was fond of Kraus, particularly because he had been her late brother Ludwig's professor at the Freiburg university.

February 5, 1899
Rome

Honored friend,
I have looked around on your account and I would think you could be satisfactorily placed in the Hotel di Milano (on Montecitorio). I saw southern rooms – right spacious for the situation – elevator, electric light, etc. Everything right at hand. The secretary said: Pension from 10 lire up or for the large room I looked at on the 3rd floor, 12 lire, everything included. Reduction of 2 lire as often as you lunch or late breakfast out of the house. The building story makes no difference on account of the lift, just because up there it is sunniest and quietest. They promised to afford you every accommodation. Only I would beg you to arrange beforehand because the rooms are very occupied, especially by deputies.

I send off this open postcard hurriedly so that – in case you are already forth – someone can dispatch it to you.

We all rejoice here heartily for you. Trauttenbergs[129] charge me with special greetings.

Therefore with God for a speedy Wiedersehen!

AVE

---

[129] Constantin Baron von Trauttenberg (1841-1914), Austrian Ambassador and Plenipotentiary, and wife Maria Uschakoff, born 1850.

February 26, 1899[130]
Sunday
Rome

Dear friend,
This evening a man and wife who supped with you at Pasolini's[131] are also coming here. Both of them are very eager to meet you and both are converts of the finest observance. He, a Mr. Gibbons (son of Lord Ashburnham)[132] has already written a life of Lammennais. <u>She</u> is a delightful former Huguenot, that is, French. They live at the Hotel Quirinale.

Therefore send your carriage forth and come as soon as you can (about 10) to your

A.E.

---

[130] This note was addressed to Kraus at the Hotel de Rome. Evidently he decided to avoid the Chamber of Deputies at the Piazza Montecitorio. See previous letter.

[131] Pier Desiderio Count Pasolini (1844-1920) 1889 Italian Senator, host of famous salon in the Palazzo Sciarra on the Corso. Kraus described him as an "addlepate adorned with cordiality and a lot of information." *Tgb*, p. 699. Contessa Pasolini, a correspondent of Paul Sabatier's, was the author of the work, *Per la formazione di una coltura sociale e civile* (Rome, 1899).

[132] Misspelling for Ashburne. William Gibson (born 1868), second Baron Ashburne, eldest son of Lord Edward Gibson Ashburne who was twice Lord Lieutenant for Ireland and ennobled in 1885.

To FXK (No. 152, Hotel de Rome)

March 1, 1899

Urgente

Dear friend,

O'Connell just left. The Archbishop[133] will expect you tomorrow at ten o'clock in the morning and O'C will be there.

A propos: all at once it struck me boiling hot that you have promised yourself to Fräulein Hertz Friday at 1 o'clock. Therefore nothing can become of our symposium unless you decline there. Pray let me know this decision at once, all right?

With cordial thoughts, wishing that you rest well, your

A.E.

---

[133] John Ireland.

to Franz Xaver Kraus 123

FXK (No. 152, Hotel de Rome)

Rome
Monday, 11 o'clock
[March 6 or 13, 1899]
Early

Worthy friend,
I am just coming from the hunt for your commission, with the attached sample that is called Molleton[134] and appears to me from all I have seen to be the best for the intended purpose.[135]

The people promised – in case no cancellation comes within an hour – since the material must be décatirt[136] – to deliver the night shirt (according to the written measurements) by tomorrow noon, ready to go, <u>for nine lire</u>.

How are you? I will come in the evening to look in. Meanwhile here are the craved lemons and oranges.

In a great hurry, your

A.v. E.

---

[134] Thick flannel.

[135] Kraus was in bed with the influenza and needed a new nightshirt. He was confined to his room in the hotel, ill, for four weeks.

[136] To have the sizing sponged off.

April 19, 1899
Rome

Dear friend,

Cordially I thank you for the quick report.[137] Hopefully sunny rest and social exchange with dear friends will soon assuage the painful exhaustion of travel. Baroness Ebner[138] would like to know how long you plan to rest by the Arno? And if you then go directly to Munich?

I miss you like a foster child!

What say you to the Bavarian duffer? Hertling was yesterday with the pope.

O'Connell missed coming here today, which I regret.

With cordial thoughts, your

AVE

---

[137] Kraus had written to her on April 17, 1899 from Florence. "Only a word to say I am here at last...A thousand thanks for what you did for an old sick man."

[138] Marie Baroness von Ebner-Eschenbach (1830-1916). "Famous writer" wrote Kraus, (*Tgb.*, p. 718). Born Baroness von Dubsky (Countess, 1843), married Moritz Baron von Ebner-Eschenbach in 1848. Her work, portraying marginal persons and the lower classes, was critical of titled society

April 23, 1899
Friday
Rome

Dear friend,
My card of the 19th, with its inquiry about the length of your stay and trip over the Brenner, you have hopefully received?[139] I was commissioned by Baroness Ebner, on behalf of her niece, Countess Waldburg.[140]

Meanwhile, have you, God willing, gotten better and improved through the change of air?

Rotenhan[141] came yesterday and inquired after you.

O'Connell has gone yesterday to Genoa to meet Archbishop Ireland and to accompany him to Milan. From there O'Connell thinks to return here in the course of the week and in fact through Florence. He asks you to expect his visit about Thursday or Friday; can however be earlier.

---

[139] Since Kraus, still in Florence, had written on April 22, 1899, she did not have the note yet.

[140] Marie Countess Waldburg-Zeil-Wurzach (1861-1941), and her sister Sophie were nieces of Baroness Ebner. Also a poet, Sophie Countess Waldburg-Zeil-Wurzach (1857-1924), in 1882 had married Karl Count von Waldburg-Syrgenstein, (1841-1890). After his death Sophie married Karl Heidler Baron von Egeregg but separated from him. With men not a factor, Sophie was the 'Burgherrin' of Schloss Syrgenstein in the Allgäu.

[141] Prussian envoy to the Vatican.

The Hampels[142] are in Florence by today. Yesterday I ate with them at Fraknoi's.[143]

God be with you...truly,

A. v. E.

---

[142] Josef Hampel (1849-1913), Archaeologist and Paleo-historian, Professor in Pest.

[143] Bishop Vilmos Fraknoi (1843-1912), Founder of the Hungarian Institute, Rome.

April 29, 1899
Sunday evening
Rome

Dear friend,
Dead tired from my reception, which brought me, among others, Cardinal Serafino Vannutelli, with the most sympathetic inquiries about you, [but overjoyed] at the news that O'Connell, coming from Milan, stops to see you Monday or Tuesday.[144] Keane informed me of this just now, as telegraphed news, and wanted to send his most hearty respects. Also Countess Kinsky begs the same.

That things go better with you I conclude from your projected excursion with Countess Maria [sic] W[aldburg]. Unfortunately her lovely aunt went away yesterday evening.[145]

Duchesne was here also today and greets you.

May this heavenly weather increase your strength and strengthen you for the journey homeward!

I am all in from lumbago.

In heartfelt thoughts,
A. v. E.
I gave the Crown Princess of Sweden your address since she planned to go today.[146]

---

[144] Kraus was still resting in Florence.

[145] The mother of Marie and Sophie Waldburg, Sophie von Dubsky, was a sister of Baroness Ebner's.

[146] Kraus wrote Eichthal on April 30, 1899. The Crown Princess took him for a trip to Venice in her carriage.

May 29, 1899
Monday
Rome

Dear friend,
You write in the most impermissible minor key![147] If I didn't know how sensitive you are, I would take your mournful dirge of sorrow for the bare sad truth, however…I will hope only the exhaustion from the trip made its painful consequences felt in your poor arms and legs and also that your heart weakness might be more of the nervous sort!

<u>In any case</u>, agitations must harm you and so it is very wise <u>first of all</u> to avoid the same by giving up the occupation with politics. This miserable politics! What does one get from it but trouble and want? What, for example, are we now experiencing from Ireland![148] Such a maddening, base, flattery and adulation of our beloved gallic neighbors as his in Orleans, no one has indeed experienced outside of the Bramarbas of Victor Hugo! And it was <u>self</u>-glorification! In Ste. Clotilde his address before the literary elite turned into a fiasco, while his speech at the workers' association sparkled with his

---

[147] Kraus had written on May 12 and May 25, 1899. Exhausted by the journey home, and still waiting for news about Ireland's proposed trip to Germany, he added, "I can never forget your care for me in the sickroom…Write and tell me how it goes behind the Great Wall of China."

[148] Ireland's speech had upset AVE greatly. To O'Connell she wrote, "Got Archb. Ireland's speech from Paris – a gorgeous magnification of France than which nothing more has <u>ever</u> been said. After such an outpouring his visit to Germany would seem to me <u>imperative</u> to dispel misconceptions only too natural after the like extraordinary adulations from the Jesuits. We must talk the matter over and no time ought to be lost. Can't you look in today about 5 PM and have a cosy cup of tea to ourselves?" (AVE to O'C, May 26, 1899, Archives of the Diocese of Richmond.)

democratic commonplaces. His true friend Bishop O'Gorman[149] (of Sioux Falls), who just came directly from him, said to me yesterday: the Archbishop had been driven unwillingly by the French clerical press, inimical to him, and their malicious insinuations, to emphasize his love for France so over-enthusiastically that he himself now feels he went too far to be effective in Germany as an impartial leader of the movement.[150]

---

[149] Thomas O'Gorman, (born 1842), friend of John Ireland in boyhood and for life, Professor at CUA, Bishop of Sioux Falls, South Dakota 1896.

[150] She eventually received a letter from Archbishop Ireland, written on stationery of the Imperial Hotel, Cork, dated; The Ocean, July 26, 1899: [In cool delay she only replied on January 8, 1900]

My dear Baroness –
In the leisure of an ocean voyage I am now passing in review the good friends I have left behind in Europe – and to the dearest ones among them sending them a word of remembrance.
 So doing, I could not leave you out. Let me then break in upon the quiet of the "Rimpetta" [sic] – to tell you that you shall be remembered by me in America & that I shall ever be grateful for your many acts of kindness during my stay in Rome.
I had the pleasure of meeting twice your brother in London – but to my great regret, I was not able to have any lengthy conversation with him.
I was not able to go to Germany. Time was lacking - & then, to be frank with you, I was so thrown in with France, that I felt I could not in good grace – either to France or to Germany – accept hospitality in Germany.
One thing, I trust you have remarked – in all my utterances, there was not one word that could offend the most sensitive German. I was constantly on my guard, & in this I was obeying the dictates of my conscience and my heart.
The next time I shall come to Europe – I must see Germany – I hope I shall not be long away - & meanwhile I am going to strengthen myself in your "theure Sprache" – so as to feel myself more at home in trans-[R]ean regions.
I thank you very specially for having brought me into close touch with Dr. Kraus. I consider my acquaintance with him as one of the most valued incidents of my visit to Europe.
Continue to serve us. You understand thoroughly the situation in the United States - & you are in a position, by your words and influence to render us most important services.
Be so kind as to write to me at times, & give me your appreciations of matters in Europe & in America.
Very devotedly,   John Ireland

O'Connell added to that very truly: "Ireland is no thinker, he is our drummer. From now on he is to be taken as no more than that. The movement of progress must from now on be advanced specially and in fact by those who live there."

Ireland had originally wanted to go from Belgium to Germany and specially also to visit you. Now he has given that up and is silent towards you out of sheer embarrassment. His winning, magnetic personality is just absolutely Celtic! Fantasy, the momentary impulse and a great susceptibility for flattery, make him into an unpredictable, unsteady element, that glows like a meteor and behaves erratically. O'Gorman makes a far more deliberative, calmer, stronger, impression. Something indefinable in him reminds me of the trustworthy Grannan.

Did you see Schell in Munich? Do you know Professor Grauert there? O'Connell thinks so favorably of his speeches in Switzerland and above all in Krefeld that he asks you: if you do not think: he would be the man to take in hand the liberal [*freiheitlich*] Catholic movement for Germany?[151] For that it must be a layman is obvious; otherwise thanks to the current episcopal servility and Vatican terrorism, it would never prosper. Please, quickly and clearly – your opinion here, and who you would select for such a difficult task?

Here, you know as well as I, on June 22 Cardinal Rampolla will get the purple auxiliary troops whom he needs for his own good eventually or the elevation of Gotti. The latter has let everyone in the Vatican be assured of continuation in their present offices, in case he should get in there as pope!

---

[151] Hermann Grauert (1850-1924), Historian, 1885 Professor in Munich, Stiftspropst of Türk. Kraus wrote O'Connell directly, "I beg you now to have no confidence in that person at Munich about whom you asked me for an estimate through Baroness Eichthal." (FXK, Freiburg, to O'C, June 3, 1899, Archives of the Diocese of Richmond.)

Yesterday the South American sheep pen beyond the Tiber was called into session with pomp by Cardinal di Pietro.[152] What will they decide? In contrast, on Thursday the 25th, Soeur Marie,[153] after three weeks presence here in strictest incognito, has gone home <u>victorious</u>! According to Cardinal Vincenzo Vannutelli (she was judged, <u>unread</u>) (as I duly could have told you) his good will won out when he heard through me of the sad situation. He was the one who procured her a special audience with Leo XIII, from which she emerged comforted and cheered up. After the pope questioned her precisely about her connections in this place, he praised her efforts, granted her to wear the habit outside the cloister, encouraged (!) her for founding her school, allowed the sale of her books (!), etc.! In short: first they strike her dead and then they bring her back to life!

The last in any case an act of courtesy which a <u>man</u> would never have had to take, and at the same time a look into the thoroughness and conscientiousness with which the congregations work and the superiors let fall their decisions. Fräulein von Castomer, who was much with her, asks me to recommend the purchase of her books urgently in all quarters because their proceeds are now her <u>only</u> resource. All right, do accept this request and recommend the purchase?

---

[152] The Latin American Plenary Council in Rome of May 28 to July 9, 1899, totalled 12 archbishops and 41 bishops, out of a potential one hundred and four. Called into being by the encyclical *Quum diuturnum*, Dec. 25, 1898, to formulate unity of church discipline and 'worthy morals'.

[153] Mother Marie du Sacré-Coeur, a religious of Notre Dame, author of *Les religieuses enseignantes et les necessities de l'apostolat*, Paris 1899. Condemned in early 1899 by the Congregation of Rites for this book which declared instruction in convent schools to be insufficient and advocated normal school training for instructors. Duchesne said her chief accuser was the Bishop of Nancy, Charles Turinaz. (*Tgb.* ,p. 719)

The worthy widow[154] of your old friend de Rossi visited me the day before yesterday and asked <u>very</u> concernedly about your condition and greets you urgently.

The sly Tarnassi is now here. How that one has understood to shuffle his cards! In Munich he will be able to quench the thirst which that Dutch cheese has caused![155]

The intriguer and blusterer von Hussar delighted Gennochi[156] and me the other day with the enthusiastic assurance: since Bossuet there has been no speech given like the one by Ireland in Orleans about Joan of Arc!

Gennochi greets you most cordially, likewise O'Connell, who has rested himself in Anzio and looks very well. Duchesne is out of sorts and criticizes everything, and thereby is as brave…as a tailor! But, 'what use to prove his heroism in tilting with windmills?' Basically…he's not so wrong!

I have personally been laid up with lumbago, which is very difficult for me, although I ought to be used to it. So I will leave Rome earlier than otherwise, probably about the 10th of June and likely travel direct to Paris where brother and wife only have a place until June 30th and expect me for 14 days. After that I need to take strengthening baths in the ocean, which makes me slightly bored. In any case however I will try to spend a while with you in Freiburg,

---

[154] Constanze Countess Bruno di San Giorgio before her marriage to the renowned Catacomb researcher, Giovanni Battista de Rossi (1822-1894). Kraus and de Rossi were co-workers in archaeology. By de Rossi Kraus had been able to inform Leo XIII about German willingness to end the Kulturkampf.

[155] Francesco Tarnassi (1848-1902), Auditor at Munich 1879, at Vienna 1882; Internuntius at the Hague, 1896. He worked to become Nuntius at Munich but failed to gain approval.

[156] Pater Giovanni Genocchi (1860-1926), Professor of Biblical Studies at a Roman seminar, driven out by Jesuit Cardinal Mazzella.

worthy friend! Take care and look after yourself right well above all, until you feel the old strength stirring in you – I beg that earnestly.

O'Gorman stays here 8 days longer. It would be very worthwhile in the meantime to receive the requested reply from you.[157] Thursday, O'Gorman, with O'Connell, had breakfast here. The former spoke of you as if he knew you…so work the actions of mind and spirit.

With hearty good wishes and greetings, your

A. v. Eichthal

---

[157] Kraus wrote on June 3, to say he would not forget "poor Soeur Marie." After greetings to O'Gorman and Rotenhan, he added, "The South American sheep herd is the most amusing comedy one has yet seen."

June 8, 1899
Thursday
Rome

My dear friend,
Through Rotenhan I obtained your last Spectator of June 2 and translated the principal ingredients for O'Connell yesterday, which he pondered over attentively and approvingly. Only about the report of the two Franciscans did he shake his head and regretted that you had in that followed Sabatier's false news, since in reality it happened quite otherwise.

In the Cloister of S. Antonio the well known Pater David (the Irishman)[158] gave lectures about Scholasticism, taught Scotus, etc. Then one day there came to the superior a fulminant rebuke from His Holiness (which likewise appeared in print): how could he be so bold, against his express orders, as to allow lectures on anything other than the sainted Thomas? He, Leo XIII, was alone the authority which according to his encyclical: In Aeturnum (?)[159] one had to obey. What was left to Father David but to request his release from the lecture desk?

The cloister prior however [saw] behind this groundless humiliation, that in truth was deserved by nothing, a malicious blow from within the order itself. And correctly, with a monkish sense of scent, he finally caught up with the two treacherous fratres who did the false tattling.

From that there followed their deserved Last Judgement. Fra Teofilo lost his reason and went to an institution; Fra Marcellino, banished to Leghorn, sits in the cloister there. One proof more about the frivolous accounts from which

---

[158] David Fleming, O.F.M.

[159] *Aeterni patris.*

the Vatican takes draconian action. As in the old Venetian Republic, a slander serves to annihilate people, but is never investigated!

Meanwhile the 55 South American sheep were called here, I), To come to agreement in disciplinary matters, II), Under the papal aegis to form an overwhelming counterweight to the hated North American Union – to pack up their respective hides already and peacefully reverse everything up till now. The "larger South America" with its Latin affinity, in its much trumpeted preponderance, compared to the Anglo-Saxon race, however, spiritually makes just such a fiasco as the Spanish did in the war.

In order not to make them, the shepherds of these Latin American nations, skittish before the outset of this Roman council, and to assure their unrestricted devoted cooperation, one let them know as a sedative beforehand, that the <u>subject of women</u> would remain undisturbed! According to natural law there, of course, they are all married *coram publico*! The state of the thermometer, in our church, sets the terms of the vow of chastity!

Bishop O'Gorman went day before yesterday to Lyon in order (with Ireland) to refresh his youthful memories of the seminary there. Within about 8 days you may expect his visit. He will then regale you with the account of his fearless openness toward Leo XIII, who – unused to such speech – from astonishment let the bulb for his electric call-bell get away from him, whereupon the bishop in his excitement forgot the Peter's Pence in his pocket! In the ante-chamber he regained his senses and turned back to smooth over the experienced disappointment. Then the pitiless one mounted up to Rampolla and informed him with his point-blank guns, totally disconcerting him! Nevertheless what use is it? No Latin wants to hear the truth, and when they hear it, they <u>don't believe it</u>!

Soeur Marie had Fonsegrive,[160] Goyau,[161] etc., behind her and that brought about the turn in her favor; for these gentlemen let Rampolla know that they want to have nothing more to do with his unholy French politics – after what has been experienced. Archbishop Mathieu of Toulouse, who has arrived for the consistory, has remarked: the church ought to be liberal toward Italianism! Words and directions for all occasions.

Friend O'Connell greets you cordially and hopes to see you soon for a brief time. As for me, on account of my lumbago, and in spite of repeated insistence, I have given up the trip to Paris and plan on the 16th to go directly to <u>Bad Heilig-Kreuz</u> by <u>Hall</u> in <u>Tirol</u> (Station at Innsbruck) where Eperjesys expect me before their return to Teheran. Everything beyond that lies undetermined in the future. I suspect that I scarcely will achieve Freiburg before September.

Your intention: after conclusion of your Christian Art to devote yourself <u>exclusively</u> to your life's work, fills O'Connell and me with deep satisfaction.[162]

The departure of Ambassador von Saurma, which finally became official, saddens me on account of his pretty daughter; otherwise one hasn't lost much in him, as a politician, I mean.

What struggles must your keeping silent as Spectator have cost you! What may the preceding things have been! Were initiatives taken from here? I definitely suppose that. Courage. Your hour draws near!
Most sincerely, your
A.v. E.

---

[160] Georges Fonsegrive (1852-1917), philosopher.

[161] Georges Goyau (1869-1939), church historian and author.

[162] Kraus had written her on June 3, 1899. The Spectator Letter of June 1, 1899 contained the announcement that the series was being brought to an end.

July 20, 1899
Pension Washeim
16/I Türkenstrasse
Munich

Dear friend,
Your recent lines[163] were marked by affliction; God knows this mark is wide spread! Do you know that I have rushed here to meet the pair of sisters, the Schleinitzes, before today (Saturday) when they will be led away by Princess Oettingen[164] to their country seat so that Alexandra can recover from the results of a serious operation?

I sought them out yesterday in Dr. Angerer's surgical clinic. Alexandra is so unselfishly philosophical that she speaks of everything that so seriously lies behind her as if it concerned a third party. Her cheerful equanimity even impressed the doctors. She still carries her arm in a sling, for since the removal of the breast an inflammation of the nerve has occurred in her arm!

Thanks to Duchess Karl Theodor's[165] intercession Adele was allowed to stay with her sister, which otherwise would be unthinkable in the clinic. God grant that Dr. Angerer's assurance will be proved correct, namely that a recurrence of the horrible suffering is not to be feared! Let this not be a pious lie!

---

[163] On July 12, 1899, Kraus wrote that he was uncertain where she was, that he had terrible pain in his hands and was depressed, and that he hoped to see her for his birthday in mid September.

[164] Marie Princess Oettingen-Wallerstein (born 1861 as Countess von Waldbott-Bassenheim), married 1884 Maurice Prince Oettingen-Wallerstein (1838-1890), Seigneur de Seyfriedsberg, the "country seat."

[165] Maria Josepha (1857-1943), the Infanta of Portugal, was the second wife (1874) of Karl Theodor (1839-1909), Duke of Bavaria. Duke Karl Theodor was an opthalmologist with a highly reputed clinic.

Both sisters live and breathe the issues of the day and commend themselves to you most warmly.

Schell appears to be played out? Who is the Dr. Müller whom I find so tartly mentioned in the Germania for several weeks![166] Does he seem a Würzburger also? Where is O'Connell gadding about? What's happening?

I had to laugh that in the end Tarnassi's struggle to get here was still frustrated at the last moment. How nice to name a Pole for here.[167] That will pay off.

I am not doing very well. Yesterday exhausted me and shook up my back afresh as if I had not for four weeks favored it and pickled it like an anchovy!

Hopefully it now goes less painfully with you? The air here is oppressive. Next week I'll go to the Alps, but where. It wants to be high, woodsy, sunny, somewhere about 1000 to 1200 meters. I am sick of searching. Everything becomes too much when one has to 'pay' for everything!

Write soon, your

A.v.E.

---

[166] Joseph Müller, born 1855 in Bamberg, priest. In the title of his book, *Der Reformkatholizismus, die Religion der Zukunft* (Würzburg 1899), he coined the new term. Kraus would have nothing to do with him.

[167] Franz Tarnassi, in the 1880's had been Auditor of the Nunciature in Munich. (*Tgb.*, p.434) The reference to a Pole is unclear. See the letter below of December 27, 1899.

August 13, 1899
Sunday
Oberstdorf über Immenstadt

Dear friend, your silence makes me concerned since your last letter was so filled with lamentations. I answered you about 3 ½ weeks ago from Munich with reports and greetings from the Schleinitzes, who now spend the summer with the Oettingen-Wallersteins at Schloss Seyfriedsberg. Alexandra writes me that the left arm is still unusable. God grant her a <u>definitive</u> healing. But what is it with you? How goes it? Where do you turn your steps between now and the middle of September?

Before I left the city 8 days ago I bought Freiherr Georg von Hertling's newest manifestation (which you naturally have known for a while) in order to enjoy it here in the silence of the mountains. How its content confirms my view of the man! Clearly – that one must concede – he knows how to lay out the obviously most confused and abstruse matters in flowing language. So much for the first chapter. But as he gets down to a discussion of particular current issues, about which his brochure stands prefixed with a modified form of Schell's title[168] — it's finished and all over! Of the intellectual scientific educated man nothing is left but a deplorable pussy-footer in felt slippers. Whoever wants to found anything on him, leans on a reed, shaking in the wind.

What a pity! To read him, one would think the church was perfect, there were no Jesuits, and the acceptance of revelation, a <u>blind faith</u>, a totally warranted scientific corner-stone! All-righteous God!

---

[168] Georg Freiherr von Hertling, *Das Prinzip des Katholizismus und die Wissenschaft*, (Freiburg 1899.) Kraus reviewed it in *Deutsche Literaturzeitung*, 1900. Schell had written a broschure titled *Der Katholicismus als Prinzip des Fortschritts*.

God save a person from counsel like that! With Schell he flirts, timidly, greenly screws up his lips, for he doesn't want to fall out with the men of science; his whole tract however is about how to be "dear child" in the Vatican and with the Ultras…Who is able to serve two masters?

Can you tell me what has become of O'Connell? Where he alights? Whether he is really in place in Bonn and tries to drum German into that head of his, so fortified with languages?

Friend Venturi, at the invitation of the Belgian Academy in Antwerp, today gives the solemn memorial address about Van Dyck. Who there will understand it? For he is not strong enough in French, therefore as a convenience has to speak Italian. He wanted (if at all possible) on the return trip to make a detour to you for a short period. If you don't see him, it means that once again he was too hurried for it.

Now, dear friend, don't let yourself be reminded once more, to reassure,[169] where possible, your, anxious

A. v. E.

---

[169] Kraus responded from Wiesbaden two days later, August 15, 1899, telling her not to complain for he had written her from Munich. Later she found the letter.

August 29, 1899
Hotel Baer
Grindelwald

Honored friend,
I write this open card so that if necessary someone from your surrounding might give me a report about you. <u>Two</u> letters to you from me have remained unanswered so that I am seriously concerned. As a result of your silence I altered my plans and followed my brother here. He has left me yesterday and now I am here first with my relatives Count and Countess Muelinen[170] and then to look for another Alpine height in case we go forth from here, since my back leaves a lot to be desired. <u>Please</u> let me know, here, how you are and where you are,

your

A.v.Eichthal[171]

---

[170] Although the name Mulinen or Muelinen is associated with Grindelwald, Canton Bern, no further identification was found.

[171] Kraus responded August 31, 1899, from Mettlach. He assured her that a letter must have been lost in the mail, since from Wiesbaden he had answered her August 13 letter promptly.

September 10, 1899
Grindelwald
Switzerland

...Thank God that only a letter was lost and not you yourself. Sent you the Times[172] to Mettlach.[173] Saturday the 16th latest Sunday 17th I hope to arrive and to greet you — all better. Yesterday I arranged with the beau Sejour and H. Schatzky[174] and sent him my trunk key for the Customs because I had my trunk shipped from Bern as freight to Schatzky. May I sincerely ask your dependable housekeeper to send to the beau Sejour to make sure that my key arrived and that I can be sure on Saturday evening to find a room ready for me there? along with my trunk key in loco?

I feel inexpressibly relieved by your news. Everything further when we talk. How many things to tell you! [175]

With faithful thoughts, your   AVE

---

[172] An article from the Times of June 28, 1899, about the plans of the Catholic Union of Great Britain to honor Archbishop Ireland, was mailed Sept 10, 1899 in a green envelope from Hall, in the Tirol. (In file Ireland, *Nachlass* Kraus.)

[173] Kraus spent the period from August 28, 1899 to September 8, 1899 in Mettlach with the family von Boch. O'Connell came there to see him and was charmed by the wealthy porcelain manufacturers. *Tgb.* ,p.725.

[174] The beau Sejour was a hotel in Freiburg. Schatzky was a freight agency. German customs needed the key to inspect the trunk.

[175] On the day of his birthday, the 18th of September, she spent the evening with Kraus at his home.

November 7, 1899
Hotel d'Europe
Sestri Levanti (Liguria)

Dear friend,
I suppose you are back home again and I hope full of good results for body and soul?[176] My thoughts were often with you and today I have sent you a supplement of printed things from Comersee[177] (for 4 weeks) from different French and English papers. What a disgrace is this Transvaal war! How one's heart yearns to see it just left alone. Politics is indeed the diametrical negation of Christianity! And afterwards how will our bishops bestir themselves? Like flies!

Damp Comersee suited me so badly that after 8 days I came here where I am splendidly taken care of and at home in heavenly nature, so in case this divine weather holds I don't want to go Rome-wards before the end of the month and can only warmly recommend to you this guesthouse, situated <u>absolutely</u> in the southern part of the bay of Sestri.

Have you seen O'Connell? Where is he? How is he?

Here there is so much warmth that one goes about in summer clothing.

Please, just a sign of life sent here for the ease of mind of

AVE[178]

---

[176] Kraus had written her on October 26, 1899, after an extended stay in Baden and Karlsruhe, which he made from October 7th to October 22nd for political and academic purposes.

[177] Lake Como.

[178] He answered on November 9, 1899. He then wrote to her on November 24th and received a letter from her brother Emil von Eichthal on November 28th. (This and an

December 27, 1899
Wednesday
Rome

At last,[179] dear friend, I come to you with the most fervent holiday wishes for now and always. May you not regret spending this bitter cold winter at home, instead of taking your ease here, forbidding the Roman floods of rain.

Not easily have nature and politics been in such pathetic harmony as now. Mountain slides, ice breaking up, ocean storms, collisions by water and land, pestilence and yellow fever, conflagrations, inundatations - - - don't they seem to correspond to the feverish greed for gold and land of all large and small states, whose logical result we witness in the edifying decomposition of age-old culture lands in the far East and the climax of all Christian hypocrisy, the disgraceful war in South Africa; to say nothing of the internal dissolution of France and Austria?[180]

Happy is the one who is able to dispense with present things, in the study of noble works of the intellect, be they of the past or of areas that stand far from the current sorrows of the day. Wherever I listen, wherever I look, I am disgusted by the lower passions, the common motivation of most public transactions! What should one say in conclusion about the deep inroads of cancer which feed on the whole entrails of Italy, as for instance, the process Notarbartolo so horribly revealed?[181]

---

earlier letter from the brother on October 7, 1899. These letters probably concerned wine deliveries.)

[179] She had had a letter from Kraus written on December 5, 1899, in which he surmised that she was back in Rome and he thanked her for "the wine."

[180] This sad resumé reflects her back pain and her serious thoughts at the turn of the century.

[181] The slashed body of Commendatore Emanuele Notarbartolo, politician, corruption fighter, Mayor of Palermo, was found on a railroad bridge on Feb. 1, 1893. The murderers' identity was common knowledge but seven years of delay saw a trial moved

I fear Dante's disconsolate saying must also stamp its brandmark on this beautiful land — abandon all hope ye who enter here!

From Dante to Petrarch is such an easy leap for you that forthwith I call on your agility for the purpose of an important find which Bishop Fraknoi has made these days in the Vatican archives, and through me, brings piping hot to your attention. In his studies of King Louis the Great of Hungary, to his surprise Fraknoi stumbled in the papal archive upon a dispatch of Pope Clement VI, wherein he notifies the Scala of Verona that on the 12th of November 1347 he sends off to him Canon Fr. Petrarch with this letter in order to prevent his [Scala's] participation in the expedition of the Hungarian king against Johanna of Naples and his relationship with Cola di Rienzi. Fraknoi adds, as becomes clear from these documents, that Petrarch's poetic enthusiasm for the people's tribune Cola di Rienzi, because of his subsequent moves, goes up in smoke and that the new light which now falls on his trip home, by this political mission, alters all at once the earlier conceptions. No wonder!

Fraknoi beamed to be able to tell you this fact, and asked me to send along his card. The good man is straight off the best example of peace of soul in the current confusion and hardship, to the confirmation of what was said above. Why should he trouble himself about the present? He has the past!

Unfortunately we are made of other stuff and so I can only quickly report on the latest, that Msgre. Sambucetti[182] (the pope's state coach as I call him partly on account of his stately exterior which brought him his special mission to the jubilee of Queen Victoria), that this narrow-minded, cold and petty, only

---

to Milan in which the son of the victim accused "Deputy Palizzolo, the head of the Mafia" in open court. During the trial members of the nobility, judges, police chiefs, etc., were implicated. Palizzolo was acquitted.

[182] Cesare Sambucetti (1838 – 1911). Special Representative of the Pope at Queen Victoria's Diamond Jubilee. Nuntius at Munich 1900-1901. The portly Roman native was close to Cardinal Hohenlohe and sealed the cardinal's papers at his death. (See Weber, *Quellen und Studien*, p. 293.)

thinking of himself, but totally devoid of any wider viewpoint and political awareness, brother of my landlord, since day before yesterday, has received his appointment as — Nuntius to Munich!

Truly it is time to set in motion the proposal of Gerontius [183] (and Barry and Company)[184] for the decentralization and de[illegible] of the hierarchy, but how?

Hertling is supposed to be here literally only for educational matters, that means in the matter of the theological chair at Strassburg. Everyone who knows the situation, and him precisely, assures me: they lead him around by the nose, always agree, raise only difficulties about the form, but they don't want the thing, in which he will not succeed. Over the holidays he is home and then returns.

But I just heard this — since the enlightened Prince Regent had struck down Tarnassi (possibly on account of his Viennese antecedents under Galimberti)[185], an unctuous churl Msgre Gasparri,[186] who enriched himself in Paris through marriage negotiations and earned his spurs in the Nunciature

---

[183] A pseudonym under which Kraus wrote three articles about 'Religious Movements in England' in the *Allgemeine Zeitung* in December 1899, and January and August 1900. He drew attention to articles in the *Contemporary Review* (William Barry) and in the *Nineteenth Century* (William Gibson) which advocated change in church law. [See next footnote.]

[184] The Rev. William Barry D.D., of Dorchester and Father John Berry of Liverpool had earlier made a plan to publicize victims of Vatican oppression. (William Barry to Denis O'Connell, Jan.21, 1898; John Berry to Denis O'Connell, Feb. 24, 1898; John Berry to Denis O'Connell, Feb. 22, 1899, ARD). In May of 1899 Dr. Barry wrote to Kraus, explaining that he had again talked this over with O'Connell. Barry urged a precise campaign in the German press to demand an end to Roman proceedings *in camera* and to the unexplained condemnations of the Curia and asked Kraus to assist him in gaining access. [*Nachlass* Kraus, file William Barry.]

[185] Luigi Galimberti (1836-1896), sometime Nuncio in Vienna, Cardinal 1893.

[186] Pietro Gasparri (1852-1934), Cardinal 1907, Papal Secretary of State 1914-1930.

in Peru, had been contemplated for Bavaria. Compared to such an individual, the morally upright and already-filled-out Sambucetti is a gain!

28th of December – Day of the Holy Innocents! An appropriate anniversary to write about Roman matters![187] I am too miserable with my back to mount up stairs and make social calls, have almost always to lie down, write even now stretched out on my back…This restriction is especially painful for a nature like mine, which needs daily activity. I was at Lovatelli's one time recently and was struck by the stony lack of sympathy which reigns there and which stifles every warm heartbeat! German faithfulness, Northern dependability – one does not seek on this volcanic ground, rich only in horrifying surprises.

Tell me, valued friend, <u>why</u> isn't it possible for you to leave the *Allg. Zeitung* without Supplements for a while? Your paw is too leonine not to be <u>immediately</u> recognized and since you once made known your reply, in the sense of silence, your glaring immediate resumption of the scarcely disrupted participation, makes bad blood. The surprise is general and that restricts and disturbs the influence of your words. Why don't you send the same things out into the world through other papers? That wouldn't seem so disagreeable and wouldn't put you in contradiction with yourself before the public, to whom just in June you so solemnly and sadly announced your going silent!

The grand ceremony[188] on the 24th in St. Peter's seems to have run off astonishingly well for Leo XIII and inspiringly for those present. One purchases postcards with the phizzes of Boniface VIII and Leo XIII side by side! May the 20 Jubilees which these encompass have found their conclusion herewith. What has happened at all times but the coarsest sort of material taking advantage of the credulous, of the need by the masses for saving blessedness? This whole lunch menu of indulgences – for whom does it not turn the stomach from disgust and indignation?

---

[187] Kraus sent her New Year's greetings on December 28th, concerned for her health and with the hope for "a better new year".

[188] The opening of the Jubilee Year.

Hügels are here again for the winter and he is supposed fully recovered. Still I haven't seen them. Cardinal Mathieu[189] has rented for himself in the Villa Wolkonstky and Gotti[190] is said in the moment to have more prospect than ever as the successor to Peter. That all heaves around however like the ground under our feet. Amusing is only this, that the pope was all prepared to relieve the contradictory Parocchi[191] of his post and to install Jacobini[192]…who is said to suffer from diabetes!

Dear friend: All love's labors I hold for lost which you apply to any reanimation of our 'petrifact.' Indeed, step forward materialistically smart like the South Americans, then you may in despite get material advantages and freedom like they did for their concubinage – freedom of the soul, of the spirit; freedom of conscience, perception and thought one does not gain by fighting, not now, not evermore!

Friend O'Connell looks after me diligently. The death of Princess Leiningen[193] has affected me very painfully. I knew her since I was born. She was a noble gentle sufferer!

God be with you, my dear friend! May you soon come back to us and may the old power of spirit and temper work to bring fortune in the new year. Always unchanged, your   AVE

---

[189] Francois-Desire Mathieu (1839-1908), Bishop, Angers 1893, Toulouse 1896, called to be curial Cardinal June 1899.

[190] Girolamo Gotti (1834-1916), Discalced Carmelite, Cardinal 1895. From Genoa, reputedly ascetic.

[191] Lucido Maria Parocchi (1833-1908), Cardinal 1877.

[192] Domenico Jacobini (1837-1900), Cardinal 1896.

[193] Marie Amalie (1834- 21 November 1899). Princess of Baden, married in 1858 to Ernst Leopold Fürst zu Leiningen.

1900
Chapter 5

January 31, 1900 [194]
Wednesday

Dear friend,
Roma locuta est! Yesterday Brunetière[195] solemnly proclaimed Bossuet's[196] modernity in the Hall of the Cancellaria, Urbi et Orbe, that is before a public of cardinals, prelates, and seminarians, lightly peppered and sugared with laity. As near as I sat to the front, those in front of me with their feathered hats and capes frequently made so much noise as to prevent me from clearly following the address, since unhappily Brunetière sat <u>exactly</u> on the same level with us, which made hearing very difficult in the crowded hall.[197] However I grasped enough of the torrent of words to hear proclaimed an emphatic exaltation of Leo XIII as Bossuet's spiritual successor (!). Rampolla's elastic smiling profile was a priceless vignette for me. [As for] Brunetière, his wrinkled hide showed from afar the nervous excitability of this litterateur, who had now found in the Vatican, in the fitting frame of the Cancellaria, the

---

[194] Kraus wrote to inquire after her health on January 14, 1900.

[195] Ferdinand Brunetière (1849-1906), critic, professor, editor of *Revue des Deux Mondes*, converted to Catholicism in 1895.

[196] Jacques-Bénigne Bossuet (1627-1704), preacher, 1681 Bishop of Meaux, theologian of history.

[197] The great Aula on the northeast corner of the Cancellaria opens off the interior balcony. Restored by Pius IX in 1866, and again in 1933 by Pius XI as a venue for lectures on public matters, the ceiling mottoes emphasize that peace is the work of justice and comes from the reign of Christ. There is no stage or dais, only a set of raised desks which line the sides, with a very low tribune on the north wall.

podium for his retrograde manifestations. The selection of the audience was carefully supervised through giant-sized cards of admission without which no one entered. I thanked friend O'Connell for mine, in that he lay in bed with influenza. Recently that has hit here mildly, and hopefully will soon be over.

Meanwhile Parocchi's successor in the Roman vicariate still has not been blessed at present, although last week two English ladies, veiled in black, appeared before him to edify themselves at his corpse.[198] Vincenzo Vannutelli told me weeks ago of his surprise that Jacobini, with his health severely undermined by diabetes, had regardless been appointed to the responsible post! He couldn't even move into his official dwelling and lies dying in the Condotti in Palazzo Lepri. Cardinal Trombetta gave the first fanfare for the departure of the three death candidates from the Sacred College, practically chained together…who now will share the honor with Jacobini![199] And what does it matter? The spirit of darkness that hovers over them all will not be lifted by such departures. One must have something else.

Characteristic for that to me was that lately Gotti anxiously whispered to the publisher[200] of the Florentine *Rassegna Nazionale*, an old friend from youth and school visiting him on a trip through here, "Perhaps you will mail me your *Rassegna* in a package? Then you don't compromise me?" What do you say to this stifling atmosphere?

During all that, Leo XIII pursues his French private-politics. Made wiser by his fiasco of an earlier epoch with the rallies, the successor to Bossuet has now

---

[198] Cardinal Parocchi, learned, vacillating, opposed to Rampolla, was dismissed in 1899 as Vicar of Rome. Cardinal Domenico Jacobini, dying with diabetes, had been appointed to the important position.

[199] Cardinal Luigi Trombetta died on January 17th, Domenico Jacobini on February 1st, and Camillo Mazzella SJ, died on March 26th of 1900.

[200] Marchese Manfredo da Passano (1846-1922), like Gotti a native of Genoa, founded the liberal *Rassegna Nazionale* in 1879.

logically united himself with the royalists through the fathers of the Assumption. He treats directly with Father Picard and Co., that way bypassing Rampolla, leaving it to that one to trumpet his own republican sentiments as the official papal one as ever before. That Rampolla stays on despite this I do not ascribe to his ambition for the Chair of Peter, which he completely frittered away, as any child can see.

Pater Esser's[201] appointment as successor to the † Ciccolini[202] as Relator for the Index pleased me at the start because I regarded him as moderate; now people tell me otherwise. Who knows reality behind all these masks?

Duchesne grows thick and round by his maxim "it is necessary that every priest should be an opportunist," and stores up honor upon honor.

Did you see that Capecelatro[203] dared in his seminary address at Capua some time back to cite Archbishop Ireland as an example for patriotism because he (himself) praises love for one's fatherland?

What, in consequence of your conclusion to stay out of the literary Supplement, will become of your review of Hertling?[204] As much as I regret that, I can only praise your decision <u>as long as</u> things remain as they are. May God improve them!

---

[201] Thomas Esser, O.Pr. (1850-1926), native of Aachen, Professor at Freiburg (Switzerland), 1900-1917 in Rome, Titular Bishop and Secretary of the Congregation

[202] Stefano Ciccolini died in 1895.

[203] Alfonso Capecelatro di Castelpagano, Cardinal Archbishop of Capua (1824-1912), conciliatory to Italy, former confessor of Queen Margareta.

[204] The review appeared in the *Deutsche Literaturzeitung*, Vol.21(1900),12-19.

The emperor's sorrow over his mother-in-law[205] was clearly demonstrated in the <u>caviar</u> biscuits after the prayer service at the embassy. Now always be considerate! An imperial virtue!

Have you heard of the vulgar writings here of the glottologue Professore Ceci,[206] which he has never tired since August of publishing in the *Popolo romano* (like and like go together)? On the occasion of the Cippus discovery, with the ancient Latin inscription at the Forum,[207] he just spewed forth in it, first at Hülsen[208] and after that at the whole of German science, Mommsen at the top, as well as a pair of Italian professors who dared to confront him — with a veritable literary flood of sewage! So what did Bacelli[209] do at the conclusion of this august series? He let this tasteless excrescence of the Italian *fará da sè* be put together as a brochure and sent it, documented with his calling card, to every embassy and legation here which he supposed to be foreign! In this way, Italy can attain to a singular respect.

Hertling has brought his spouse with him from Munich and seems, despite the experienced failure of his mission, beamingly content. How so? Why? Does he believe he still has something to accomplish?

Stallo's sudden death of a heart attack on the morning of the 5th of January has touched me deeply. He was a rare character and spirit! His daughter was

---

[205] In 1881 the future Wilhelm II married Duchess Augusta Victoria of Schleswig-Holstein. Her mother, Victoria of Schleswig-Holstein, born in 1840, had recently died.

[206] Luigi Ceci (1859-1927), specialist in linguistics and the etymology of Roman law.

[207] The recently discovered *cippus* in the Forum was a short five-sided column, inscribed with archaic Latin law from about 510 B.C.

[208] Christian Hülsen (1858-1935), renowned specialist for the Roman Forum at the German Archaeological Institute in Rome, 1887-1909.

[209] Guido Bacelli (1832-1916), doctor and politician, in 1900 was Italian Minister of Education for third time.

fortunately on hand when he collapsed. Her alliance with B.P. seems pushed far to the back according to her latest report, since she now must devote herself entirely to her poor mother. An existence filled with renunciation!

Dear friend, you must come here in March-April. There's still too much for you to study near by, as you well know.

I scrawl lying down, and almost as illegibly as the Freiburg Seer, whose hand I warmly press, Your

    AVE

February 23, 1900
Friday
Rome

Dear friend,
Everything thankfully received,[210] much pleased at the continuation of March 1st. Sickel[211] remarked that he had been disappointed by it: what did he expect then? To find the Spectator *redivivus*, who with the opening words pours his satirical caustic lye over everything? Only after the pudding is cooked, then comes the *chaud' eau*, poured over it boiling hot! And while such culinary practices also apply to the rest of things, it doesn't dare happen with the genesis of the Anno Santo.[212] There the clear methodical historical presentation serves, and when one is at the end of this rosary, one knows even without the *chaud' eau* what must be thought of it. Some salt and pepper-corns were nevertheless sprinkled about and F.X. Kraus has so coyly winked at the devil in No. 1 that already one has some pepper-corns in one's teeth. Would they have been too fine for Sickel's palate?

Friend O'Connell loves and honors and greets you; the writing however he leaves to me. God only knows what troubles him! I believe his proud characteristically reserved nature suffers today almost more than in the moment itself from Ireland's ingratitude and want of appreciation for that which he accomplished here for the cause. Gradually that forces itself out into the open with him. He is a noble, selfless character but <u>sadly</u> without any

---

[210] Kraus wrote February 7, 1900 and included his latest newspaper article. He had not heard of Stallo's death and he asked if O'Connell was still ill because he had not heard from him.

[211] Theodor von Sickel (1826-1908), 1881-1901 Director of the Austrian Historical Institute in Rome.

[212] A six part-series, 'Anno Santo,' by Kraus in the *Allgemeine Zeitung* in the first half of 1900. Signed with his name.

talent for judging human nature. Through that he makes many blunders and then becomes unsure and dejected.

He brought to me on Saturday 8 days ago the Bishop Spalding (Chicago)[213] whose open, energetic, earnest countenance won me over at once. You perhaps remember that the selection for the first Rector of the new Catholic University in Washington lay at that time between him and Keane. Even now it seems that Spalding's knowledge and clarity of mind would have been better there than our unsteady speechifying good Keane of limited personality. I expect the bishop today for longer conversation and I will write to you the conclusion of this letter after that.

Meanwhile Hertling has left Rome for the second time, possibly to return again for a third. As I pointed out to you then, this pussy-footer has achieved exactly nothing![214] Do you know that the Strassburg chapter even sent a deputation here to thwart the concession of the Catholic chair? What do you think of that business? Just as little has Hertling succeeded in enthusing the Vatican for influencing the Center [party] in the naval question. In regard to his diplomatic bowings and scrapings, one comported oneself courteously, rejecting everything as a matter of course. With the Curia only a strong start and appearance and cunning persistence wins the victory.

Jacobini's final release has brought the important Vicariate question into the foreground again, after a brief interregnum. I hear that Satolli's nomination back then was dropped because he spoke out to Leo XIII about the intention: to introduce a more vigorous regimen among the Roman pastors. "*Che innovazioni non ne voglio,*" growled His Holiness and so he picked the easy

---

[213] AVE is in error. John Lancaster Spalding was Bishop of Peoria.

[214] Hertling's business in Rome concerned the establishment of a Catholic chair of history at the Strassburg University. See Christoph Weber, *Der Fall Spahn (1901)*. (Rome, 1980.)

going and deathly ill Jacobini, the Roman landlord's son, about whom he knew that he wouldn't stir himself.

Remarkably enough Svampa's[215] name emerged for the important position. Since his summons here from Bologna could increase his chances at the next papal election, that appears doubtful since it became known that the aforementioned had sinned with an epistle to Bonomelli! Formerly one would have dared write off one's soul to the Devil rather than to traffic with the poor Bishop of Cremona!

Saturday early

Spalding lets you know that it would be urgent for someone like you to write up in factual tones the history of the intercourse of the Roman Congregations with important Catholic individuals in the course of the last 100 years. He thought that would kill off this organization. Spalding commends himself to you most warmly and will immediately start to read your principal works, hopes to find them at Loescher's[216]. Beloved friend! <u>He</u> and not our *charmeur* Ireland is your man! While that one subordinates everything to his personal ambition and swings the censer toward all sides in order thereby to be censed in return, vanity slides off Spalding like rain off a waterproof coat. Of all the American bishops whom I know he distinguishes himself through his <u>absolutely</u> <u>un</u>-Celtic-Irish, strong, independent, bolt upright, essential character. In politics he is very reassuringly contrasted, compared to our Ur-Jingo friend Keane, or Ireland.

I believed I heard Stallo speaking, as he gave expression to his justified indignation over America's lusts for expansion and aired his complete displeasure about England. Yes, he maintained that the latter has in fact only

---

[215] Domenico Svampa (1851-1907) Archbishop of Bologna, 1894 Cardinal.

[216] Bookseller, "Loescher and Co.," Via del Corso 307.

been behind America in its newest phase and unfortunate occupation of the Philippines, in order then not to stand isolated before the world with its own lusts, which show up with the Cape ablaze in flames, and to hide its voracious imperialistic appetite behind the American one.

He spoke golden words to me, from the heart! Further, I was able to hear from him astonishing particulars about Ireland's compacts with the Holy See, reaching back over years — everything out of regard for the hoped for cardinal's office. Do you know that Ireland has in mind to come to Europe once more? And what for? To help in the unveiling on the 4th of July of Lafayette's statue in France with a big speech. With him, sadly, there is nothing serious to be done, nor moreover, with Gibbons!

Accidentally, Spalding came to Schroeder's dismissal and related to me how Gibbons, frightened by Cardinal Steinhuber's[217] letter, then came out once more for Schroeder's retention and the others wanted to break away with him, until Spalding raised a loud protest that stigmatized Steinhuber's letter as an unprecedented interference and so won the victory. He sticks to his principles! That is a character!

Imagine this – that Gibbons, the last time he was here, in his inconceivable limitation, knocked down the offer of the pope to name the American Bishop Elder as Papal Delegate.[218] Spalding still shakes with fury that this reasonable beginning to a more rightful understanding of the American circumstances by the Curia, so tragically miscarried.

About Satolli's mission no words need be lost by men of wisdom generally, so you can picture to yourself this thorough man's text concerning that

---

[217] Andreas Steinhuber, SJ (1825-1907), 1867-1880 Rector of the Germanicum in Rome, 1894 Cardinal.

[218] William Henry Elder, born 1819 Baltimore, 3rd Bishop of Natchez 1857 (Civil War), 2nd Archbishop of Cincinnati 1882, demonstrated ability at Cincinnati after the bankruptcy of Archbishop Purcell.

bygone mischief. Before O'Connell brought Spalding to me he acknowledged in a whisper that this one could not now or ever forgive him for taking Satolli across to over there. "I believe that easily," was my answer, "I could hardly grasp it then as a simple observer and still haven't managed to get over it."[219] On this subject, Spalding afterwards came to this: with deep indignation he stamped this chess play as an intrigue of Ireland's, who then believed he could make use of the language restricted delegate as a tool. Naturally this was so; a blind man could see it. Well, that took its bitter revenge!

Spalding assured me that Ireland, with all these maneuvers, has so damaged the cause to which as a reasonable priest he also adheres, that in America it suffices to hear that he, Ireland, has been named as the sponsor of an undertaking, to prejudice it with the public. He is only popular in <u>political</u> administration circles. After our experience I don't wonder, but it is too bad for the gifted man.

How much there is to talk about. So surely come. The weather improves, the influenza disappears, and Spalding stays for several weeks. He converses a great deal with Hügel, Genocchi, and naturally O'Connell is with him a lot. O'Connell has become the victim of his fascination for Ireland and Keane!

It's miserable with me: I write lying on my back, this excuses the mess. Do you know that Schleinitzes are again back in Munich, Briennerstrasse 13, with Princess Oettingen-Wallerstein, to see Dr. Angerer? Adele writes that he has relieved her anxiety and has reduced her sister's new swellings through

---

[219] The initial Satolli trip to America in 1892 was viewed as a move of expansion by the pro-French (and thus pro-Russian) Secretariat of State under Cardinal Rampolla, at the expense of the Propaganda which had hitherto managed the American church. Count Mieceslaus von Ledochowski, a conservative Pole who became Prefect of Propaganda in January 1892, feared danger to Polish interests from the French-Russian alliance. Baroness Eichthal's sympathies were with the 'pro-German' Propaganda, to which both Cardinals Vannutelli belonged. Some of the background for this is explained in Gerald P. Fogarty, SJ, *The Vatican and the Americanist Crisis*, Ch. VIII, 'The European Diplomat, Institution of the Apostolic Delegate,' (Rome, 1974), pp. 227-250.

poultices. But what a Sword of Damocles! They hoped to see you soon in Meran? They are only staying 14 days in Munich.

Write good things. What should I say to Spalding from you? Countess Taube greets you most cordially, also the other friends.

Always, your,   AVE

March 22, 1900
Thursday
Rome

Dear friend,
What is new?[220] That Bishop Spalding, greatly bothered with rheumatism, leaves Rome next Monday to seek healing in Aix-le-bains and <u>on your account</u> wants to stop over in Florence 24 hours or at least for the day. I am pleased beyond measure to have secured this for you. Yesterday Spalding preached here at 4:30 <u>in the Gesù</u>[221] (oh the irony of the circumstances!) His theme was <u>Education</u>. The way he presented and developed it was so powerful that I am sorry to say it openly, one could hardly believe oneself at a Catholic sermon right in the center of Roman Jesuitism. How redemptively sounded his enlightened words about our century and its incumbent tasks. How skillfully he set forth that our Saviour only directed his anathemas at unjust stewards, etc., but not against art and science! How manly and courageously this resounded from the pulpit; that not in dead forms, but in the living model of a distinguished educated clergy lies the power of our church! I am so accustomed to the rarefied local air that while blissful over his openness, I was also startled practically at his daring! Now he travels off right soon and can enjoy the luxury of his convictions.

Golden words had he for the higher education and formation of women; indeed the more he spoke of the present and future of the Teutonic, energetic races in contrast to the more quietistic Latin ones, the more enthused he became and closed with such a marked emphasis on confidence in the assumed development of Catholicism, in which the education of the

---

[220] Kraus wrote to her from Nervi on March 13, 1900, and then again when he arrived in Florence on March 20, 1900, "sick on Italian soil" but eager to arrange a meeting with Spalding.

[221] The Jesuit church in Rome.

individual would be carefully cultivated, that one felt how everyone was deeply moved. Italians clapped in applause the way they do every day at the Lenten sermons.

I write lying down, miserable, but this page must bring you the good news without delay. Through Spalding I will write again. Please when you get this send a note and report whether you are better? Rome would be better than Florence. Pope lets himself be painted by Father Laszlo,[222] thinks not on the kingdom of Heaven as anything other than here down below! O'Connell greets and comes.

Always faithfully yours,

A. v. Eichthal

---

[222] Fuelop von Laszlo (1869-1937), Hungarian portraitist.

March 24, 1900
Saturday noon
Rome

Dear friend,
Spalding writes me this minute that he wants to come tomorrow to afternoon tea to chat privately since his departure here is put off for several days.[223] His visit to you is assured in any case.[224]

Recently I wrote to you, tired to death from boring but unavoidable visitors and completely in semi-darkness. After that it came to me how I neglected to emphasize from Spalding's sermon, the flailing clarity with which he said of Christ: he had no word of rebuke for the men of learning, but well he portrayed the Pharisees, the so-called learned of God, for their empty dabbling in words and their arid system of formulas.

Oh friend! Since the days of the Reformation such truths have never been proclaimed inside the Eternal City, and this right in the middle of the Gesù, at whose opulent marble pulpit they had to occur. Verily, signs and wonders come to pass!

Unfortunately, whether from ineptitude or because some other machination stood behind it, the organizers of the devotion (which was supposed to be followed by a collection for local religious schools for the poor)(which Spalding characteristically forgot to announce at his conclusion – no wonder

---

[223] "Dear Baroness: I shall be detained in Rome a few days longer than I had expected and hope to call to see you Sunday afternoon about half past five. I am very glad to know that you liked the sermon.
Very truly yours, J. L. Spalding, Bp.Peoria, 24.3.1900, Rome"
(*Nachlass* Eichthal, Spalding file)

[224] Kraus, still in Florence, had written on March 23, 1900, delighted at Spalding's impending visit.

with his mighty excitement!) kept the matter so secret that not even Spithoever[225] got wind of it. The audience was correspondingly small, but breathlessly and silently they followed a full hour of the splendid presentation.

Spalding's audacity – the more I think it over, the more unrestrained I find it. You know what it can mean, <u>in the midst of the Gesù</u>, without that eye-rolling playing upon the Madonna, to praise the ennobling influence of woman on man, "be it as Mother, as Spouse, as Sister, or as <u>Friend</u>!" This noble word, what does it mean to the southerners other than an earthly lover?

Further, not to shrink from calling attention to the current superiority of the Teutonic races over the Greco-Latin ones, and, as an American, to the great advantage of the free church in the free state, that is to emphasize the separation of both. It was a deed that here would earn a funeral pyre as its reward if everyone were still nice and proper as in times gone by. Well for him that he leaves soon, otherwise — woe to him!

Duchesne lies at the feet of the peasant-sly and peasant-looking Cardinal Mathieu, who last year publicly uttered those winged words: Esterhazy[226] should serve as the model for every French officer! Now France's enemies can indeed rub their hands together.

Duchesne is newly occupied more with his preparation for the Christian Archeology presidency, and the resulting cardinal's rank. Accordingly the "scarlet fever" breaks out on him. Already he has explained that he will write

---

[225] A bookstore, library and meeting place for Germans, then at Piazza di Spagna 84.

[226] Marie-Charles-Ferdinand Esterhazy (1847-1923), born in Austria, died in England. As a French army officer, he sold military secrets to Germany, a crime for which Alfred Dreyfus was wrongfully convicted in 1894. When Esterhazy was accused of the deed in 1897 he was acquitted by his fellow officers. He fled from Dreyfus' supporters to Belgium and then to England. He later admitted that he had been a spy for Germany, and the German military confirmed his guilt.

<u>nothing</u> more that even at the remotest could make the Curia suspicious of him! Much good may it do!

O'Connell recovers slowly, was here yesterday, and greets you from the heart, as does your

    A. E.

Baron Rotenhan wanted to be most cordially remembered to you.

March 26, 1900
Rome

Dear friend,
Just two words with the news that Bishop Spalding – who was here yesterday – will be held up here this whole week and possibly, as of today, can go forth in 8 days – Monday. He will be staying in Florence 2 days, doesn't know which hotel, since he travels with his filthy-rich ward, a former Miss Caldweg[227] presently Marquise de Monstiers, and doesn't bother himself with details.[228] (This for your private orientation.)

I found Spalding happy with the success of his sermon and fortunately roused from his earlier quietism. He is only fearful about the limited help of like-minded in Europe, particularly in Germany, where other than you he finds no one since Schell fell silent.

---

[227] Mary Gwendoline Caldwell, Marquise de Monstiers-Mérinville. The major benefactress at the founding of the Catholic University of America.

[228] In Rome Spalding stayed at the Grand Hotel d'Europe, Piazza della Terme, described in the 1897 Baedeker as "a large establishment …with a good but expensive restaurant, handsomely fitted up." [A note from Spalding to AVE is on the hotel stationery. *Nachlass* Eichthal, Spalding file.]

He studied in Freiburg[229] and spoke glowingly of the intellectual life that Alzog,[230] Alban Stolz,[231] Staudenmaier,[232] enlarged for him. Now, see, it is still not the end of our days!

A pro pos: do you know who awaited Spalding's entrance into the sacristy of the Gesù after the sermon? Pater Brandi![233] – He [in English] <u>did not look pleased</u>! remarked Spalding, laughing lightly as he related this.

Cardinal Mazzella[234] will likely succumb to his typhus-like lung inflammation. But what does it matter? Every toad always grows back a new tail!

Give news of yourself and varia[235] — your   A.E.

(I enclose a page for Fräulein Stallo.)

---

[229] In July 1864 the young Spalding attended lectures for three weeks at the University of Freiburg im Breisgau where he met Alzog and Stolz. See David F. Sweeney, *The Life of John Lancaster Spalding* (New York, 1965) pp. 59-60.

[230] Johann Baptist Alzog (1808-1878), 1853 Professor of Church History in Freiburg I. Br., Kraus' predecessor.

[231] Alban Stolz (1808-1883), 1847 Professor of Pastoral Theology in Freiburg i. Br.

[232] Franz Anton Staudenmaier (1800-1856), 1837 Professor of Dogmatics in Freiburg i. Br., significant member of the Catholic Tübingen School. Professor Staudenmaier was no longer living in 1864.

[233] Salvatore Maria Brandi (1852-1915), Jesuit, 1891-1905 Director of the Civilta Cattolica.

[234] The Jesuit Cardinal Mazzella died March 26, 1900.

[235] Kraus wrote that day to say he was grateful for Spalding's sermon, and awaited him eagerly.

April 16, 1900
Rome

Dear friend,
Your delight over Bishop Spalding was of great satisfaction to me. Do you know that I myself, yesterday in his Easter sermon at S. Silvestro, first had a glimpse into his deep mind? Shall I confess to you, that yesterday for the first time in my life, words coming down from the pulpit, through their deep, passionate conviction, have so moved my innermost soul, so touched and strongly affected it, that my eyes overflowed with tears? If his sermon in the Gesù about education was a deed of highest courage and great significance, just so his eloquence of yesterday, in comparison, was a revelation of his inner faith, his warm love of mankind, and his truly apostolic mission.

Even though that slights his address, which otherwise did not lack for a strong line of thought and betrayed, always beneficially, his philosophical schooling — even in this situation of greater intimacy, Spalding's deep force of conviction, his overpowering appeal from the heart, came through all the more clearly. When he, moved by his efforts to make the word of God real, wringing his hands, spoke breathlessly the first petition of the Lord's Prayer with muted voice to show how far we still are from the true grasp of its meaning — there, I assure you my friend, I was filled with awe, as with a holy revelation!

How rightly he separated politics from religion like the goats from the sheep, and emphatically stressed the hollowness of a civilization which is only nominally Christian, which in reality only pursues the struggle for its own existence in envy and mistrust, that that civilization should turn into such an opposite society, in which Christ's word counts for nothing more than a clanging noise!

Yes he should be our pope! He smiled happily when I read to him this from you,[236] and on his side, could not say enough about his satisfaction at your acquaintance, which was joined with his deep sympathy for your health.

He charged me with all good wishes for you. He will scarcely leave before Wednesday. Today or tomorrow he comes to me again.

That finally golden sunny weather arrived, as God wills! helps your pains and enables you to linger in Florence, for that damp Venice doesn't suit you at all! Adele Schleinitz urgently questioned me: whether you are not thinking at all of coming back through Meran? She pleads pressingly that I let her know! What say you about that?

Who induced you then to designate my stupid back pain as rheumatic? If it were that, how happy I would be, for that can be improved! Unfortunately the evil lies elsewhere. The doctor says, only lying down is to be applied. I know his apathetic manner and in summer I will look around for a more energetic cure. In June I am going to Paris to my brother where he has taken a house for the year (in Passy) and from there I go surely to the sea.

Maria Waldburg breakfasted with me Tuesday, with – Bettina Ringseis (!)[237] and told me enchantedly of her hours with you.

Day before yesterday I delivered salutations from you to Baron Rotenhan which I had solicited for him, for he inquires after you steadily and always sends greetings, etc. I like him very much as of a dear, cheerful character, who additionally works uncommonly hard to do honor to his position.

---

[236] On April 4, 1900 Kraus wrote to thank her for arranging Spalding's excursion to see him in Florence. "He is a total person, clear intelligence, great knowledge, strong character. No single flaw, not one. If he is not our pope, he would be very papal."

[237] Bettina, born 1833, youngest daughter of Johann Nepomuk von Ringseis, distinguished Bavarian patriot.

Weeks back I ate with him and Genocchi, Denifle,[238] and Fraknoi. Duchesne had held off. Have you read the last's protest in the *Allgemeine* against the degeneration of the Christian Archaeological Congress into an exclusively Catholic one? Privately sometime more about that. For the protest the non-Catholic scholarly world and the remaining civilized participants can thank — your humble servant. He, with so sharp a tongue, so anxious about the business, Duchesne, would never himself, without my push [*spinta*] have decided about it, and the Congress would have been all crumpled together into the Vatican incense pot!

Just now O'Connell sent me the newest *Voce!* with a <u>lead</u> article about the Congress. The stupid sheet is a bell-wether for clerical, lying chaplains of the chase — a disgrace of the hour and of the Curia.

O'Connell also wants to go to you truly after the 20th! Enviable, because, away, he can speak with you. Write soon to your

A.E.

I saw the Lovatelli recently. Couldn't you, after your return home, cause my translation of her "Ancient Roman Fire Brigade" to appear in some respectable sheet? The Supplement of the *Allgemeine* has, in spite of all, recently published a long-prepared matter of hers.

---

[238] Heinrich Denifle, O.Pr. (1844-1905), Church historian, 1883 Sub-archivist of the Vatican Archives.

April 20, 1900
Friday evening
Rome

Dear friend,
I wrote in detail on Tuesday.[239] Bishop Spalding just got away yesterday (direct to Paris) on account of the enormous retinue of his ward, who will have made on you as well as on me the impression of the most superficial nobody.[240] Friend O'Connell was just here, exhausted to death. The doctor says it is anemia of the brain and he must rest and breathe country air. But along with that there are so many people from America, commended to him by Ireland and Keane, to whom he doesn't want to seem disagreeable, that he just can't get away, not even once to <u>you</u> and that annoys him so severely that I promised to report this to you to prevent any misinterpretation. Duchesne spoke brilliantly yesterday at the Christian Archaeological Congress. Hopefully you have given up on damp Venice and instead go to Meran? 1000 wishes.

---

[239] Kraus was still in Florence.

[240] The gallant Kraus was a bit kinder toward the wealthy woman. He found Mary Gwendoline "a remarkable mixture of esprit, uneasiness, creed." *Tgb.*, 734.

May 26, 1900
Saturday
(S.Filippo Neri)
Rome

Dear friend,
Countess Sophie Waldburg has transmitted to you my commissions 8 – 10 days ago. Today I hasten to report; that I travel next Friday evening June 1 to Paris direct in a sleeping car, to comply at last with my brother's invitation. He and his wife have set themselves up there since the first of the year in a pied-a-terre (in Passy) <u>79 rue de la Tour</u> and have offered me their guest room for the month of June.

Fortunately I am better for a short time now, even if I still can't make any leaps, and so I hope to be able gradually to obtain an overall impression of the exhibit.[241] You also want to go thither, as I hear? Reasonable, I find it not, but if one were always reasonable, where would be the bold moves, the elixir of life?

Friend O'Connell, who loves and honors you, but who has become simply anemic and neurasthenic as a result of frugal nutrition and overexertion of all kinds, causes me worry. Every American bishop requisitions him here for guidance through this labyrinth and for other motherings and he cannot resist letting himself be used up.

To fill up that cup, Ireland has drawn him back into his magic net and laid him at his feet. After all that he has experienced from him, he is today dazzled enough to believe that the 65 year-old can still change his character, dismiss his two royal Hussars [body guardsmen] – Ambition and Vanity – and will put himself selflessly into the cause (*viribus unitis* with Spalding!) I have

---

[241] The Paris Exhibition of 1900.

laughed at him and scolded him severely, but I still fear that he remains an incorrigible optimist, to experience ever newer disappointments.

Ireland wants to come to Rome <u>after</u> his formal speech of the day in Paris, as far as I know. But the affable Archbishop of St. Paul is too much forfeited to the French, too through and through a Celt, to be useful <u>in the long run</u> for the lofty goal of international concerns rather than particular ones, regardless of his two personal guards [*Leibhusaren*] who watch over the entering and the exiting at his door.

Your article in the Supplement of the *Allgemeine Zeitung* has brought great joy.[242] Presently our choice Genocchi is enjoying it, who, beaming, just returned from his 4 weeks journey, shortly ago informed me of his appointment as <u>Examinator</u> at the Appollinaire, as the first happy result of Cardinal Mazzella's death.

As much as I was pleased by your German article, so little was I edified by your letter in the *Times*,[243] which I was instantly sent at the time. I wanted to be silent about it, but you mentioned it to me,[244] and now I openly acknowledge my sad discontent. And besides it was badly translated. It is neither chopped nor stabbed; you wanted to mediate, where I fear it is love's labor lost, and now – out of tune – you have celebrated England's <u>religious</u> sentiment in the very moment when at the Cape it is so bloodily contradicted, where at all cost they have thrown out their opponents, <u>also</u> religious – that, worthy friend, cannot find acceptance. What good does it do when finally you

---

[242] "Über Erziehung," ["Concerning Education"] Tuesday, May 8, 1900, four page article in the *Beilage* to the Munich *Allgemeine Zeitung*,, subtitled 'A voice from America,' about Spalding's sermon. Unsigned, but in Kraus Bibliography.

[243] "To the editor of the Times: Mommsen on the war." In the London *Times*, March 30, 1900.

[244] In a letter of May 9, 1900, Kraus had asked her what she thought of the *Times* letter.

concede that not everything in Albion is to be marveled over, it comes as a lame messenger – the [negative] impression has resulted long before.

When Genocchi wanted to visit Bishop Spalding in Paris, he lay sick in bed with the influenza, but will now be back for some time in Peoria. His ward, the Marquise, has not helped much with O'Connell's condition. Imagine this, that the silly skirt was really hateful and small enough, in her anger over a well-deserved correction by our friend (because of her stupid public abusive language about the church and gossiping), to make her way to his notorious opponent, the current Rector[245] of the North American College, in order to complain to him about his namesake! The pure and simple scandal monger! O'Connell became just raving mad with indignation when he learned it. Quaking with rage, he told me about it. And then…before they left, she had O'Connell invited through Spalding to a reconciliation dinner and met him as if nothing had ever happened! God protect us from women like that!

O'Connell yearns to go to the sea shore and then – to you. Letters are first a burden for him to receive and above all to answer and on that account he feared himself sickly, as I let you know.

Duchesne beams over the success of his Congress and ….over….his….lilac….neckband! You would have to see it to believe it! "*Monsignore je vous prie*," he corrected my greeting. As I looked at him astonished, he laughed, "Must I unbutton my front [*me decolleter*] to prove it to you?" And he did just that on the terrasse of Santa Prisca, *coram publico*! I couldn't restrain myself from saying, "There are however so many monsignori but still only one Abbé Duchesne."

---

[245] William O'Connell (1859-1944), 1895-1901 Rector, North American College, later Cardinal Archbishop of Boston . See James M. O'Toole, *Militant and Triumphant: William Henry O'Connell and the Catholic Church in Boston ,1859-1944* (Notre Dame, 1992).

He has scarlet fever all over. Oh gallic vanity! So he will know nothing of Spalding because of his incautious emphasis in his sermon on the future primacy of the Anglo-Saxon races over the Latin ones. "It is allowed to think it, but one must never say it," he blustered, in spite of my remarking that <u>he</u> was not touched since the French are no <u>Latins</u>, and Bretons count even less as such. At the same time he paid eternal homage to the totally [illegible] Cardinal Mathieu.

Last year, after he became ecstatic about him as the morning star, I inspected the clumsy crafty peasant in purple, with his frying pan of a mouth, and found him 'as a tinkling cymbal.' Later Duchesne looked at me askance and very embarrassed here, as I suddenly pointed the pistol at his chest, teasing: "A pro pos of your cardinal; of course you find him much superior to the others?" "I don't know what you want of me? What a strange way to question me!" Yes, that's it: Not now or evermore can one <u>count</u> on such keen opportunists!

Because the Vatican makes golden business with its Jubilee, the ventilation was life threatening on account of the colossal throng, and yet these theatrical displays of allegiance affect Leo XIII as pure life-prolongers.

Please write <u>where possible</u> to here or later to Paris. Beyond June there is still no firm place for your friend,

AVE

July 22, 1900
Sunday
Dieppe

Dear friend,
The more one would say, the more monosyllabic one becomes. Since your letter[246] I have seen Ireland and was — with Gibsons in England! There we wanted to send you a greeting together; it did not happen.

First of all about our archiepiscopal *'charmeur'* (as I call him.) Scarcely had he heard from me, he begged me to excuse him from visiting me before the Lafayette celebration, but to come to visit him at a determined hour. He lives <u>like a prince</u> in the Palace Élysée Hotel, unaffordable by Europeans (surely as the honored guest of the Parisian Americans) and one ante-chambers with him just as with a ruler, or — a dentist!

To my astonishment I met in the corridor – dancing attendance since an hour ago – as he himself assured me – Msgre. Straniero from Rome. As Ireland soon appeared in the doorway with his previous visitor and finished with Straniero in five minutes, to gossip with me at length, there flowed round him the magic of his lively and happy personality like an electric stream and so worked on everyone, that requests for receptions, made through the servant, only broke off our conversation for a while, until he put a stop to them.

You, my honored friend, succumbed in Rome <u>blindly</u> to this magic and enthused for Ireland as somewhat mighty, made of bronze. <u>Mighty</u> is only his totally overpowering unpredictable personality, whose warm-blooded truly Irish impulsive nature constantly leads him to go beyond the bounds, to say in the current moment the seemingly most imaginable affable things, to create the most pleasant impression and <u>where possible</u> to leave the same behind. He is only to be taken seriously – as I believe – in the labor question, which he

---

[246] Kraus wrote her on June 30, 1900.

has made into his own particular field and in which he has produced something real.

Also as a theologian he's risky. How our Spalding towers as high as the heavens above him there, not only in knowledge and thought generally, but completely in steely determination and fearless courage!

Ireland soon asked me if I had heard Spalding's great sermon and what did I say about it? Upon my marveling appreciation he laughed, pleased, and thought he would tell that to Spalding. I instinctively kept quiet about my personal dealing with Spalding, for he did not know it, as I saw.

After a while I resolutely questioned him closely and asked him straight out, how in all this world he could have sent off such a letter to Rampolla? That had flatly perplexed not only me but all of us and bewildered us about him, and totally and painfully where it touched you. If you only could have seen that big old child, as he laughed in embarrassment, looked at me good naturedly, and finally came up with, "you see, I wrote that off so rapidly one evening, didn't look at it the next day before it went to the mail … <u>How could I also have suspected that they would publish it</u>! If I had had you at my side, it would not have happened, you would have held me to moderation!"[246a]

That shows him just as he is! One cannot be angry with him when he stands before one. But grace and God be with the one who would count on him. Golden quicksand — that he is!

After his official glorification of the silly enthusiast Lafayette (which naturally he achieved beyond all measure) he came to talk to us and ex officio conquered all present from head to toe![247] While that took place, O'C might

---

[246a] Ireland's "Letter to the Duke of Norfolk," thanking the duke for his recent pleasant reception by the Catholic Union of Great Britain, had been construed by the Roman correspondent of the *Journal de Genève* as a disavowal of the necessity of the Temporal Power. On May 25, 1900 Ireland wrote to Cardinal Rampolla to say that he had not even mentioned the Temporal Power in the letter to the duke and that "as a Christian and a bishop,… in that matter so serious and so intimately bound up with the life of the

fry in Rome, expecting him, and it never occurred to him to leave pleasant Paris one day sooner in consideration for the latter. On the contrary he prolonged his sojourn handily, and filled with unease, shoved Rome into the distance. In the end, he is still here!

In any case, the Gibsons did not hurry to Paris till last Monday night to see him for three days, after I had been with them for five days. We spoke of you a great deal and wished you with us in that idyllic country life which would <u>have</u> to suit you. Do you know that Gibson, for the latest whim, cultivates things "Irish," prances up and down in Irish kilt and makes propaganda for the same, evenings prays the <u>rosary</u> aloud in Irish in his chapel before a pair of poor Irishwomen into whose heads he has previously drummed the responses?

Thus each has his lunatic streak. Recently he went on that account with his wife to Ireland for the summer and came back afterwards as a full-blooded Celt, to free Ireland from the British, in culture and outlook!

Holy Church," he had never had any other thought than that of the Pope. Rampolla gave Ireland's letter to the Catholic press, and consequently it was read with disgust by Eichthal and Kraus. (*Tgb.*, p.739, Aug. 24, 1900.) In this incautious expression, Ireland could be seen as endorsing the claim to sovereignty by a Pope-King.

The central paragraph of Ireland's letter to Rampolla reads, "Certes, jamais un mot ne s'est èchappé de ma plume ou de mes lévres contraire aux idées du Souverain Pontife sur le pouvoir temporel. Je connais, Dieu merci, assez mon devoir comme chrétien et come évêque, pour ne parler et penser, que comme parle et pense le Souverain Pontife sur une matière si grave et si intimement liée avec la vie de la sainte Église."(Quoted in *Rassegna Nazionale*, 114 (1900), July 16, 1900, p. 410.)

[247] There is a note from Ireland to AVE about admission to the stands for his address: "Élysée Palace Hotel, My dear Baroness – I enclose tickets admitting to "enclosure."...Once admitted, please have my card forwarded to Mr. Peixotto....John Ireland." George Peixotto was Director General of the Equitable Life Insurance Co., Paris.

I ride at anchor desperately here for 3 – 4 weeks of sea bathing. After that I have to have good strengthening mountain heights for myself! You are also going to Schöneck (as you wrote Gibson?) I need something higher, but don't want to travel far. Advise me and write soon to your

A. E.

O'C wanted to go with Zahm to Denmark before the Munich Congress, as I hear. Please greet the excellent Grannan warmly for me.

FXK is in Schöneck[248]

August 13, 1900
Carsbach – Sonnenberg
(Ober Elsass)

Dear friend,
Probably you made a mistake by this sudden decision not to use a carriage in your vicinity? That is, perhaps this served your economy better than your health, which I suspect will be greatly improved at any mountain height, with good air and pleasant company, and from the gastricism, which fortunately you are getting over, you will be recovered.[249] In Dieppe such storms raged that after 13 baths I sat on the dry ground. Thus I decided to pursue my healing in this Kneipperei[250] which caters with proven results to nervous and poor circulation conditions (which are the basis for my lumbago.)

Whether I will persevere? That alone is the question. Pastor Ellenbach, Kneipp's best student, appears clever, serious and experienced. The establishment however suffers from over-occupancy and a lack of efficient management. The woman in charge is not up to the task and so there is a delay in all matters of order and cleanliness, about which everyone complains. Air and spaciousness alone would be outstanding. But one would hardly believe oneself on German soil. There are only French papers lying about in the salon and indeed in the style of the *Verité française*, an enchanting example

---

[248] Where he had gone August 8, 1900 for the "Frey" treatment for rheumatism, etc. O'Connell and Grannan were nearby.

[249] Kraus had written her or August 2, 1900, about his "gastric fever," which he ascribed to the heat.

[250] A form of residential treatment using the hydropathy and cold water method of 'Father' Sebastian Kneipp.

of which I enclose. The respected *Croix* has its offshoot here in the "*Croix de Belfort*." Besides that the *Gaulois* and the '*Moniteur*' — (the old petrefact).

It totally swarms with French divines. Thank God they eat – like their predecessors at Sais[251] – behind a light board wall (instead of the curtains of their ancestors). An honorable cheerful Rhenish pastor from Koblenz sits by himself, separated from them, and among us laity, and allows himself to enjoy his food respectably before all eyes.

The German element seems to be represented more in the lower classes. At the table one hears only French — with the many defeats which their vanity has suffered everywhere one can certainly not begrudge them the attempt to make themselves believe that here they are still <u>at home</u>.

Yesterday in the house chapel one of these abbés preached so movingly about Our Lady of Lourdes that I could think myself in Rome.

But now dear friend, what do you know of O'Connell? Ireland wants to be again in September in Paris, where it was <u>very</u> good for him and he was paid colossal homage. Doesn't O'C write anything about Zahm, who indeed wanted to come this month and in September to do the Congress in Munich with him? And how is it with Grannan? Do we all meet at your place on the 18th of September?

Constantly I wanted to ask you about Countess Waldburg-Syrgenstein.[252] She fell ill in Rome with the measles before I left, was too sadly miserable (exhausted from the packing) to be able to let me see her. Did she completely recover? A sympathetic personality! She had proposed to me to visit her with

---

[251] An allusion to the priests of Neith, goddess of war and the loom, at Sais in Egypt, mentioned by Herodotus, II, 59 ff. It was their custom to do honorable things in the open streets, but to do less worthy things in privacy behind their walls.

[252] Sophie, the 'Burgherrin.'

you for 8 days in Syrgenstein. That will probably happen for neither of us both?

And now let me know which Siemens shall have died suddenly in Baden-Baden? I read it in Dieppe in a paper. Would it have been the blind brave husband [253] of our lovely fresh Eleonore? Or his father? What do you know about it?

In Italy the "Left" have conducted themselves neatly! The young king[254] however has hair on his teeth and will certainly know how to get a grip on the machinery of government more energetically than his apathetic father, who always let problems remain as they had developed.

Write soon, something gratifying about your happenings, to, in this spiritual desert, your

A.v.E.

---

[253] Werner Siemens, the young husband, died in Russia. (*Tgb.*, p.738)

[254] Victor Emmanuel III, had succeeded Umberto I, assassinated at Monza on July 29, 1900.

FXK is in Schöneck
August 23, 1900
Tuesday
Schloss Sonnenberg
(Ober Elsass)

Dear friend,

I send forth to you more than a miserly postcard, not only to thank you for your last lines,[255] but also for your punctual dependability in taking charge of both enclosures for Grannan and O'Connell. Good heavens, how I am on fire to be with you three! Can't you make it possible for Grannan, O'C and Zahm to help celebrate your sixtieth on the 18th of September? That would be splendid.

I earnestly fear that for O'C this miserable protracted sojourn in Rome has greatly damaged his already shattered health. I cannot conceal from you my fears about him and want to ask you urgently to talk to him so that he will disclose his critical condition to a German authority of the first order so that – <u>in case it is still possible</u> – an end can be brought to these unbearable discomforts which increase from year to year. As you know it has to do with the adhesion of a bowel to the peritoneum (in consequence of the peritonitis ten years ago). Most unfortunately that steadily turns into cartilage and thereby the torturing pains of each digestion increase in such measure that he constantly has to lie down to relieve the hurt.

In order to lessen the pain he hardly trusted himself to eat anything much last winter. Through that he lapsed into such anemia and nervousness that he became totally apathetic until finally the doctor helped him out with a diet of milk and eggs. O'C is a peculiar fellow, most quiet about himself. One time he told me all this and moaned dolefully about this God knows! pitiful condition. Would it not then be possible to help this poor man?

---

[255] Kraus wrote only a card on August 21, 1900.

I am curious about all the – 'new' and 'important' – things he will report to you. If only his Irish one side has not allowed itself to be 'papered' by the Enchanter of St. Paul!²⁵⁶

Such a loss for the visitors to the Arcadia … at that terrible train wreck by the Castel Giubileo, the Dominican father V. Vannutelli (brother of the mother of the chancellor) was also wrecked! For years he read all winter in the Arcadia sull' Oriente! That was his favorite dish!

The young King of Italy has plenty of spirit [hair on his teeth], that I know. Nevertheless what would a <u>single person</u>, ever so spirited, be able to straighten out in the midst of universal laxity and undependability? Was not the bloodiest illustration of that alone, in and of itself, the wretched train accident before the gates of Rome?²⁵⁷

You ask whether I have seen the *Allg. Ztg.* of August 1ˢᵗ and your contribution therein? How would that have been possible <u>in Dieppe</u>?

And there after all it might have been more likely (because of the casino, which however doesn't aspire so high) than here!!! *La Verité, la Croix, le peuple français, le Moniteur,* and *le Gaulois*! This is the summary step-ladder of the day's press in the salon! In the restaurant one can have at hand at all holy times, the *Elsässer,* the *Lorrain* and either a Mühlhaus or a Strassburg local rag!

---

²⁵⁶ A letter from AVE to O'Connell that same day begins: "Well, Propeller mine, let loose at last from dancing attendance on our Charmeur of St. Paul's? Got him safely piloted thru' the eddies of Rome? Fancy you have succeeded in capping him once more and passing a rope thru' his nosering fastened to your belt? – You poor dear Innocent abroad! Anyhow I feel for you since this prolonged broiling in Rome must have been detrimental I fear to your poor constitution so sadly shaken already last spring." (A. von Eichthal to Denis O'Connell, Schloss Sonnenberg, August 23, 1900, Archives of the Diocese of Richmond.)

²⁵⁷ Shortly after Victor Emmanuel's accession there was a terrible train wreck in the outskirts of Rome. The young king and queen quickly took a cab to the scene and comforted the injured.

Much enjoyment in Waadtland.²⁵⁸ May my task here at least come out successfully. Could you not send me the *Allg.*, against honorable return in Freiburg?

With heartiest greetings and wishes, your   AVE

---

²⁵⁸ The German version of the Swiss Canton de Vaud.

Addressed to FXK in Freiburg
September 8, 1900
Carsbach-Sonnenberg
(Ober Elsass)

Your disturbing news[259] about your state of health, precious friend, just adds to my own prospects, to tell you that my current cure ties me down here <u>unfortunately</u>! <u>for at least six weeks</u>, so that as far as meeting with you on the 18th, which I have so long awaited with joy, <u>nothing</u> can be done! The director in fact thinks that I should stay here the whole month, which was hardly to be doubted. As far as the outlook for gaining strength ...it doesn't help one for that! I expect O'C day after tomorrow[260] and send this card to your home since you gave me no other address. Now I urgently would ask for news, as well of your health as of how long you will remain at home, since I want to and must see you <u>in any case</u>. Schleinitzes expect me in Meran in October, can scarcely get away from there because of Adele's gout, as I learned from them today.

Warmest wishes and greetings,   AVE

---

[259] Kraus wrote from Clarence, Switzerland, on September 5, 1900, telling her he was ill.

[260] "I think it is very likely that we shall meet and talk next Monday. Details later. Saluti. Prop[eller]."(Denis J. O'Connell, Weggis, to AVE, Sept. 5, 1900, ARD) "Propeller" was her pet name for O'Connell.

To FXK in Montreux, Suisse, URGENT
September 9, 1900
Carsbach-Sonnenberg
(Ober Elsass)

Yesterday I wrote you a card, to Freiburg, to say that I sadly! had to stay nailed down here the whole September! Today O'Connell's words horrified me that he knows you seriously ill in Switzerland[261] and so I rush (since thank God he gave me your address) to offer my services to you without a moment's loss. What a person might not give up on behalf of a joyful celebration, illness demands that one do so. Be silent, as it is about something more serious. One can "Kneippen" any time and find such establishments elsewhere. Therefore, understood? Precious, honored friend! through O'C, if possible, let me know by telegram whether you can use me.[262] Then I'll come at once! As far as 'out' goes, know that it would happen with pleasure. God be with you. AVE

---

[261] "Our friend Kraus is very ill at Hotel Royal, Montreux, and I go to-morrow to see him. I shall see you anyhow if my stay there be not long, but will write. Saluti. Prop[eller.]" (Denis J. O'Connell, Weggis, to AVE, Sept. 8, 1900, Archives of the Diocese of Richmond.) On August 31st, Kraus had hemorrhaged badly while visiting near Montreux. Old friends came from Germany and took him home. (*Tgb.*, p. 743)

[262] Kraus wrote her from Freiburg on September 11, 1900, "Thanks for your card of the 9th. 'Pellegrino.'"

November 5, 1900
Hotel d'Europe
Sestri Levante

Dear friend,
I thought you long ago had been given the news of my deep misfortune[263] through my notice in the *Allg. Ztg.* which you receive daily. The pompous and detestable so-called "notices of partings" I only sent where I had to think that neither the *Allg.* nor the *M.[ünchener]N.[eueste]N.[achtrichten]* were read.[264] One month was I in that desolate Schloss with the widow, in <u>fearful</u> loneliness! Then an old friend summoned me to 8 days in Paris and from there I came here last Wednesday (reduced to the absolute depths of my nerves) where an old dear friend slowly and painfully met death. In spite of that I hope, here in the sight of the ocean, to collect myself and to get stronger. May God give that! — And you? A "ruin" of your variety is worth more and stands stronger that most new constructions! Letters[265] to here are implored as well as detailed news of yourself by your

AVE

---

[263] Suffering from renewed loss of blood, Kraus wrote her, ("I am a ruin,") on October 26, 1900. He reproached her for not informing him that her brother, Emil von Eichthal, had died on September 18, 1900.

[264] Newspaper clipping "München September 24, Marie Christine Freifrau von Eichthal, geborene Gräfin von Bronno-Bronska, Augusta Freiin von Eichthal und Luise Freiin von Eichthal geben hiemit Nachricht von dem sie tief erschütternden Hinscheiden ihres theuren Gatten und Bruder des Freiherrn Emil von Eichthal. Versehen mit den Tröstungen unserer hl. Kirche, entschlief er nach kurzem, schwerem Leiden am Morgen des 18. September aus seinem Gute in Südfrankreich. Chateau de St.-Selve (par Castres-Gironde) 21 September 1900." (*Nachlass* Eichthal, file Emil von Eichthal)

[265] Kraus replied November 7, 1900. "At last a sign of life from you...Meanwhile our friend Ireland has revealed himself more and more as a Vatican Bajazzo [clown], his recent American speeches are almost unbelievable. These Irish! I am very interested to see whether these new events can get him sent the red hat. I still don't think so..."

November 14, 1900
Hotel Europa
Sestri Levante

Dear friend,
In these sorrowful weeks I have written to <u>no one</u> who urgently begged me for news. You appear not to grasp <u>how deeply</u> this loss affects me.[266] I just counted on this brother, the sole person who was near to me by the bond of blood and similar in temper — with all the strength of my heart.

That your birthday should become his death day will remain with me from here on as a deeply sorrowful memory. Here in this quiet little ocean bay I seek to steel myself for going on, and to bring my deeply shattered nerves into some semblance of order.

Sadly this death was followed by yet other troubles which surrounded me, troubles that at first so disgusted me that I almost succumbed to them. Still, a true friend saved me in the eleventh hour, summoning me to Paris to obtain for myself a legal advisor and watching with him moreover, to see, that because of the greed of the widow, I was protected from the beggar's staff! – I was a full month in the Gironde and have turned my back on that unholy Schloss forever, leaving it behind on the 19th of October. Nevertheless, should you ever again want the product from there, just write to the Regisseur there, M. <u>Bernardin</u>, and they will gladly be at your service.

You think that in the meantime I would have experienced and heard lots of things? Only what was to be read in the papers, like now in Cologne the nice revelations about Msgr. Stahlnacky's opinion about the [illegible] outside of the government scarcely anyone else should have been disappointed. O'C, that real true soul, presses me to return to the Ripetta so he can be near and

---

[266] Kraus' letter of November 7 assumed that she could return to normal matters and recent news.

distract me.²⁶⁷ He exults over the departure of the del Vals²⁶⁸ and justifiably so.

That our great deceiver from St. Paul carries out still further Vatican capers since his return home, I learn from you, but it doesn't surprise me. Since last year we know what to think of his Irish dependability. But would you actually believe that he has now succeeded so completely in captivating both of the magnificent Wards²⁶⁹ that they now swear only by him? Wonder if Spalding knows that? What an experience of the heart for that high-minded serious man! I wrote him from Dieppe, without getting any reply.

Baeumler²⁷⁰ should only cure you just thoroughly enough so that you can quickly head south and visit your friends in Rome. What do you say to the endlessly renewed Neapolitan and other scandals? A land filled with cancer in which one ulcer breaks open after another… What could possibly help there when there is lacking the strong hand of a surgeon, so that the blood poison

---

²⁶⁷ "…I was hoping that you would come soon to Rome so that we could chat & chat & chat….I imagine what a void his departure has made for you in this world. Come on here, and let us try and fill it. In me I hope you will find something of him….You will find the atmosphere of Rome changed a little bit better; the del Vals will be out of it…Come on to Rome soon, dear friend, and let us poke up the oil and make life's lamp burn brighter." (Denis J. O'Connell, Rome, Oct. 21, 1900, to AVE, *Nachlass* Eichthal, O'Connell File)

²⁶⁸ The Merry del Vals, parents of the Spanish/English monsignor Raffaele Merry del Val.

²⁶⁹ The wealthy Caldwell sisters, Mary Gwendoline,"Mamie," Marquise de Mérinville, and Mary Elizabeth, "Lena," Baroness Zedtwitz. Kraus had now met Lena as well, when both sisters entertained him at dinner in Luzerne, August 28, 1900. He described Lena as aspiring, well educated, not like her 'very sick' sister.(*Tgb.*, p.742.) Eichthal's expression, about Spalding's "experience of the heart," has intuition.

²⁷⁰ Dr. Christian Baeumler, Professor and Director, Medical Clinic, Freiburg.

becomes general ... Bonomelli[271] does the right thing in turning to Italian colleagues in other countries and to try to heal worse things there.

You ask about the food here. Last year it was outstanding to begin with, this year frightful and just now bearable through a change of cooks. The protected location and the little southern bay, the exemplary cleanliness and the obliging attitude in the house make it still very worth recommending, and — 7 lire[272] pension, everything included, even the wine.

Next week I go back to 176 Ripetta. I look forward to your "*Allg.*" with impatience. In old friendship, always yours -

AVE

---

[271] Geremia Bonomelli (1831-1914), 1871 Bishop of Cremona, advocated a reconciliation of the Vatican with modern culture and with the Kingdom of Italy.

[272] Equivalent to $1.40 or RM 5.00 at the time.

December 12, 1900
Rome

Dear friend,
I hear that you asked the Sickels about my address. I answered you on Nov. 14 from Sestri and enclosed several lines to Princess Liechtenstein[273] with the request to give them to the city post office. Also I asked to have the promised newspapers sent <u>here to Rome</u> at the soonest since I would leave on Nov. 19th. And so it was, but from you since then – Nothing? As my letter to here, announcing my arrival, never got here, so that at 1 o'clock in the morning I stood, in an unbearable storm, in front of a locked house, in the torn-up, impassable Ripetta, wet as a dog, and pounded until <u>finally</u> somebody woke up — I am concerned that something may have gone astray,

Friend O'C greets you intensely, it is bearable with both of us, and you? *Sale et salve* —

AVE

---

[273] Probably Marie Henriette, born Princess von und zu Liechtenstein (1843-1931), married 1865 to Alfred Aloys Edward Prince von und zu Liechtenstein (1842-1907).

December 31, 1900
Monday – noon
Rome

My dear friend,
We thank God that this Jubilee year draws to an end in a few hours! It has been a year of horror for the world on all sides! The immortal ancient in the Vatican alone can rejoice with a look back at the deification and enrichment experienced during the Anno Santo. Do you know what the Romans say? All the evil spirits shut up behind the Holy Door are unleashed by means of its opening and that is why we have seen all that we have!

On the eve of its conclusion, using the silver masterkey, I penetrated the hermetically sealed St. Peter's, walked about, saw the Veronica sections with the reliquary balcony decked out in purple and hung with crystal chandeliers, the carpet already spread out in the middle church, readied for the end of the pope's prayers, and at the end stepped three times over the threshold of the famed holy door (whose walls are being worked on in the atrium, where the last nails were even being driven into the papal throne) and doing so I was astonished to see the ancient golden inscription of Gregory XIII[274] standing out from the shadow!

That is a spot for philosophical historians and historically minded philosophers! What will become further of this hocus-pocus? Who would not there comprehend the idealistic foolishness: to want to pour pure wine into these old tarred wineskins?

---

[274] The nave of St. Peter's has a frieze of biblical quotations in tall gold letters referring to Peter. As one steps through the Holy Door, the only quotation visible, to the upper left, is the passage based on Luke 22:32, EGO ROGAVI PRO TE, O PETRE, etc. ["But I have prayed for thee, (O Peter) that thy faith fail not."] AVE attributes this decoration to Gregory XIII, Ugo Buoncompagno, 1502-1585.

Our friends (O'C above all) let their heads hang down in gloom, for the reason that Ireland, in a fulminating sermon in Washington, announced *orbi et urbi* [sic], short and sweet, his brand new leap into another saddle and with full ceremony proclaimed his characterless eloquence. The hoped-for gratuity would truly come to him, if it only depended on Leo XIII and Ledochowski, who sincerely would like to give him the purple. The remaining *porporati* nevertheless are of another mind and work so cleverly against it with their objections, delivered one spoonful at a time – that since nothing is ever eaten as hot as it is cooked and the next Consistory is <u>not</u> at the door, — very possibly between Ireland and Corrigan, Msgr. Chapelle might be the *terzo gaudente* [third gay dog].

Do you know that Ireland is now numbered among Don Albertario's saints?[275] That the former editor of the *Moniteur de Rome*, Msgr. Boeglin,[276] thrown out of here back then, and Goyau[277] and Lorin,[278] in Paris, are now his [Ireland's] inspiration? What miserable politicians, these Celts take the cake with their lack of internal balance.

When Cardinal Oreglia (as Dean), after the closing ceremony on the 24th, maliciously wished the pope, "*di riposare bene*," the pope gave right back to him that he was not thinking about observing the "*riposo eterno*" which Oreglia wished for him, but only to astound everyone with his tenacity on life!

---

[275] Editor of the Milan *Osservatore cattolico*.

[276] Eugen Boeglin (1854-1914), 1877 ordained priest in Strassburg, worked in Rome 1882-1896 as editor of the *Moniteur de Rome*. Boeglin played a double role with the Americanists, using them for his own ends. He was thrown out of Rome in 1896 for taking bribes and keeping a woman.

[277] Georges Goyau (1869-1939), French writer on church history and politics.

[278] Henri Lorin (1858-1914), French socialist-catholic politician. Friend of John Ireland from school days.

Venturi wants to greet you a thousand times and asks you to excuse his silence about your flattering reference to him. In September he so stupidly overworked that he became ill and incapable for a long time. Then came renewed overloads of work through the approaching appearance of Vol. I of his art history at Hoepli. If I am not wrong the book has arrived in the stores just now. Venturi promises himself to write to you soon.

The Ripetta will be raised higher.[279] What mud, dirt, and near impassability of the street that involves, is not to be expressed. The loose stones serve additionally for the street urchins as throwing materials, with one of which I was almost killed recently. The stone caught me just above the ankle; all day long I suffered from the results.

Gibsons come in February. How happy I am about you in March! Until then take care of yourself.

May the new century bring us good things, as God allows!

In true thoughts, your

AVE

---

[279] Eichthal lived by the ancient stepped harbor, the Porto di Ripetta, now disappeared into the eastern base of the Ponte Cavour. An elevation of the steps and river wall in 1900 was for protection against flooding by the Tiber.

1901
Chapter 6

[In Italian]
January 30, 1901
Rome

Dear friend,
For some time I have wanted to thank you for sending the most interesting printed things, however I am overwhelmed by such annoyances as to render me incapable of almost everything. Moreover our friend O'C suffers not a little through the change produced in him in consequence of the pronounced about-face of Ireland. He feels dejected to such a degree that it consequently results in his withdrawing himself so seriously as to have reduced him almost to a misanthrope. The poor one won't give himself any peace about the lost illusions, and, what is more, from the tremendous abuse done to his bona fides, and also to his self confidence. We'll talk more, face to face. He needs to be uplifted, to regain faith in himself, and for that to happen, he needs things of which only you are capable ─────────

We look forward to March with impatience. For the greatness of your vitality, the elasticity of your nature, we will just have to survive [until you arrive], of which I am convinced.

So hurry to leave that district of cold and fog, and give your precious news[280] quickly to, affectionately, your
AVE

---
[280] Kraus wrote to her on February 2, 1901. "At last I come to make answer to your letter of December 31 and your card of January 30. I was disturbed by what you reported about affairs related to your brother's departure and now also about O'C's condition. After two weeks in Nervi, I expect to be in Rome by mid-March."

February 19, 1901
Rome

Dear friend,
Unfortunately I am not able to write more than this brief thanks for letter and papers since Alexandra von Schleinitz's death has disturbed me too deeply. A lung inflammation (well gotten over in December) had aroused the old evil … Beginning of January she lay down never to get up again! On the 14th this noble great soul passed away. What will become of Adele? It is too heart rending.

Since yesterday we are snowed upon here, still I hear little or almost nothing said about influenza. The cold air is quite healthy.

In Nervi you will hopefully find a warm oasis where you can recover and wait for further things. All of us here are happy for you and send heartiest greetings.

AVE

Postcard to FXK
Eden Hotel, Nervi[281]
March 7, 1901
Rome

Dear friend,
Can't you speed up your coming hither by going now to Florence?[282] Florence is for you the same as toward Rome; I on the other hand must unfortunately leave soon, can not make up my mind about that before I see you again for a little bit. Poor Adele asks for me and in fact <u>soon</u>! I offered to her to come at the time of Alexandra's death. After so long a silence she just first wrote that she accepts and very much wishes it, she was too crippled by grief 'til now to write.

There is so much for me to set in order, but <u>at the latest</u> I must leave in 10 – 12 days.

Meantime we have given Ireland check and mate. This clever thing I believe to have accomplished and am justly proud of it.[283] Already all odds were for him, it needed only a hair's breadth more and the purple would have flowed around his figure ... only: [in English] 'there's many a slip between the cup and the lip!'[284] <u>Finished off</u>, I say to you, is he, for whom the reflection of the

---

[281] Nervi, the oldest resort on the eastern Riviera, 14 miles east of Genoa.

[282] Kraus had written to her on March 5, 1901, to say he was hurrying to Rome, and to add: "I don't see or hear anything more about the consistory for the red hat for friend Ireland. I think Rampolla will give the matter more time."

[283] This stroke against Ireland was probably accomplished by working on her friends in the German orientation, the Propaganda, Ledochowski, and the Vannutelli,brothers. She would have drawn attention to Ireland's lack of dependability and his likely vote for Rampolla.

[284] This saying occurs also in a letter from Sabina Parravicino di Revel to Denis O'Connell of February 23, 1901, written in the same moment, as she inquires about Ireland's fate.

scarlet hat had so blinded the eyes, that he no longer knew how to distinguish between friend and foe! *Sapienti val*!

I expect you next week definitely.[285] Good luck in the south.

AVE

"But what comes then with the red hat? I recollect a famous phrase said by <u>you</u> in that previous time of a downpour of deliberation: [in English] 'From the cup to the lips there are many slips.' Is it perhaps again true this time? It would be cruel, too cruel and undeserved." Quoted as Sabina to O'Connell, 23 Feb 1901, Archives of the Diocese of Richmond, in Ornella Confessore, *L'Americanismo Cattolico in Italia* (Rome, 1984), 233, n. 13.

[285] Kraus wrote to her the next day, March 8, 1901: "With Ireland you have done well. The time is past when one puts up with tight-rope walkers...allied with the gentlemen of the Parisian society, of the left and the right."

to Franz Xaver Kraus

FXK is in Florence[286]
March 24, 1901
Sunday
Rome

This time it is a real gestation of hindrances until you succeed in coming here! Through our friends Gibsons (who travel to you tomorrow) you will learn that my departure must now be put off to the 2nd half of April because of the total impossibility of finding the simplest lodging in Meran-Obermais. Adele suspected it herself and finds it better for her as right now she is plentifully surrounded.

I see Countess [illegible] a great deal and will deliver your message. Better not to write about that, since written things only strain your poor eyes and their improvement can only be assured by extreme care. Anyway, Roman living is more bearable for you for the last ten days than it would have been until now because of the dreadful weather, and so I am twice as glad to see you here again, and on the mend.

Rotenhan, Sickel, etc., diligently inquire after you, thought that you were already here, and wish you speedy recovery and timely arrival, in union with, your

AVE

---

[286] Kraus wrote to her from Nervi on March 14 to say that he had caught cold in the rainy weather and hoped to be in Rome by the 21st. He wrote from Florence on the 21st to say that he was still sick and would remain in Florence until the end of March.

FXK is in Florence
March 27, 1901
Rome

Dear friend,
A real comedy of errors! It seems definite that we are not to come together! While you – alas, alas! – lie in bed,[287] and Venturi, before his departure to Naples, fruitlessly and repeatedly sought you out in the Hotel de Rome (which he asked me to tell you with his sincerest regret and wishes) – now I am hit with news that I must go, at breakneck speed, to Paris!

You well know with what miserable warfare I have been pursued from there, since my good brother's death. I believed myself, thanks to an incomparable friend who gave me her notary and I conducted all with him, to be now finally at an end and in peace ... there it appears to my friend's horror and my absolute petrifaction (which was only momentary, rest assured!) that my notary, <u>in my name</u>, has signed a stipulation which is <u>completely</u> contrary to what was arranged with him and gives consideration solely to my grasping sister-in-law! Think about my situation! He had my power of attorney and misused it in this manner right under the eyes of his lifelong patron and client! She called me herself urgently in order now to bring the notary under attack ... I fear the game is lost, it would be that he would fear my threat to have the document legally annulled, which would damage his, up till now, respected name.

And after that ... I have to contemplate going to London where the administration of the property lies in the hands of a narrow-minded, vain, 'snob,' who previously has prepared endless annoyances for me, with whom however I must deal gently, whereas vain narrow-mindedness is the most

---

[287] Having caught the flu in Nervi, Kraus arrived ill in Florence on March 16, 1901, suffered and socialized until April 30, 1901, when he was strong enough to make a trip to Milan, spent five days, and was back in Freiburg by May 6, 1901.

difficult opposition which can come to one. Oh, dear friend, what a ticklish, serious, situation!

Gibsons will first come Sunday to you, in between they drive themselves up and down in Umbria and Sienna. Please give this brand-new news to both, because possibly we will soon see each other again in London, and greet them, for this sobering discovery dates only from yesterday.

I travel Saturday night, to be in Paris early Monday, where letters reach me *aux soins obligeans* de la Duchesse Caracciolo,[288] 94 rue de l'Université.

Keep your fingers crossed for me and let me at the earliest know about your condition and your plans.[289] The beloved Countess Waldburg I see often, read Harnack to her and sincerely regret to have to leave her so soon and for what? All righteous God!

In true friendship, always your

A. v. Eichthal

---

[288] Born Stephanie Weg, an old friend of AVE's.

[289] Kraus answered from Florence on March 29, 1901: "I am deeply troubled about your departure from Rome and the reason for it. Today I can write only a card for I am still suffering as ever and my situation is very confined. I still intend to go to Rome after Easter, but whether that will work, depends... Give me your address for April... after Pentecost I go to Berlin."

FXK is in Florence

April 6, 1901
Holy Saturday
94, rue de l'Université
Paris

Dear friend,
May tomorrow's Easter Day be likewise the day of resurrection for your good health! Here it is <u>terrible</u> in every way. My business is irretrievably bungled. Don't know how it will end — probably in surrender.

Yesterday afternoon in the theater of the 'Capuchins,' J. Claretie[290] gave a memoir filled lecture about Bossuet,[291] interspersed with selections from his sermons, which Monnet-Sully[292] read perfectly dramatically before the packed house. — Something like that one can only experience in this land of actors! [Yet] if all roads lead to Rome, so also all roads lead to God!

When the abominable weather permits, I must go to England. Gibsons have most cordially invited me, but it is too far from the city. Could you send Loisy's[293] address right back to me? Klein,[294] whom I wrote (with no answer) is in Italy now.

---

[290] Jules Claretie, writer and memoirist, whose works spanned 1870 to 1940.

[291] The famous Bishop of Meaux.

[292] Popular French actor, known for his portrayals of Oedipus and Hamlet.

[293] Alfred Firmin Loisy (1857-1940). Ordained priest in 1879. Principal French representative of Modernism. Excommunicated 1908.

[294] Felix Klein (1862-1953), Priest, 1893-1907 Professor at Institut Catholique in Paris. Deeply involved in Americanist controversy, translator of life of Isaac Hecker.

I have no idea what will become of me in May. Couldn't we meet in Baden or Munich?[295] The above address is always certain for your A.E.

---

[295] Kraus' reply of April 8 was re-addressed in Paris by Duchess Caracciolo (she favored purple ink), and forwarded to 18 Bayswater Terrace, Kensington Gardens, W. London. He supplied AVE with Loisy's publisher's address, informed her that Klein was in Milan, and although "suffering greatly," said he still hoped to be in Rome at the end of the week.

May 1, 1901
94, rue de l'Université
Paris

Dear friend,

<u>Where</u> are you hiding? O'C writes that you are returned home (instead of going to Rome) because of your poor condition. That upsets me <u>very much</u>. I have just come back from England where I got a bronchitis under which I still labor. Gibsons are here for a few days. Tomorrow I go with him to see Loisy because she is holding a bazaar for the benefit of Soeur Marie. Zahm should hit here soon. My affairs, through so much evil intent and such phenomenal avarice, were dragged out so and confused so, that their end seems not to be in sight. God help it! Please, for a word here about your condition![296]

AVE

---

[296] Kraus replied from Freiburg on May 9, 1901 that he had been in great pain in Florence, lying in bed most of March and April. "Today I can only find strength for a card...I think about the important matters visited upon you and hope to God that He came to your aid against all Manichaeans, Pharisees and Sadducees... In the period May 29 to June 10 I anticipate to be in Baden if I can travel...Let me hear from you."

May 20, 1901
94, rue de l'Université
Paris

Dr. frnd!
With great sympathy do I learn about you suffering so. And I hope that with your elastic nature, with the final arrival of warm weather, you will rise up like the phoenix, out of the ashes of the cast-off weakness, to new powers. About me, it is best to be silent … was made so sick from moral infection that I had physical stomach upsets, which I cured with 'Chinese wine.' How long the human ill will and greed will hold me fast here is unfathomable…

Sadly therefore I don't know how to establish a finish at this location. How gladly I would come to Baden at the end of June…

Saw Baron Hügel here at Loisy's one afternoon. Otherwise everything the same.

AVE

June 6, 1901
94, rue de l'Université
Paris

Dear friend,
Where are you? How are you? – Why so long no sign of life? – Today only so much, that, tired out from the fruitless waiting, I will go forth next Monday (10 June) and if possible by the night train (because of the heat.) Tuesday early I hope to get into Baden, to stay 2 days. Then I <u>have</u> to go to Munich.

For the final development I come back to here … when? Chi lo sa! Should you be in Baden, please – your address. I always stay across from the Badischer Hof in the "lange Strasse" with Frl. Luise Siefert en garni.

God be with you! Please a word to here and as God wills! it will sound more encouraging than the last.

AVE

June 12, 1901[297]
Baden-Baden

Dr. fr.
As assailed and kaput as I also am, I am coming, like the oriental saying, if the mountain doesn't come to the prophet, etc., so the valley [*Thal*] comes to the professor tomorrow <u>Thursday</u> to Freiburg and in fact I hope to be there 11:42 minutes mid-day. Would you be so good as to request for me a room in Hotel Thomann at Hecht's? Tante grazie! I stay until Saturday evening, to be in Munich early on Sunday. Auf Wiedersehen tomorrow.

Yours, sincerely,

AVE

---

[297] Kraus wrote to her on June 10, 1901, that although he could not come back to Baden-Baden because of University matters, he was a bit better. Eating more and happier. "I beg you give me your news, better to bring it."

June 19, 1901
Türkenstrasse 6
Pension Washeim
Munich

Dr. frnd.,
Today only a quick request to send the conclusion about de Lagarde, whose Part 1 I read yesterday with such intense interest that I was beside myself lest I miss the end.[298] You know the beginning is of the 1st of May. The July number contains Anglo-Saxon things, as is known. It must therefore be hiding in the Part 2 number in May.

Adele Schleinitz came through here last week. Today I'll write her. We sit here in Heine's "green painted winter" right up to the eyes! May it be better with you and may you be spared this beastly weather, which nearly freezes your

AVE

---

[298] "Paul de Lagarde,"Parts I and II, the last subject in a series by " Xenos" (Kraus Pseudonym), entitled *Centenarbetrachtungen*, which appeared in the literary supplement of the *Allgemeine Zeitung* during the first half of 1901.

June 29, 1901
6 Türkenstrasse
Pension Washeim
Munich

Dear friend,
How I thank you for quickly[299] forwarding the 2nd of May. Xenos is a fine fellow and now he and Gerontius[300] revive the friends in Rome, from whence O'C has written me this day. He seems depressed to me although he doesn't say it. No wonder after the rude disappointments!

He announces the departure of Cardinal Gibbons, whose sojourn was passed in the loveliest ways with reciprocal affability between him and the Curia. About that, O'C noted how different it was from the last visit, and also thinks that Ireland wakes up to insight into his situation ... Somewhat late, don't you think? Scarlet fever all gone, he awakes from the crash and cries ouch!

The 1st Vol. of Klein's translation of the Spalding speeches has appeared. O'C will stay in Rome till mid-July, then to Paris with the rector of the Baltimore seminary to spend a few days together, then to Nauheim and afterwards going to the Schwarzwald with several American friends. In so doing he shoves along near us and quite naturally within hailing distance of you, of which he will take advantage as he is able.

Here I repeatedly see the Nuntius, who lives nearby.[301] What a conception these gentlemen have of their mission, as the simple *gradus ad Parnassum*

---

[299] Kraus answered her request on June 20, 1901, pleased that she was comfortable in Munich and that she liked Xenos.

[300] Kraus pseudonyms in the *Allgemeine Zeitung*.

[301] Msgr. Cesare Sambucetti, the brother of her landlord.

(*vulgo ad riposo cardinalizio*), it is enchanting: "These fine Germans! What dullards!" "*La nostra baronessa*, who is already half Italian in all other things."

Meanwhile yesterday I was at Schloss Seyfriedsburg with Prince Oettingen-Wallerstein[302] and found our Adele waiting for me at the [railroad] track. Her features have grown smaller, thinner, otherwise she doesn't look bad, considering what she has been through. Her grand earnest nature protects itself in almost superhuman self-control and resignation in her hard lot. Her sister lives <u>in</u> her and further surrounds her invisibly with her nameless love. Praise God! she receives it, to me, in a natural way and finds therein trust and strengthening for further living as God wills. To me the poor one, masterful in this uncomplaining destitution, is unspeakably touching. Through her gout she is so seriously restricted in her movements that she thanks you through me with all her heart for your exceedingly sympathetic letter. Much I had to tell her about you. Till about the middle of August she will remain there. Then she turns back to the Tyrol to set up for the winter at Vahrn, far from Meran, to steel herself for the return to Meran. How I understand that. Prince Wallerstein still stays at Marienbad.

Here it has finally grown hot and sultry, and for you hopefully the sun also beams down life-giving warmth? The 90 year old, extremely vigorous, Herr von Hefner-Alteneck wants to send by me his most devoted greetings. He regrets having met you only 2 times in his life, but has treasured an indelible impression thereof. Do you know the only thing he complains about? That his lynx eyes are giving way when he does very fine painting and he has to get used to glasses! I recently ate with him and am astounded at his inexhaustible liveliness.[303]

---

[302] Prince Maurice Oettingen-Wallerstein, born 21 Sept 1838, was the Seigneur of Seyfriedsburg.

[303] Jakob Heinrich von Hefner-Alteneck (1811-1903), 1868 General Conservator of the Art Monuments and Antiquities of Bavaria. Lost his right arm at age five. In paintings and drawings he recorded countless examples of applied and decorative arts of the 10th century to the 16th.

I will surely travel off to Jordanbad in a few weeks. Hopefully it goes bearably with you and you are able to move about enough? Oh, say goodbye to an anonymity which fools no one and sign yourself henceforth in a new way with your own name!

In constant faithfulness, your

AVE[304]

---

[304] Kraus responded on July 14, 1901: "Dear friend, An indescribable number of visitors has prevented me from answering your dear lines. Meanwhile Grannan was here, who wanted to be remembered to you. He is now in Tarasp after days in Luzern with O'C, who has gone again to Paris. ... I go the 23rd [of July]...to Berlin...to the *Reichskulturamt*...and then on August 15th to Wannsee & then to Munich. To promise days after that for Syrgenstein is very questionable. Things go slowly better with me... How I would like to have you write good news about your Parisian matters..."

July 14, 1901
6 Türkenstrasse
Pension Washeim
Munich

Dear friend,
I forgot to ask you recently in the last letter, whether the Ceylon Tea Co. delivered to you the price list and tea samples, and whether it asked your preference in an eventual order in German or French? For I wrote immediately from here.

Since then I have received from friend Venturi a whole pound of his lines of worry, wherein the following is found for you; "poor Kraus. How much it distresses me to know the state of his health! The power of the warmth of summer will succeed in helping him and benefit him really. Say to him however that I have thought of him, that I have been many times to ask about his arrival at <u>albergo Roma</u>,[305] and finally that I have been happy to make for him a sign of my admiration and my friendship, proposing him as a member of the Academia di S. Luca, where very few historians of art are inscribed. He will already have received the act of nomination."

He said this to me from Paris a few days ago, where he has betaken himself for renewed manuscript study, and then will hurry to London for the same purpose; this as preparation of the critical studies for the 2nd Vol. of his Italian art history. He added that if time allows he would like to go to Spain to compare the Arabic with Hispano-Arabic art. The man works himself to death. You see how conscientiously he carries on and will comment on nothing which he has not seen with his own eyes in the original (where at all possible). He must be back in Rome in 14 days and then he proceeds to the composition of the 2 volumes.

---

[305] Hotel de Rome.

Meanwhile O'C has left Rome on the 11th. He wrote me days before in obviously depressed mood, wanted to go to the 4 [Vier] Waldstätter See and keep in touch with us both. The climate in July holds nothing for him in Rome; only cold blooded salamanders like Donna Ersilia can stand that!

Loisy (according to his newest resolutions) will leave them in peace in Rome. That Keane takes the cure in Nauheim is nothing new to you and in any case immaterial, I suspect. People say to me, he is as transformed, since he became his own master again, free from Roman pressure.[306]

The Nuntius after a time came to speak of the Americans, of Hecker, Ireland *e tanti altri*. Forthwith he whined nasally, à la Leo XIII, "'We do not consider him <u>ripe</u> yet for the purple.' Thus the Holy Father spoke à pro pos of Ireland!" <u>The Moor</u>!

Here I am recovering visibly in spite of the chicanery which is brought to my ears from beyond the Anglo-French border. <u>Never</u> have I felt so intensively the good feeling of being in the homeland as this time in contrast to France!

The Renaissance Private-Exhibit (opposite the Glyptotek) charmed me through its rich complexity and selections from far off. To be sure, in this enjoyment, there sounds the gloomy death knell of the Leipzig crash,[307] which naturally will pull in after itself a collection of others from all German territories. The solid banker Finck assured me that such a shameless bankruptcy had <u>never before</u> been experienced in Germany.[308]

---

[306] Now made Archbishop of Dubuque, Keane returned to Bad Nauheim for treatment of a heart ailment. He had left Rome for good in the late fall of 1899.

[307] Recent bank failure.

[308] Banking matters came naturally to an Eichthal.

Has the brochure of a certain Stahly (a Swiss naturally) – 'The Mafia and Monarchy in Italy' – Berlin, at Dr. John Edelheim – come to your attention? Notwithstanding the contrary hateful tone and many overstatements, also small inaccuracies – there is, only sad to say, so much truth in it! It is a badly written, bungling piece of work but based on a great number of facts all too well known to me. The beautiful poor land … I long have given up any hope for a better future there.

On the 28th I happily follow up on an invitation to Bayreuth at the Palais Württemberg, stay about 8 days, and then back here for Jordanbad.

Hügels are from Milan all together up at Airolo[309] for summer refreshment, from where they want to be in Rome on the 15th of October for the winter.

How are you? The present heat has made it easier for you, God willing! to get about and as a result your physical condition has improved? This [good news] hopes soon to learn in 2 words, your faithful

AVE

Can't you please ask around [for the Stahly brochure] at Förster Bursengang?[310]

---

[309] In the Canton Ticino, Switzerland.

[310] A shop in the *Bursengang*, a pedestrian way in the center of Freiburg.

August 13, 1901
Tuesday
Post Immenstadt (Württemberg)
Jordanbad

Your lines from Berlin,[311] my dear friend, greeted me Saturday evening at table. The comfort received from this reception was of course reduced by the information about your renewed stomach bleeding ... The Berlin doctors nevertheless happily confirm my intuition so completely about the wonderful, if not to say wondrous, tenacity of your vitality – about the soundness of your organs – that a new lease on life seems certain for an incalculable duration. May God give his blessing to that! (A special compensation for your Vatican friends!)

How much your satisfaction with Berlin pleased me, needs no comment. Indeed we can all share therein ever so enthusiastically, since your influence alone succeeds in greatly benefiting *real* progress, enlightened Christianity, and the patriotic outlook. I view the occupation of Metz,[312] etc., as a compromise expertly advised by you, and do I err in that?

I have been fascinated by the three different sorts of announcements of the death of Empress Frederick[313] to their dioceses by Kopp, Stablewski,[314] and

---

[311] Kraus wrote on August 8, 1901, "Berlin, Reichshof: Dear friend, only a few words. I hope that Prof. Renvers [Rudolph von Renvers (1854-1909), Director of the City Hospital, Berlin-Moabit] will let me travel off tomorrow. [The doctors] find my heart and vital signs extraordinary. Tell that to friend Rampolla, he will enjoy it...I will be in Bad Steben (Parkhotel) from 9 –18th and then 18-22 in Munich (Bayrischer Hof)."

[312] Willibrord Benzler, OSB (1853-1921), 1893 Abbot of Maria Laach, in 1901 was made Bishop of Metz. Known as one with whom Wilhelm II, patron of Maria Laach, was very comfortable, his appointment was encouraged by Kraus.

[313] Victoria (1840-1901), daughter of Queen Victoria and wife of Emperor Frederick III who reigned only from March to June 1888). She and her son Wilhelm II were largely estranged.

— Simar![315] The strictly official/episcopal notice by Breslau's prince-bishop; that of the Archbishop of Gnesen-Posen, with true Polish charm, connecting it with the personal appearance of the Empress during her 99 days of rule, on the occasion of the drought in Posen, and praising her personally (and if I may say, from one who is the true product of a German couple); compared to the cringing fawning letter of the Archbishop of Cologne to the emperor!

Should one not believe that the weakling's imperial heart is broken in two and that everyone makes intercessions for its healing? When a person knows how the two long stood in relation to each other, how only the last years just began to improve and smooth over the relationship, provocation to laughter combines with nausea [at Simar's letter.] I had thought better of Simar before that. Do you know him?

Has the *Allgemeine* meanwhile brought out anything further from your *doppelgänger* Gerontius or Xenos! Please, please! Is it for that that you go for four days, 18 – 22 this month, to the site of the *Allg*.? I fancy that very meaningful!

May Steben[316] make you stronger meanwhile, so God will! to further misdeeds! What do you say about Italy? 'The beautiful land where sounds the yes (but nothing else!)' [*Il bel paese ove suona il si (ma nient' altro)*]

---

[314] Florian von Stablewski (1841-1906), 1891 Archbishop of Gnesen-Posen.

[315] Hubert Simar (1835-1902), 1864 Professor at Bonn, 1891 Bishop of Paderborn, 1899 Archbishop of Cologne.

[316] On the way back from Berlin to Munich, Kraus spent five days at Bad Steben to recuperate.

The struggle for Crispi's[317] soul on his deathbed produced a tragi-comic effect. Didn't he remember Heine's insolent death-joke?[318]

In Bayreuth I met D[on] Roffredo Caetani[319] at Wagners and learned through him that Rosalia Lovatelli-Gabrielli[320] was blessed several months ago with a little boy. Meanwhile the gardens of the Quirinal apparently threaten to fall in, thanks to the slovenly tunnel[321] digging! Thus all is as ruins down below — materially and morally!

I also spoke with Thode[322] in Bayreuth. Never before have I found his appearance so good, since he abandoned Athens on the Spree and the art squabbles about the modern there, for the benefit of Heidelberg.

Where are Grannan and O'Connell hiding? Have you seen the latter anywhere? And what is it with Syrgenstein? Whither do you turn your Mercury staff after Munich?

Here it is quiet, clean and comfortable, appropriate for recovery, for which basically needy feels your, true
AVE

---

[317] Francesco Crispi, (1819-1901), twice premier of Italy, anti-clerical, advocate of Triple Alliance, 1896 compelled to resign after the Abyssinian disaster at Adowa..

[318] Heinrich Heine (1797-1856), on his death-bed, "God will pardon me. It is his trade."

[319] Don Roffredo-Michel-Ange-Francois Caetani, born Rome October 13, 1871, nephew of Donna Ersilia.

[320] Rosalia was the daughter of Donna Ersilia.

[321] Work done to extend the Babuino/Due Macelli thoroughfare southward under the Quirinal hill and to create the tunnel which connects to the other side.

[322] Henry Thode (1857-1920), Art Historian, Prof. In Heidelberg 1893-1911. Married Daniele von Bülow, Richard Wagner's step-daughter.

August 30, 1901
Jordanbad (bei Biberach)
Württemberg

Dear friend,
When on Tuesday early I telephoned the Mainau castle management to hear about your health after such a burdensome trip,[323] I got the dumfounding answer: you had already journeyed off. The mistake was so obvious that I telegraphed to Kissleg[324] for clarification. From there I first learned of your, too terrible to mention, layover in Lindau where there is no covered train station as far as I can remember, so that you, poorest one, really must have had a watery test of your health. If <u>that</u> didn't damage you, it shows that obviously your physical aspect is just as <u>armored</u> as your moral one. If the train conductor at Hergatz had given any indication of this miserable waiting period, I would have abandoned all applicable hesitations about the [hotel] Bayrischer Hof in Lindau, naturally to get on the train with you and to be useful for that atrocious wait. And after that for you to set down on the damp Mainau ... the will of man is verily his Kingdom of Heaven.

I have devoured your Gioberti with admiration.[325] Admiration without end over the material you have marvelously seen and which you have at your command – like a keyboard to a musician – admiration at your fine and

---

[323] Kraus left Bad Steben on August 18, spent several days in Munich, then arranged to meet AVE and the Waldburg-Zeil-Wurzach sisters, Sophie and Marie, at Sophie's Schloss Syrgenstein near Lindau in Bavaria. Several days later, in the rain, they put him on the train at Hergatz, only to learn afterwards that he, quite weak and susceptible, had a layover in the pouring rain at Lindau, waiting for the train to the grand-ducal island Mainau in Lake Constance.

[324] Kissleg was the Zeil-Wurzach chateau on the Danube in Württemberg belonging to the sisters, Sophie and Marie.

[325] "*Die Centenarfeier für Vincenzo Gioberti*," three installments in the *Beilage* of the *Allgemeine Zeitung* in mid-1901, signed with Kraus' own name.

measured weighing and evaluation of such a disposition, filled with Sturm und Drang, so truly southern, so overflowing with froth, who fundamentally would only fit in on the Island Bimini[326] with his dreams of Latin supremacy. Poor, poor, illusionary!

What? You have even read D'Annunzio's '*Fuoco*'?[327] Good dinner! There admiration for the speculative splendor of the portrayal is still outdistanced by several horse-lengths by revulsion at such prostitution of a truly loving wife!

The devil with such a despicable fellow! With that sort there is only more to spit out! What lamed fantasy, what is more. He manages to discover nothing, only to exalt the particular experience, enveloped and swarmed with a shower of intensive sparks.

Should Grannan or O'Connell emerge near you, heartiest greeting to both. After the chilling downpour of rain of the previous four days, it looks as if it finally wants to get basically better. Please <u>one word</u> about the course of your rosary of travel adventures.

Since the pen flies over the paper as nimbly as ever, and despite all, you are still a sly-boots, and henceforth you are the unburnable Spaniard,[328] for whom, highly satisfied, the hand is pressed by this faithful

AVE

---

[326] Contemporary expression for unreal, extreme, illusory.

[327] Gabriele D'Annunzio, (1863-1938), published '*Il Fuoco*' 1900, "Grace, voluptuousness, affectation, characterize this apostle of a new Renaissance."

[328] Signor Lionetto, "The Incombustible Spaniard," a native of Toledo who performed in Paris in 1803 at the age of twenty- three. He handled red-hot irons, drank boiling oil, and plunged his fingers into melting lead. See Harry Houdini, *The Miracle Mongers and Their Methods*, (New York, 1920), pp. 38-41.

[In Italian]
September 5, 1901
Jordanbad

Dear friend,
What does this mean, to let me suffer so much for your news, in spite of my request? The mistakes which ruined my finances telephoning to the Mainau for <u>well over three quarters of an hour</u> without result call for that?

That deserves for itself a least a little card, I think. Calm me with only one word, to here, please, and that right away.[329]

I read these days your essay about M. Ducamp[330] and finished it with a first rate impression. It is wonderful, your gift to balance things so equally, taking pen in hand in the moment to characterize the quality of the individual, a true pleasure for whoever reads it!

I hope in God that your Grand Ducal excursion may be a success! La Lovatelli salutes you. Here we have such bad weather as to make me think to leave these

---

[329] After this scolding in Italian Kraus replied pitifully the next day, September 6, 1901. "Dear friend, I have been back here from the Mainau for some days, exhausted almost to death. I had in mind to answer you…but friend O'C demanded all my time for two days. On the Mainau I have absolutely not known of any telegram or telephone inquiry, even though that same day other telegrams arrived for me. How did you like the September letter about the Rosminian movement? O'C was in good spirits, greets you heartily, goes today to Zurich. Does it look as if the Santa Sede falls more and more into disgrace?…Don't be so impatient, if I, in my total exhaustion, and pursued every day by a thousand men and matters, can hardly find a moment for a letter. What I can tell you of my person is that it is now more of a museum of pathology. *Addio, addio per oggi* – your F X Kraus."

[330] "Abenddämmerung. Errinnerung an Maxime Du Camp," in *Deutsche Rundschau*, 1895. Reprinted in Essays, Vol. I, 1896.

parts next week unless we have a miracle Appolinare (not Appolinaris[331] for goodness sake)!

I am still hesitant about my movements. However that does not disturb the constant faithfulness of your

AVE

I hope you know how to tell me to get together with friends Grannan and O'C.

---

[331] Appolinaris of Laodicea, + c.390, heretic, slighted the human nature of Christ.

September 17, 1901
Villa Friedheim (Obermais)
Meran, South Tyrol

Dear friend,
Yesterday evening, an eight day spell of rain, marked by cloudbursts right up to the end, finally concluded, and I hurry to send you, for tomorrow, the 18th of September (a day so painful for me), my and Adele Schleinitz's sincerest birthday wishes. May the chilly weather have assailed you less than I must have feared.

All very well for you to say, "don't be so impatient." I had to see you travel off adventurously, obviously suffering seriously, to the wet Mainau, and then to hear by the telephone: you had just left, and although I took this for nonsense, I would never have believed in a <u>lengthening</u> of your stay, as it finally turned out.

If one is <u>indifferent</u> to her closest ones, then one is untroubled. If one <u>takes trouble</u> however, then one is scolded. That, I suppose, gives satisfaction to somebody!

Adele came here with me at the same time. She seems smaller in her features and is again right troubled with the gout. This noble sister of suffering is <u>magnificent</u> in her isolation. One feels oneself as with two interwoven human souls, the surviving one basically imagines herself loosed from this earth and yet simultaneously a poor self longingly oriented toward the beyond. What strength of character is needed to hold out uncomplainingly to the end and yet take part in the life of those still here!

More than ever her holy indignation has flared up over the Vatican and the Romelings, and humorously she pondered with me early today the possibility of a Pope Rampollus I who then fortunately would let the bark of Peter be so steered that out of this shipwreck could follow a re-birth of the church, in the religious sense … In any case the Holy Ghost would have to throw down a wall placard beforehand on which was clearly written, that having had enough of his imprisonment in the Vatican, and having been hypnotically misused, he had fled his papal birdcage, in order from now on to let his light shine everywhere. What do you think of that?

I don't really believe that the Holy Father has returned to a state of childish innocence …that was unknown to him from the beginning!

Otherwise, what do you hear?

Will the so-called civilized world not finally unite in the instinct for self-preservation to make common and pitiless war on Anarchism? This product of burned-out brains and the most idiotic envy – if not destroyed like weeds and uprooted – will gradually exterminate everything that gets in its path. There is just not a single idea, other than the pure lust of murder toward anyone who has things better or who is anything in himself.

May I soon learn that you spent the 18th happily and feel generally better?

Your faithful AVE[332]

---

[332] On September 28, 1901, from Freiburg, Kraus replied in the last letter she kept:

"Dear friend, Only a few words to give you a sign of life when I am almost so constantly suffering, that writing seems very difficult for me. The pains in the stomach don't let up… my regards to Baroness von Schleinitz." Mentioning a possible trip to Egypt as a gift from the government, he sorrowfully tells her of the death of his best friend. "On the very day that I parted from my friend von Sicherer, with the intuition that I would never see him again, I got the news of his death…Seldom has a loss touched me so painfully…Freiherr von Rotenhan was here and brought news. You know that O'C visited me…My Essay about Cavour is almost ready. I fear that it will make a particular spectacle. The child is already born…Please don't be cross with me, I didn't say anything evil about you, you took me amiss, [but] no damage to your soul's health. Where shall I send the Pellegrino Rossi Part I of October 1?"

October 9, 1901

Rundegg
(Obermais) Meran

Dear friend,
I have received the 1st part of Pellegrino Rossi, devoured it and regurgitated it (not as the doves do!) to the intense satisfaction of Adele Schleinitz and all present. Where however is No. 2? I am afraid you grabbed the wrong thing when bagging it for the mail and sent me, instead of P.R. No.2, a repeat of your Rosmini from the month before – Isn't that so?

It concerns me especially to get No. 2 quickly because Adele inaugurates her hibernation next Wednesday, the 15th – that is, following her innermost need to withdraw to a farm at Vahrn near Brixen, to – as she rightly says – make up her mind about her affliction, which is not possible for her among people. Adele greets you most respectfully and with full thanks for your expression of sympathy. What an astonishing nature! Deeply mystical, self-contained, more at home in the beyond than here and nevertheless … a clarity in conceiving and judging earthly matters which many could envy who only live and breathe earthly things.

I would to God dear friend, that you decide soon about the South, if Egypt doesn't appeal to you in the moment, there is still a rich selection … toward Sicily, for example. In Girgenti[333] there is a superb guest house and there or at Syracuse there prevails a really ideal climate in winter.

---

[333] Since 1927, Agrigento.

Happily, I would follow you to wherever it might be more comfortable for you to establish yourself, and to look after you <u>physically</u>, which your disciple Sauer[334] could hardly understand.[335]

About the 'Cavour,' I pray to you with uplifted hands. My soul's salvation in the <u>Roman</u> Olympia is thus done for.

Do you know that Revertara[336] once again succeeded in squeezing out a year's extension for Rome? Done is done and Count Szecsen[337] reserved this post for himself after that, (since he now has it totally in hand already at the Ballplatz,[338] as the section chief of this division.)

Constantly I forgot to ask you, whether in Berlin things have been totally reversed, in allowing the establishment side by side of protestant <u>and Catholic</u> history professorships? Since when is history a matter of confessional parity in academic institutions? I lack the key here, and you, political cellar-master, please send me pure wine about it.[339]

---

[334] The plan had been made for Kraus' protégé, Dr. Joseph Sauer, to accompany Kraus to San Remo.

[335] Kraus declined her offer on October 11, 1901, with a letter which is not in her *Nachlass*.

[336] Friedrich Count Revertara y Salandra (1827-1904), 1888-1901 Austrian Envoy to the Vatican.

[337] Nikolaus Count Szecsen de Temerin (1857-1926), 29 Nov. 1901 – 23 Jan. 1911 Austrian Envoy to the Vatican.

[338] Site of the Austrian Foreign Ministry in Vienna.

[339] Martin Spahn was specially appointed as a Catholic to the faculty at Strassburg.

When I learned of the death of your friend, von Sicherer,[340] I painfully felt this loss for you and understand what a void this means for you. 1900 and 1901 have been horrible years for us all ... That calls for us to draw closer together and hold together all the more intimately, don't you think?

In a flying rush, most affectionately, your

AVE

---

[340] Hermann von Sicherer (1839-1901), Jurist, 1868 Professor at Munich. A lifelong and most intimate friend.

Epilogue

ON OCTOBER 11, 1901, the day that Kraus informed AVE that her offer to accompany him to a warmer clime could not be accepted, he wrote to his protégé Joseph Sauer that the mid-December trip for the recovery of his health would not be to Egypt or Sicily but to the Riviera, to San Remo.[341] On December 12 the two began the journey, with Kraus joking about his impending death. A two-day delay in Milan was caused by a snowstorm, and many of Kraus' northern Italian friends came to pay their respects and to talk bravely about the future.[342]

The professor and his student reached San Remo shortly and Kraus was given over to the care of German speaking religious sisters. On the 19th Sauer left for Rome to return to his studies. In the late night of December 28 he received the news of Kraus' death and began to send notice to friends. Baroness Eichthal was one of the first to be notified.[343]

Kraus' friends knew what his death meant for her. Typical was the note from Baron von Hügel on January 31, 1902, to express his deep sorrow over her personal loss and the loss to the church and Catholic learning. Kraus had dictated a postcard to the Hügels as late as December 27, 1901. The baron wrote to her, "We got news from him of his illness with a few words written by himself at the end. And how terrible his being all alone. I feel so much for you knowing what a long intimate friendship yours with him has been. Please accept my sincere and deep sympathy."[344]

---

[341] Claus Arnold, *Katholizismus als Kulturmacht, Der Freiburger Theologe Joseph Sauer (1872-1949) und das Erbe des Franz Xaver Kraus* (Paderborn, 1999), p. 81, F.X Kraus to Sauer, Oct. 11, 1901, *Nachlass* Sauer.

[342] Hubert Schiel, *Im Spannungsfeld von Kirche und Politik, Franz Xaver Kraus, 1840-1901-1951* (Trier, 1951), pp. 55-56.

[343] Arnold, *ibid.*, p. 89.

[344] Friedrich von Hügel to Ave, Jan. 31, 1902. *Nachlass* Eichthal, File von Hügel.

Appendix

THE BARONESS AND THE GENTEEL PAGAN

MOST PEOPLE WILL BE ACQUAINTED with Baroness Augusta von Eichthal in connection with Denis O'Connell, Franz Xaver Kraus, John Ireland, or John Keane, or from works related to the "Americanists" in the early days of the Catholic University of America.[345] Recently an excellent article devoted to the Roman 'saloniste' appeared in the 1998 volume edited by Hubert Wolf, *Antimodernismus und Modernismus in der katholischen Kirche*. A chapter by Claus Arnold, "Frauen und Modernisten. Ein Kreis um Augusta von Eichthal," gave readers a good understanding of the lady. In his subsequent work about Joseph Sauer, *Katholizismus als Kulturmacht. Der Freiburger Theologe Joseph Sauer (1872-1949) und das Erbe des Franz Xaver Kraus*, (Paderborn, 1999), Arnold has twenty-five citations which outline the role in Sauer's career played by this remarkable woman who lived from 1835 to 1932. Her *Nachlass* in the Bavarian State Archive in Munich contains one hundred and eighteen files of correspondence from people ranging from Franz Liszt and Ignatius Döllinger to —— Charles Warren Stoddard!

For Baroness Eichthal's associations with American Catholic academia pre-date her 1890's Roman friendships with O'Connell, Ireland and Keane. In 1874 she entered into friendship with Charles Warren Stoddard, a poet and writer who was destined to teach at both Notre Dame and the Catholic University of America. The bohemian Catholic convert[346] was in London

---

[345] Gerald P. Fogarty, S.J., *The Vatican and the Americanist Crisis: Denis J. O'Connell, American Agent in Rome, 1885-1903*, Rome 1974; Christoph Weber, *Liberaler Katholizismus: Biographische und kirchenpolitische Essays von Franz Xaver Kraus*, Tübingen 1983; Robert C. Ayers, The Americanists and Franx Xaver Kraus: an Historical Analysis of an International Liberal Catholic Combination, 1897-1898, unpublished dissertation, Syracuse University, New York 1981.

[346] A nominal Presbyterian, Stoddard is said to have been baptized on November 2, 1867. Among the Francis Davis Millet letters to Stoddard in the Arents Research Library at

serving as secretary for Mark Twain. The famous American author was lecturing in London for six weeks and needed someone to help with his mail and to provide relaxation from the social demands of the English city. Stoddard's California background and association with wild-Western writers like Ambrose Bierce, Bret Harte and Mark Twain afforded him a definite cachet in 1874 in London, where, he recalled,

> We chat as well as an American is supposed to do under the circumstances; we talk dirk and gulch and wild, wide West, because this is the sort of thing we are bullied into by bevies of London maids who have never heard anything better of California. We grieve that we have never 'dropped our man,' for this is expected of us.[347]

The thirty-nine year old industrialist's daughter, a resident of Rome, was visiting London with her brother Emil and his wife in 1874 and met the thirty-one year old Stoddard through mutual acquaintance with Lady and Sir Thomas Duffus Hardy (1804-1878) and their daughter Iza Duffus Hardy (1852-1922). Sir Thomas, Deputy Keeper of the Public Records since 1861, was a renowned editor of (English) Rolls and Catalogues. Iza Duffus Hardy is remembered for her novels and travel accounts, among them a *circa* 1870 description of Arlington National Cemetery. Stoddard attended Lady Hardy's "Saturday Evenings" in St. John's Wood, charmed and instructed by English manners.[348] The notes from Stoddard to the baroness written in this brief period show that when he wanted to visit the Eichthals,[349] he inquired about

---

Syracuse University, there is a single letter from Peter Richard Kenrick, Archbishop of St. Louis, dated August 11, 1867, acknowledging Stoddard's conversion and congratulating him.

[347] "A London Drawing Room," *Ave Maria* 41, (26 October 1895), 463. Cited in Austen, p.66, see footnote 350.

[348] Austen, p. 66, see footnote 350.

[349] "I hope you will prepare your brother and his wife for my very brutal appearance. Should I come in a coat of many colors, will it shock them beyond expression?" Stoddard to Eichthal, 'Saturday am,' n.d.(1874), *Nachlass* Eichthal.

them at "the Hardy's" between his comings and goings to Chester. Chester was the home of young Robert W. Jones, who was passionately attracted to Stoddard, and whose passion was returned. Roger Austen, in a posthumously edited biography, *Genteel Pagan: The Double Life of Charles Warren Stoddard*,[350] makes clear that the bohemian Californian was firmly and contentedly homosexual.

In Baroness Eichthal's correspondence from Stoddard, a series of fourteen letters in ten months between June 1876 and April 1877, some written only a day apart, makes it clear that sometime before early summer of 1876 she and Stoddard were together on an extended excursion up the river Nile. They had made "wonderful friends."[351] As a reminder of their time he sends her a blank piece of papyrus.[352] He frequently interjects the expression "Mashallah!" as a sort of theme-word of their mutual experience, and asks her for her photo and the autograph of "D," a fellow traveler. She kept his letters for fifty-six years.

Any details that we may ever learn about this lengthy holiday have to be extracted from the book which Stoddard published in 1881, *Mashallah! A Flight into Egypt*.[353] Most of the book consisted of travel accounts sent by Stoddard to American journals, including the final chapter in 1878 for the Atlantic Monthly.[354] However when the full book appeared in 1881 it bore the dedication: "To Mme. La Baronne A——— d'E———." Her reaction to this dedication may only be inferred, as Stoddard replied to her Christmas

---

[350] Roger Austen, *Genteel Pagan: The Double Life of Charles Warren Stoddard*, edited by John W. Crowley. (Amherst, 1991.)

[351] Stoddard to Eichthal, Venice, July 25, 1876, *Nachlass* Eichthal.

[352] Stoddard to Eichthal, Capri, Sept.11, 1876, *Nachlass* Eichthal.

[353] New York, Appleton, 1881.

[354] "The Moolid of the Prophet," Atlantic Monthly, vol.42 (August 1878).

letter in January of 1882, with the salutation, "Lovable but exceeding cross and very spoiled person!"[355]

Mashallah! is principally about a tour up the Nile by a small party of first-class travelers in early 1876. Stoddard's style, which caroms from subject to subject with elliptical logic and has few references to persons other than those who come into direct view, provides little detail about his fellow passengers.

The sailing and rowing barge, the Nitetis, was a *dahabeeyah*, "the most luxurious of river boats,"[356] a broad flat-bottomed craft one hundred twenty feet long,[357] two-thirds of whose deck was covered by a cabin with two saloons, several single and double staterooms, a bath-room and "all the luxuries of first-class hotel life."[358] It was powered upstream by a large sail set forward on a short mast and a slanting spar one hundred seventy feet long, and a smaller lateen sail over the rudder at the rear. When the barge needed to be towed, the crew drew it from a towpath, "as tamely as if this were the Erie Canal."[359] When rowed downstream, the oarsmen were seven to a side.

As a crew this elegant barge had a captain, second captain, fourteen sailors, a cook and a vice-cook, two cabin boys, the captain's small son, and a dragoman and his assistant. Served by these twenty-three men were the ten cabin passengers, four ladies including the spinster baroness and her friend "D," plus

---

[355] Stoddard to Eichthal, Honolulu, January 1882, *Nachlass* Eichthal.

[356] Wm. W. Loring, *A Confederate Soldier in Egypt* 1884, no page.

[357] *Mashallah!*, 128. (Hereafter M 128)

[358] M 129.

[359] M 153.

five "adamantine bachelors;" two priests, Stoddard, and two others, and, the tour conductor Mr. H———.[360]

The boat was plentifully stocked with wines, cigars, dainties, books, and easy chairs. In the evening the ladies played the piano provided. An especially appropriate rendition one moonlit night was the "Moonlight Sonata" played by "Madame" — possibly Eichthal, the friend of Liszt. Bookshelves[361] were supplied with Herodotus, Diodorus, Strabo, and English and German books about Egypt and the Nile.

Stoddard's ephebophile eye is constantly drawn to the muscular physiques of the sailors and other natives whom he watches as they shed their loincloths to hop in and out of the water, but he has little to offer about the four ladies in the group. Once he remarks on "the ludicrous spectacle of a party of modern tourists in cork helmets, puggeries, white cotton umbrellas and green goggles strutting among the ruins of an Egyptian temple."[362] One assumes it is the ladies with the white cotton umbrellas. The men visit the "fleshpots" in a river village and "by and by we return to the Nitetis, where the ladies sit and wonder at our delay."[363] Stoddard had not been very taken by the belly-dancers of the "*ghawazee* tribe ... pale moon-eyed women of ample flesh and the reckless grace of drowsy pards."[364] He preferred the drumming and singing of a "handsome boy" at Luxor, who

> skipped nimbly to and fro along the bank, singing his song of love. He had the limber spine of a cat, this agile *gaish*, and all his muscles quivered responsive to the rhythm of a ballad so iniquitous that a full translation of it were impossible

---

[360] M 129,139.

[361] M 151.

[362] Thebes, M 175.

[363] M 185.

[364] M 184.

in a language suited to the requirements of a less passionate people like our own.[365]

Upon reaching Assoan [Aswan] the Nitetis is re-rigged as an oared vessel for the downstream trip, and after an excursion by donkey and by boat, "through the iron gates of Nubia"[366] to the island tombs of Philae, "fairy templed Philae," the travelers float back to Cairo. There they say goodbye to "the dear old Nitetis, my home for two of the happiest months I ever hope to pass. But there is a consolation in the thought that the remembrance of this voyage must be a joy to me for ever and a day."[367]

The closing chapter of the book, "The Moolid of the Prophet," is a gripping narrative in great contrast to the previous atmospheric and wordy scenes. Stoddard describes a demonstration of faith to observe the birthday of "Mahomet," in which Zikkeers, the whirling dancing dervishes, in "tall brimless felt hats,"[368] arouse long-maned howling dervishes into a frenzied state which climaxes with a human carpet of prostrated fanatics, the 'howlers,' upon whose bodies a sheik rides his horse.

From among the "grim, mean-eyed, filthy" dancing dervishes Stoddard spots one,

> a lad in his teens, soft-eyed, oval-faced, touched with a color that went and came like a girl's blush – how he whirled, with his outstretched arms floating upon the air! His head was inclined as if pillowed on some invisible breast: his soft, dark eyes dilated in ecstasy: he swam like a thistle-down, superior to the gravitations of this base world, ascending in his dream, by airy spirals, into the seventh

---

[365] M 186.

[366] M 198.

[367] M 217.

[368] M 218.

heaven of his heart's desire. What wonder that his heart melted within him; that his spirit swooned, overcome by the surpassing loveliness of the mysteries now visible to him![369]

On the day of the Doseh (the Pressing), Stoddard and E [ichthal] go from the residence of the Austrian Consul to the garden park where the path for the testimonial treading is lined with tents for visitors and officials. By mistake they are ushered into the pavilion of the hereditary prince, whose harem, "under glass as usual," is set a-flutter by the presence of Stoddard's lady friends in the precincts of his Highness.[370]

There they are in position to observe four hundred howling dervishes, "of the lowest orders of the East, impoverished, fanatical, forlorn,"[371] paving the roadway with their bodies. The "sheik" proceeds to ride his horse over this human mattress. The unsteady horse, "shod with large flat shoes, like plates of steel, that flashed in the sunshine," finds it difficult to maintain balance on the bodies and is supported by attendants on all sides.

After completing the ordeal, the sheik, "stupefied with opium, for he performs this act, much against his will, in deference to the demands of the people," having passed the length of the "avenue paved with human flesh," retires to his tent and the homage of his people. Most of the dervishes rise, but some, Stoddard notes, "showed no sign of life" and some, "writhed in horrible convulsions."[372]

The "Moolid" was a thrilling finale to two solid months of common experience that united Eichthal and Stoddard for a long time. After they

---

[369] M 220.

[370] M 225.

[371] M 226.

[372] M 229.

parted, she for Rome and he for Venice, the thirty-two year old writer showered the forty-one year old heiress with letter after letter, in one of which he tells her,

> Your admirable letter is more welcome than I know how to tell you. It is so full of news, so full of yourself, it has been a source of such pleasure and profit to me. How much you have experienced in these last few weeks! The death of your friends touches me almost as deeply as if they had been friends of mine — I know so much of them from your lips![373]

Two and a half years later he was still writing fondly of the "days when we were in the East."[374] She sent him a New Year's greeting on January 6, 1879.[375]

In 1881 came the publication of the book *Mashallah!*, which was dedicated to her. When he wrote from Honolulu to her in January 1882 ("Lovable but exceeding cross and very spoiled person") he asked once more for a photograph. She wrote in return, because his next letter, December 11, 1882, says, "your letter filled me with delight."[376]

Stoddard began to teach at the University of Notre Dame in January 1885.[377] After a year there he responded to Eichthal's New Year's greeting with a six page letter in which he asked her to send him a Wagner autograph and said

---

[373] Stoddard to Eichthal, Venice, July 25, 1876. *Nachlass* Eichthal.

[374] Stoddard to Eichthal, San Francisco, September 10, 1878. *Nachlass* Eichthal.

[375] Notation by Eichthal on letter above.

[376] Stoddard to Eichthal, Honolulu, December 11, 1882. *Nachlass* Eichthal.

[377] Austen, p. 108.

he still treasured the Liszt photo and signature she had given him.[378] He added, "how old I feel with all these big boys calling me professor."[379]

Two letters from Stoddard came close together in April 1889. He had been in Munich for most of the winter and had just missed seeing her on a March visit to Rome. He wanted her to know that he had a new position.

> Have you heard of the new Catholic University of North America about to be established? The Rector, Monsg. Keane, is my most loyal friend, as are most of the American College in Rome. He said to me — you must join me — in Washington in November next, and become a lecturer in English literature.
>
> You will wonder why I am no longer at Notre Dame? While there I heard from you. It is two years this summer since I was driven out of that state, a victim of the malaria which abounds there. As you know I nearly died of the malarial fever - ...friends are now dragging me about in the hope of restoring my health...I narrowly missed seeing you.[380]

Mr. Theodore Vail and wife and son David had taken him from Munich to Italy in March of 1889, where he visited the American College and friends.[381] Apparently it was this chance excursion to Rome that brought him to John Keane's attention as one who might fill the need to have an American teaching English literature at the new graduate school in Washington.

Somehow Stoddard managed to get a loan of 2500 Reichsmarks from Baroness von Eichthal. Her circumstances at that time were comfortable and she is known to have made loans and grants.[382]

---

[378] There is a Liszt file in the *Nachlass* Eichthal, containing a lock of Liszt's hair.

[379] Stoddard to Eichthal, Notre Dame, January 22, 1886. *Nachlass* Eichthal.

[380] Stoddard to Eichthal, Munich, April 1, 1889. *Nachlass* Eichthal.

[381] Austen, p. 118.

[382] Claus Arnold, *Katholizismus als Kulturmacht*, p. 273.

Three years later the loan had not been repaid. When Archbishop John Ireland was in Rome in 1892 he discovered that Stoddard, a faculty member from an institution of which he was a trustee, had an overdue loan from the revered baronessa who was so useful to him and to his friend Denis O'Connell, the Rector of the American College. The archbishop urged her to dun Stoddard at once. Ireland was in a position to know that Stoddard received free board and room in Caldwell Hall and that moreover, from the university's rector, Bishop Keane, the professor had just had a substantial raise from eight hundred dollars to two thousand dollars a year. Roger Austen states that Stoddard earned an additional six hundred dollars annually from his articles in the Notre Dame periodical, *Ave Maria*.[383]

Friends are well advised to "neither a borrower nor a lender be" for the matter of the loan seems to have been the final chapter in the history of the bond between the Bavarian banker's granddaughter and the bohemian Californian.

A letter by Augusta von Eichthal to Denis O'Connell, written in the first stage of their long friendship and before she called him by his nickname "Propeller," tells the story in her excellent English. O'Connell had just left John Ireland in France and she was about to leave Rome for the summer.

> [Rome] 176 Ripetta
> Thursday, June 30th, 1892
>
> Dear Monsignore,
>
> Preferring to be in time on the safer side of things, I pen this note lest you should not return in time for me to see you before my departure which is fixed on to-morrow afternoon.
>
> First of all honour to whom honour is due. On the 28th inst., i.e., by return of post, Mr. Charles W. Stoddard sent me a check for 1690 lire, begging to be allowed to take his time for the rest. He explained how having an aged father

---

[383] Austen, p. 122. "Bishop Keane remained a dependable friend, and in 1892 he gave Stoddard an eight-hundred-dollar raise, bringing his yearly salary to well over two thousand dollars."

to provide for besides a widowed sister who keeps a home & takes care of the old father on 50 dl. (a month of settled income) he is obliged to divide his income with his family. Moreover he tells me how illusory the free board and lodging is in so far, at the University, as its vacations last for four full months a year during which period the establishment is closed & everyone has to provide for himself. Nevertheless Mr. Stoddard hastens to say late enactions mended his old drawn wages enough to enable him to pay the aforesaid 1690 l. [equal to $325,Ed.] out of his savings.

It is time after this [period of] time, my wrath is abated, & I mean to let Mr. Stoddard know not to trouble about the rest of the 2500 marks. For serviceable as the return of this outlay was to me, I do not want to be hard on the poor man.

How did you find our dear Archbishop? I was with both of you in mind & in the spirit ever since Saint Peter's day & am fully prepared to hear that you remain with him till he sails for America. Would you kindly give him notice of Mr. Stoddard's willingness to pay, the moment he was called upon to do so? I owe him this fairly since it was the Archbishop who compelled my claiming the debt, knowing Stoddard able to answer the call.

The Pope's political letters seem to meet but a poor reception in various parts. Times are hard with the successor of Gregory VII & the peoples now-a-days apt to apply the division of labour likewise to the Holy See: you look out for the wheal [sic] of the [church] and leave politics to the various worldly governments! they cry out.

I need not tell you how pleased I should be to receive an ever so brief an account of your excursion & further projects. Letters are sure to find me addressed to Baronne A. d'Eichthal, chez Mme.de Z...-W..., 14/II Barerstrasse, Munich (Baviere).

God speed you dear Msgre.

Yours very truly, Augusta d'Eichthal[384]

---

[384] Augusta von Eichthal to Denis O'Connell, Rome, June 30, 1892. Archives of the Diocese of Richmond, Virginia.

Bibliography

Acton, John. "The Munich Congress," *Home and Foreign Review*, No. 7, January 1864, pp. 209-244. Reprinted in John E.E.D. Acton, *Essays on Church and State*. London: Hollis and Carter, 1952.

Ahern, Patrick H. *The Life of John J. Keane, Archbishop and Educator, 1839-1918*. Milwaukee:Bruce, 1954.

Arnold, Claus. "Augusta von Eichthal," *Biographisch-Bibliographisches Kirchenlexikon*, Band XX (2002). (http://www.bautz.de/bbkl/e/eichthal_a_h.shtml)

Arnold, Claus. "Frauen und 'Modernisten,' Ein Kreis um Augusta von Eichthal," in: Hubert Wolff (Hrsg.), *Antimodernismus und Modernismus in der katholische Kirche*. Paderborn: Schoeningh, 1998.

Arnold, Claus. *Katholizismus als Kulturmacht. Der Freiburger Theologe Joseph Sauer (1872-1949) und das Erbe des Franz Xaver Kraus*. Paderborn:Schoeningh, 1999.

"Banking," Jewish Encyclopedia.com (http://www.jewishencyclopedia.com)

Bedeschi, Lorenzo. *Modernismo a Milano*. Milan: Pan Editrice,1974.

Binchy, D. A. *Church and State in Fascist Italy*. Oxford, 1941

Caine, Hall. *The Eternal City*. New York: Appleton, 1902

"Coat of Arms," Jewish Encyclopedia.com (http://www.jewishencyclopedia.com)

Des Houx, Henri. *Histoire de Leon XIII – Joachim Pecci (1810-1878)*. Paris, 1900.

Döllinger, Ignatius. *Römische Briefe vom Concil von Quirinus*. Munich, 1870.

Colonna, Vittoria, Duchess of Sermoneta. *Things Past*. New York: Appleton, 1929.

Confessore, Ornella. *L'Americanismo Cattolico in Italia*. (Religione e società, Vol.10) Rome, 1984.

Fogarty, Gerald P. *The Vatican and the Americanist Crisis: Denis J. O'Connell, American Agent in Rome, 1885-1903*. Rome: Università Gregoriana, 1974.

Fogazzaro, Antonio. *Il Santo*. Milan, 1902.

Fogazzaro, Antonio. *Piccolo Mondo Moderno*. Milan, 1901.

Gay, Ruth. *Jews in America. A Short History*. New York: Basic Books, 1965.

"Geschichte der Wiener Gasometer," (http://wiener-gasometer.at/de/geschichte/geschichte)

Graf, Michael. *Liberaler Katholik – Reformkatholik – Modernist? Franz Xaver Kraus (1840-1901) zwischen Kulturkampf und Modernismuskrise*. Hamburg: Lit Verlag, 2003.

Harris, James F. *The People Speak! Anti-Semitism and Emancipation in Nineteenth Century Bavaria*. Ann Arbor: Michigan, 1994.

Hauviller, Ernst. *Franz Xaver Kraus. Ein Lebensbild aus der Zeit des Reformkatholizismus*. Colmar: Roock, 1904.

Houdini, Harry. *The Miracle Mongers*. New York: E.P. Dutton, 1920.

Kraus, Franz Xaver. *Cavour*. Mainz: Franz Kirchheim, 1902.

Kraus, Franz Xaver. *Tagebücher, herausgegeben von Hubert Schiel*. Cologne: Bachem, 1957. [Cited as *Tgb.*]

Maignen, Charles. *Father Hecker, Is He A Saint?* Rome: Desclée, 1898. [With Appendix of extracts from Denis O'Connell's July 1898 letters to Alberto Lepidi, O.P., Master of the Sacred Palace.]

McCabe, Joseph. *The Totalitarian Church of Rome*. Girard, Kansas, 1944. (www.textfiles.com/conspiracy/mccabe)

"Montefiore, Sir Moses," Jewish Encyclopedia.com (http://www.jewishencyclopedia.com)

Moynihan, James H. *The Life of Archbishop John Ireland*. New York: Harper, 1953.

Münz, Sigmund. *Römische Reminiscenzen und Profile*. Berlin, 1900.

O'Connell, Marvin R. *John Ireland and the American Catholic Church*. St. Paul: Minnesota Historical Society, 1988.

O'Toole, James M. *Militant and Triumphant. William Henry O'Connell and the Catholic Church in Boston (1859-1944)*. Notre Dame, 1992.

Rieger, Susanne. "Traces of the Jewish-Christian Banker Family Seligmann-Eichthal at Munich's Old Southern Cemetery," (Article and

Photographs by Susanne Rieger, October 30, 2001.) http://home.t-online.de/home/RIJONUE/eichthae.htm,

Rodd, Sir James Rennell. *Social and Diplomatic Memories, 1902-1919.* London: Edmund Arnold, 1925. (http://www.lib.byu.edu/~rdh/memoir/rodd/rodd)

Schiel, Hubert. *Im Spannungsfeld von Kirche und Politik. Franz Xaver Kraus. Gedenkschrift zom 50. Todestag auf Grund des unversiegelten Nachlasses.* Trier:Paulinus, 1951.

Schnee, Heinrich. "Die Familie Seligmann – Eichthal als Hoffinanziers an den süddeutschen Fürstenhäusern," *Zeitschrift für bayerische Landesgeschichte*, Band 25, 1962.

Stoddard, Charles Warren. *Mashallah! A Flight into Egypt.* New York: Appleton, 1881.

Stoddard, Charles Warren, Letters from Frank Millet et al., (George Arents Research Library for Special Collections, Syracuse University).

Sweeney, David F. *The Life of John Lancaster Spalding.* New York: Herder and Herder, 1965.

Underwood, F. M. *United Italy.* London: Methuen, 1912.

Venturi, Adolfo. *Memorie Autobiografiche.* Milan: Hoepli, 1911.

Voss, Richard. *Aus einem phantastischen Leben.* Stuttgart, 1923.

Weber, Christoph. *Der Fall Spahn 1901.* Rome: Herder, 1980.

Weber, Christoph. "F.X. Kraus und Italien," *Quellen und Forschungen aus italienischen Archiven und Bibliotheken,* 61, (1981), Tübingen, 1981.

Weber, Christoph. "Italien, Deutschland und d. Konklave von 1903," *Quellen und Forschungen aus italienischen Archiven und Bibliotheken*, 57 (1977), Tübingen, 1977.

Weber, Christoph. *Kirchliche Politik zwischen Rom, Berlin und Trier 1876-1888.* Mainz: Matthias-Grünewald-Verlag, 1970.

Weber, Christoph. *Liberaler Katholizismus. Biographische und kirchenhistorische Essays von Franz Xaver Kraus.* Tübingen: Max Niemeyer, 1983.

Weber, Christoph. *Quellen und Studien zur Kurie and zur vatikanischen Politik unterLeo XIII.* Tübingen: Max Niemeyer, 1973.

Wolff, Hubert, Hrsg., *Antimodernismus und Modernismus in der katholische Kirche.* Paderborn: Schöningh, 1998.

Zola, Émile. *Rome.* New York: Macmillan, 1901.

About the Author

Robert Curtis Ayers is a native of Roanoke/Salem, Virginia, where he attended Andrew Lewis High School and Roanoke College. Graduating from the Lutheran Theological Seminary in Philadelphia in 1950, he became an Episcopal priest in 1953. He served for 22 years as the Episcopal Chaplain to Syracuse University, and was awarded the doctorate in Philosophy in 1981 for his groundbreaking research of "The Americanists and Franz Xaver Kraus: An Historical Analysis of an International Liberal Catholic Combination, 1897-1898." He lives near Cazenovia, New York, and is the Rector Emeritus of the historic Church of Saints Peter and John, Auburn, New York.

www.ingramcontent.com/pod-product-compliance
Lightning Source LLC
Chambersburg PA
CBHW022110150426
43195CB00008B/343